The Unhandy Man's Guide to Home Repairs

The UNHANDY Man's Guide to Home Repairs

A complete guide to home maintenance · improvements
and remodeling · for men and women · handy or not

Barbara P. O'Neill and Richard W. O'Neill

ILLUSTRATIONS BY BARBARA P. O'NEILL

The Macmillan Company, New York | Collier-Macmillan Ltd., London

CONTENTS

2 Electricity

3 Appliances

4 Heating

5 Cooling

6 Walls and Ceilings

7 Floors and Stairs

8   Doors and Windows

14   Using Your Attic

15   Using Your Basement

16   Storage

17   Remodeling

Index

INTRODUCTION:
ARE YOU UNHANDY?

If you think you are all thumbs, you've probably just been going at things the wrong way. Many people feel that home repairs are just too difficult. They think that carpentry, plumbing, and electricity take a lot of skill and knowledge—and that it's all too much trouble anyway. Well, these things do require a certain amount of know-how, but they are not really difficult. Anyone who is even reasonably intelligent can easily learn all he needs to know so as to manage most of his own home repairs, maintenance, and remodeling.

This book is written specifically for people who *aren't* handy—people who don't know a nut from a gasket or a tank float from an inlet valve. The instructions have been made clear and easy to follow, even for people who have never before done anything even remotely handy. If you can follow a recipe in a cookbook or change a tire on your automobile, you can repair a toilet or paper a wall by following the simple directions in this book.

Women can be as handy as men. In most households, men do the handy jobs—or women complain because they don't. Women tend to regard home repairs, even the simple ones like fixing a broken light cord, as out of their domain. But if men can wash dishes and baby-sit, there's no reason why women can't venture into the mysteries of faulty light plugs and cracked ceilings. In most cases, women can be just as good at these jobs as men. Some women can be better.

Why be handy? Maybe you don't even want to be handy—you'd rather leave it all to somebody better qualified. If you can afford that attitude, fine. However, if you've ever been faced with an overflowing toilet or a broken-down washing machine, and been unable to get a repairman at once, you know it would be a convenience to be handy enough to do it yourself.

Whether you live in a house or apartment, whether your home is the most modern or the most antiquated, there are frequent occasions when a repair job is needed. And a repairman is not always on the spot. Obviously, you can save yourself a great deal of money by doing much of your own repair work. You can't eliminate all professional repairs, but you can certainly do the simple jobs yourself. If a job is too difficult or complicated for you to manage, this book will tell you *not* to try it.

How to use this book. You'll find this book easy to understand. Whenever possible, every term unfamiliar to the average person has been described or diagramed when it first appears. If you do come across a term you don't know, refer to the Index.

By using this book, you can find just what you need to know when you need to know it. You don't have to study up in advance if you don't want to. Whenever a problem comes up, you can look it up in the Index or Contents.

We, the authors, have personally done nearly every job described in these pages. We ourselves have repaired leaky faucets, hung wallpaper, installed electrical fixtures, built built-ins—and we have completely remodeled two houses. Most of what we have done can also be done by any intelligent homeowner who is willing to follow directions.

This book tells you how to do things the easy way—and, at the same time, how to do them right. We have described the newest methods and the newest products now on the market, but constant improvements in the home repair field are being made by manufacturers—which means that your best source of information on new products is, in many cases, your retail dealer.

And that brings us to another word of advice: make a friend of your hardware dealer, for he is usually handy himself, and can often give you valuable suggestions. If you carry out even a few of the repairs detailed in these pages, you will be making many trips to the hardware store (not to mention the lumberyard, the plumbing supply house, and the electrical goods dealer). If you can't get what you need locally, you can order from a mail-order house, such as Sears Roebuck.

The law and your house. There is just one legality you must keep in mind when you are about to do some work on your house: If you are making electrical or wiring changes, or adding on to the basic structure of your house (by adding a room, porch, or dormer, for example), you must draw a plan of the structure and get a permit for the job from your city building department. (A building department is one part of local government charged under the Constitution with insuring public health and safety.)

If you put in a new electrical outlet (and the wiring that goes with it) without a permit, your fire insurance could be voided. If a fire started because of faulty wiring, you would be out of luck. If you put in new waste lines for a new toilet or basin without a permit, you might later be ordered to take them out and redo the work if it does not conform to local regulations. If you are adding a room or other basic structure, obviously materials and workmanship must meet basic requirements for safety.

A building permit signifies that (1) the work conforms to local building codes and zoning ordinances; (2) you are competent to handle the work (if a contractor does the job, he takes out the permit); and (3) the work will be inspected by the building department to see that it has been done correctly and safely.

The Unhandy Man's Guide to Home Repairs

1 PLUMBING

BASIC FACTS ABOUT PLUMBING

1.1 | You can make simple plumbing repairs yourself, even if you are completely inexperienced. Dripping faucets, leaky pipes, and clogged drains are not difficult to fix. All you need is patience and the proper tools. The tools are not expensive—a matter of a few dollars—and they'll save you hours of inconvenience and many dollars in plumbers' bills. You probably already have some of the tools required for ordinary plumbing jobs.

You'll need an adjustable wrench; Stillson wrench (sometimes called a "pipe" wrench because its jaws have teeth to grip the pipe); screwdriver; pliers; hacksaw; plunger, or "plumber's friend" (a rubber suction cup on a stick, available in several sizes: 4 inches for drains, 6 inches for toilets); spring-type auger (frequently called a "snake") for clearing out stopped-up sink and basin drains; and a special, long-handled toilet auger. (See Fig. 1-1.) The most common

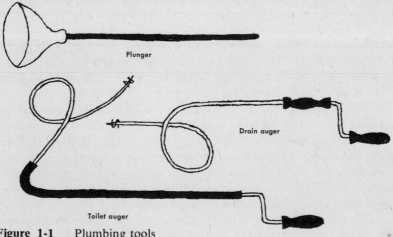

Plunger

Drain auger

Toilet auger

Figure 1-1   Plumbing tools

1

size of toilet auger is about 5½ feet long, which will easily reach all the way through the toilet trap. Plungers and snakes should be washed after each use.

Don't be afraid of your plumbing system. When you take a good look at it, it's really amazingly simple. It involves two systems: one for fresh-water supply, with hot and cold water; the other for waste disposal. (Study Fig. 1-2 carefully.) The thin pipes take the hot and cold water supply to basins, toilets, tubs, and sinks. The big pipes are the waste lines that take used water from those fixtures to sewer or septic tank. Tied into the waste lines are vent pipes that permit the sewer gases in sewer or septic tank and waste lines to escape through the roof. Notice that there is a trap under each fixture. Traps always have water in them to seal off sewer gases so they cannot escape into the house through the drains in the fixture.

1.2 | How to shut off water for repairs or emergencies. The easiest way is to close the main shutoff valve at the water meter. (See Fig. 1-2.) There are two of them, one on each side of the meter. Closing either one will do the trick. If you get your water from a well, close the shutoff valve on the house side of the pressure storage tank, not on the well side.

There are usually a number of shutoff valves in your water supply lines that permit you to shut off the water to just one fixture, or to the bathroom only, without shutting off the water to the whole house. It's a good idea to locate all the shutoff valves before trouble arises, and to label them clearly if there is any question about what fixtures they control.

1.3 | How to repair damaged or stained sinks and basins. Sinks and basins are usually made of cast iron or steel coated with glazed porcelain enamel. They should be cleaned regularly with a mild cleansing powder. A sprinkling of cleanser or a solution of Chlorox left standing overnight will usually remove stubborn stains.

Rust stains on fixtures or faucets can usually be removed by rubbing with a slice of lemon, vinegar, or commercial rust remover.

Never use harsh abrasives or steel wool, oxalic acid or muriatic acid, Sani-Flush, or Drano to clean basins or sinks. If you do, you may wear off the glaze and make the surface more susceptible to staining than before. When cleaning drains with Sani-Flush or Drano use a funnel to avoid getting any on the enamel.

Chipped basins, tubs, laundry tubs, and toilet tanks (but not the toilet itself) can be repaired or refinished with epoxy patching enamel.

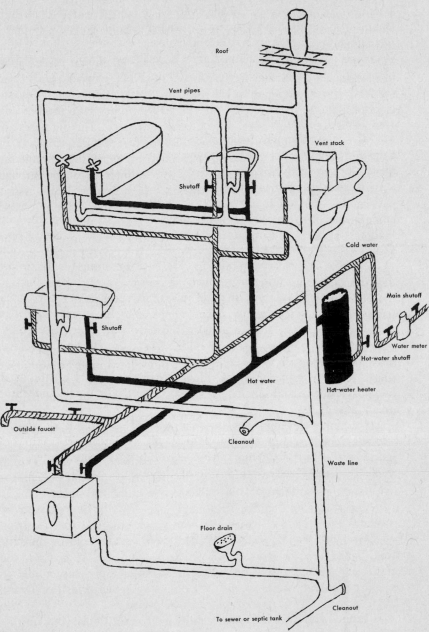

Roof

Vent pipes

Vent stack

Shutoff

Cold water

Main shutoff

Shutoff

Water meter

Hot-water shutoff

Hot water

Hot-water heater

Outside faucet

Cleanout

Waste line

Floor drain

To sewer or septic tank

Cleanout

Figure 1-2   A typical plumbing system

There are several brands on the market; ask your hardware dealer. Damaged spots are first washed with benzene (synthetic paint thinner) to remove grease and soap, and the exposed cast iron is rubbed with sandpaper. Be sure the chipped area is perfectly dry before applying the epoxy patching material, and follow manufacturer's directions closely.

If a toilet bowl cracks it cannot be repaired, but must be replaced. (See Secs. 1.11 and 1.12.)

1.4 | How to repair leaks at stoppers, strainers, tub walls. If the stopper in your basin won't hold water, it probably needs cleaning. Most stoppers can be removed for cleaning by simply giving them a twist and lifting them out. In some basins it's necessary to disconnect the horizontal rod at the joint under the basin before the stopper can be removed for cleaning. You can tighten the nut holding the horizontal rod to the vertical shaft to make the stopper fit more snugly. (See Fig. 1-3.)

Strainers on older bathtubs and basins sometimes leak around their edges, letting water run down the outside of the waste lines to the floor or ceiling below. If there is a screw head in the top of the strainer, use a screwdriver to remove the strainer; then caulk with putty (a thick paste sold in cans at the hardware store) all around under the edges of the strainer. If there is no screw head, you will have to use a wrench to unscrew the big flat nut (just under the basin) that holds the strainer in place. Then loosen the top nut on the drain line just under the basin so you can raise the strainer and caulk under its edges.

If a crack develops between the side of a bathtub or shower and the wall, it can be easily repaired with tub caulking. (Ask your hardware dealer what kind.) This is a puttylike material that you apply by simply squeezing it out of the tube.

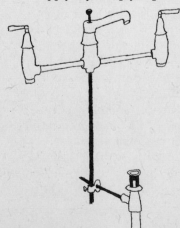

Figure 1-3   How a basin stopper works

DRAINS

1.5 | **If the drain is sluggish,** it can probably be cleared easily by using a chemical cleaner, like Sani-Flush. Such cleaners are primarily lye, which reacts with soap curds, grease, and fat—responsible for most stoppages—in a churning fashion usually sufficient to clear out the drain. Kitchen and bathroom drains can be kept in good condition by regular (every few weeks) use of such cleaners.

Follow directions on the container carefully, since lye mixtures are dangerous. Pour the cleaner into the drain through a funnel to avoid damage to porcelain—and wear rubber gloves. Don't let the cleaner touch skin or eyes, and make sure children are kept away from fixtures in which the solution is being used. Never use a chemical cleaner if the drain is completely clogged.

Excessive sudsing sometimes clogs drains. You can prevent this by using a low-sudsing detergent. If suds do back up in a drain, you can dissolve them by sprinkling with table salt.

1.6 | **If the drain is completely clogged,** make sure the stoppage is at that particular drain before you set about clearing it. First check other fixtures in the house. If they are draining properly then you know the stoppage is right near your stopped-up drain. Until you are sure of this, avoid flushing toilets; if the main drain is clogged, they will overflow.

If stoppage is general, see Section 1.13. If it is local, remove the strainer or stopper—if it is removable—before proceeding. In some lavatories, it is necessary to disconnect the ball joint under the basin at its back and remove the joint and the short horizontal level. (See Fig. 1-3.) The stopper will then lift out easily.

Remove accumulated hair and sludge. In some cases, this alone will clear out a lavatory drain. If stoppage is not in the strainer or stopper, try using the plunger. (The plunger can be used right over a nonremovable strainer or stopper.) You'll get a better "seal" by coating the flat bottom edge of the suction cup with petroleum jelly. If there is an overflow outlet (small holes in the porcelain near top of back wall of sink), hold a wet rag over it so you'll get better suction as you work the cup up and down.

Don't be impatient. You may have to repeat the pumping a few dozen times. If you achieve sluggish drainage by this method, you can often use a chemical cleaner to finish the job. But never use a chemical cleaner unless you are certain the drain is partially clear.

If the plunger won't clear the drain, you will have to open the trap.

1.7 | Opening the trap in sinks and basins. If there is a cleanout plug, remove it carefully with a wrench. (If the plug is stuck fast, loosen it by lightly striking the lower end a few times with a hammer.) If there is no plug, remove the entire trap by unscrewing the two slip-joint nuts holding it in place. (See Fig. 1-4.)

Be sure to have a pail handy to catch the waste water. If the sink contains much water, bail it out before removing the trap. If a chemical cleaner has been used, wear rubber gloves and avoid splashes.

If stoppage is within the trap itself, you can remove it with a wire hook made from a coat hanger. (If your basin has a non-removable stopper, clean it from underneath with this wire hook while trap is out. To reach it, you may have to remove the short piece of pipe above the trap as well.) The trap may then be cleaned thoroughly with a bottle brush.

If stoppage is farther on in the drain, you will have to use a snake. (Fig. 1-5.) Insert about a foot of the snake through the cleanout opening or trap (if plug is too small, remove the entire trap), heading it away from the sink. Then slide the snake handle up to the trap, tighten handle with setscrew, and turn it—always turning in the same direction. If the tip of the snake pierces the obstruction, or if all of the snake is in the drain, pull it out while continuing to turn in the same direction.

Figure 1-4   Opening a trap   **Figure 1-5**   Using a snake

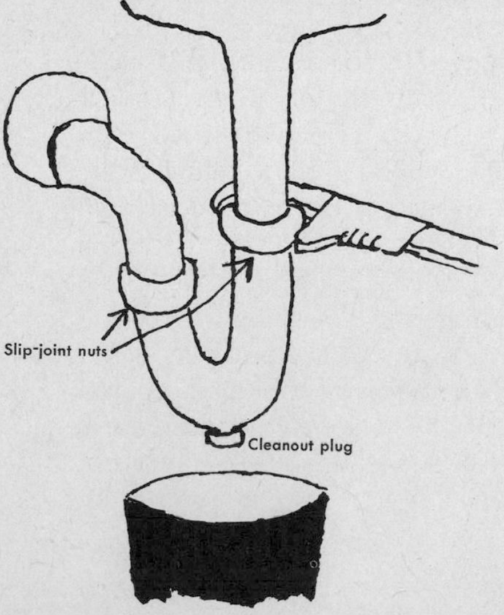

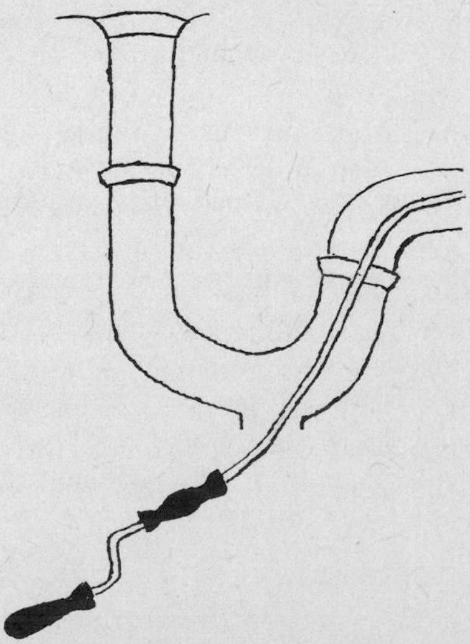

Slip-joint nuts

Cleanout plug

(It is sometimes possible, though not as effective, to work a snake directly through the sink opening after removing strainer or stopper.)

After removing the snake, replace trap. (If rubber washers at joints are worn, replace them with new ones.) Then pour boiling water in the sink. If the drain works slowly, you can now use a chemical cleaner. If the drain still does not work at all, remove the trap and try again.

1.8 | Using the snake in a bathtub drain. Some bathtubs have a drum trap, with an access cover set even with the bathroom floor. (It may be covered with a metal plate, which must first be removed.) First-floor bathtubs sometimes have drumtraps with access from underneath, in the basement.

Unscrew the cover by using a wrench on the nut at center of the cover. (Fig. 1-6.) If the nut is worn and cap sticks, it may be opened by using a hammer and screwdriver or small chisel around

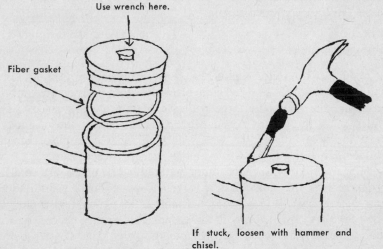

Use wrench here.

Fiber gasket

If stuck, loosen with hammer and chisel.

Figure 1-6   Opening a drum trap

the edges. Applying machine oil to threads may help. If the fiber gasket is worn, replace it with a new one before reassembling the trap.

Clean out the trap and, if necessary, use your snake.

If there is no drum trap and the strainer cannot be removed, you will have to work the snake directly through the strainer. Do the same thing with shower drains and floor drains if there is no access to the trap.

1.9 | What to do if a drain backs up. Sometimes laundry tubs, washing machines, and floor drains in the basement may back up because of very high ground water or flooding conditions outside. (If basement drains back up all the time, even when no flood conditions are apparent, your septic system may be clogged and overflowing. See Sec. 1.48.) In multifamily dwellings, excessive use of suds in one apartment may cause fixtures to back up in another.

If any of these conditions prevail, you can install backflow valves, which allow waste water to flow into the drain but permit no flow in the opposite direction. They come in standard sizes to fit in drain lines just under sinks and basins. They can be installed in washing machine rubber drain hose with grip-type connectors. Backflow valves for floor drains are placed under the drain cover, fastened with setscrews, and when water rises in them a spring-released rubber plunger closes the drain. Consult your plumbing supply house about these valves if you need them.

TOILETS

1.10 | If the toilet is clogged, or overflows when flushed—or if you notice that it is not draining properly—first remove the tank lid and raise the float (the large round ball on water's surface). This will shut off the water. You can bend a coat hanger into a hook to keep the float up and the water shut off while you make repairs. Or you can turn off the water at the nearest shutoff valve.

Then check to see if the other fixtures in the house are draining properly (try the sinks first, not toilets—you don't want another one to overflow). If they are not draining, the main drain is clogged. (See Sec. 1.13.) However, if the stoppage is local, you can be sure that something has been thrown into the toilet that doesn't belong there. Any paper other than toilet tissue may clog the drain.

Before attempting to remove the stoppage, try waiting half an hour or so. Paper, soap, or similar material may dissolve or soften by itself. If the water in the toilet is draining somewhat, you can try flushing again after a few minutes.

The first tool to use is the plunger. A large one (6 inches) will be most effective in clearing a toilet. Work it up and down several times.

If this doesn't do the trick, you'll have to use a toilet auger. (See

Fig. 1-7.) It is possible to use the drain auger, but it isn't as easy or as effective. Most stoppages are at the top bend of the trap and can be easily removed with a toilet auger.

When using the auger, fill the bowl to the rim with water. This helps clear out the trap and will enable you to tell easily when you have unclogged the toilet, for the water will run out. To use the auger, draw the end of the snake up to the curved end of the steel tube and put the curved end in the curved trap of the bowl. (Be extremely careful not to scratch the bowl or let the tool strike it, as it will damage the porcelain.) Turn the steel crank, always in the same direction, and force the snake through. If the stoppage is a rag or diaper, you can probably pull it out after the auger has pierced it, by continuing to crank in the same direction while you are pulling the auger out. If the stoppage is toilet paper or some other soluble material, push the auger through several times.

Even when water runs out of the bowl, the trap may not be completely clear. Put several feet of toilet paper in the bowl and try

Figure 1-7   Using a toilet auger

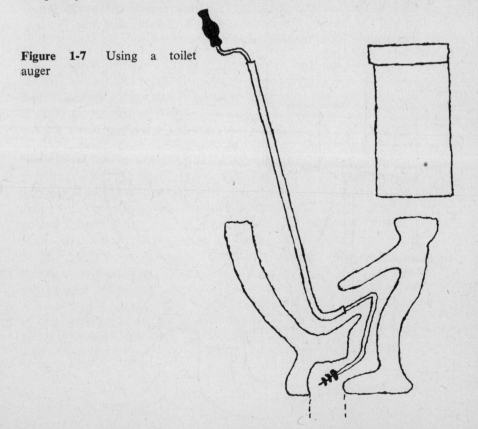

10   The Unhandy Man's Guide to Home Repairs

flushing it down. If water goes through but solids will not, there is still an obstruction. Try the auger again.

1.11 | When it's necessary to remove the toilet bowl. Once in a while an object gets so securely lodged in a toilet trap that the only way to get it out is to take up the toilet bowl and turn it upside down. Remember that this is a heavy fixture that must be handled carefully to avoid breakage. Make sure you have a ring of bowl wax on hand to use when you replace the bowl. Bowl wax looks like a 6-inch doughnut made of beeswax, and can be obtained from plumbing supply houses. If you can't get any bowl wax, a lot of putty or a sponge rubber gasket will do.

Shut off the water supply to the toilet tank and bail out both tank and toilet. Put down newspapers on the floor to catch the water left in the trap of the toilet.

On older toilets where the tank is screwed to the wall and connected to the toilet by a plated elbow, unscrew the packing nuts at tank and bowl, and work the elbow loose. If the tank rests on the back of the toilet, unscrew the nut that fastens the water supply pipe to the bottom of the tank, unscrew the nuts that hold the bottom of the tank to the toilet, and remove the tank. (See Fig. 1-8.) In

Figure 1-8   How a toilet is installed

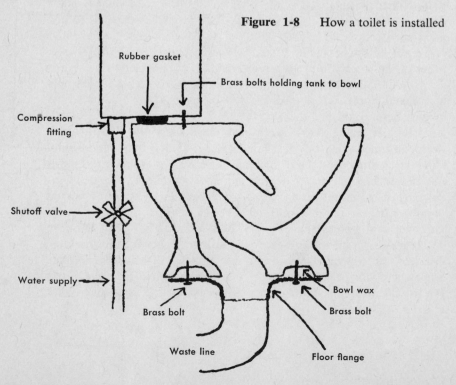

Rubber gasket

Brass bolts holding tank to bowl

Compression fitting

Shutoff valve

Water supply

Brass bolt

Waste line

Bowl wax

Brass bolt

Floor flange

single-piece and wall-hung toilets, disconnect the water supply with a wrench, and take off the tank top.

Now you can unbolt the bowl from the floor and floor flange by unscrewing the nuts and screws in the base of the toilet. (These are frequently covered with porcelain caps simply puttied in position.) Ease the toilet away from the floor and turn it over to remove the obstruction with a wire or an auger. If you can't reach the object, take the toilet outside and pour a bucket of water through it from the bottom.

Caution: A wall-hung toilet must be blocked up securely underneath before it is unbolted from the wall. Your best bet with this type of toilet is to call a plumber, as it is very difficult to remove.

1.12 | How to replace the toilet bowl. Remove old putty from the bottom of the bowl with a putty knife, and clean and dry the floor under the toilet. Clean all old putty from the closet flange. Center the ring of bowl wax or sponge rubber gasket on the closet flange, flat side up. If you can't get bowl wax, you will need approximately three pounds of putty to replace the joint between floor and toilet bowl. Spread putty generously on bottom of the toilet bowl. Set bolts in closet flange, replacing badly corroded or worn-down bolts with new ones. Place the bowl in position, and tighten hold-down nuts until bowl sits level on the floor. If you used putty, scrape away the excess with a putty knife. If you had to remove the tank, replace it before replacing plated elbow. Reconnect toilet in reverse order of the steps you took to disconnect it. (See Sec. 1.11.)

If your toilet tank was connected to the bowl with packing nuts and plated elbow, you should use new packing, like graphited string, in nuts before you put them back.

1.13 | If snake won't work and more than one fixture won't drain. In ninety-nine out of a hundred cases when the snake cannot eliminate a stoppage, you'll find that a number of your fixtures will not drain. This means that your main waste line is clogged. Unclogging it is a messy, dirty job—one best left to a professional plumber. It may require removal and replacement of pipes as well. However, if you must tackle the job yourself, here's how to go about it.

Trace the drain to the basement and find where it joins the large cast-iron or copper house drain into which all waste lines flow. Somewhere along the line you'll find a cleanout plug. (See Fig. 1-2.) It's usually near the foundation wall. Place a large container under the cleanout to catch water, and remove the plug with a wrench. Probe with your snake to locate and remove the stoppage.

If stoppage is too solid for the flexible snake to penetrate, you may be able to use a peice of pipe or a garden hose (nozzle and all) to break it up. When nozzle reaches the stoppage, stuff opening with rags and turn on the water briefly. In many cases, particularly in seashore homes, clogging is due to sand accumulating in the drain, and the hose will wash it out.

If the cleanout hole is too small to use a pipe or hose, you will need a "sewer rod"—a stiff, flat steel snake, available at plumbing supply houses and some hardware stores.

You may have a house trap at the point where the waste line leaves the house. This is a U-shaped trap with covers that can be removed with a wrench. (These traps are now illegal in most places in new houses, but do not have to be removed from old houses.)

Place a large container under the trap to catch any water that may be standing in it, unscrew the covers, and probe trap and waste line with a snake or bent coat hanger as far as you can in both directions. If you find no stoppage here, either at the trap or cleanout, the stoppage is almost sure to be outside the house.

1.14 | Clogging of sewer pipes outside the foundation often results from tree roots that enter the pipes through joints. A snake may clear such growth temporarily, but roots will grow back in time. Sometimes they may be killed by dissolving a commercial root killer (ask your hardware dealer) in a plumbing fixture, and letting it go down the drain. Of course, this is likely to work only if the drain is just partially clogged. You may have to repeat the treatment at intervals.

You can also get a plumber to come and drill out root growth with an electric snake, but this is only a temporary expedient. The only sure solution is to excavate the present pipe and replace it with cast iron. This is a big job, but a homeowner can do it himself if he doesn't want to hire a plumber. Section 1.40 tells you how to install cast-iron pipe.

1.15 | How a toilet tank works. Once you understand how a toilet tank operates, you can easily make repairs and adjustments when needed.

When a toilet is flushed, the handle or push button on the tank raises the flush ball, or the small plastic bucket in the tank. (See Figs. 1-9 and 1-10.) Water then rushes into the toilet bowl through

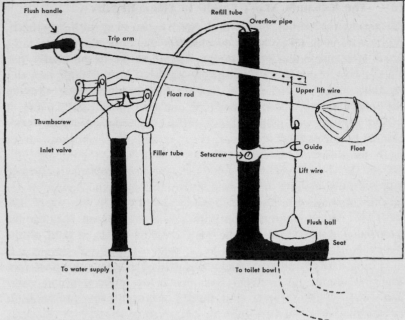

Figure 1-9   Conventional flush tank

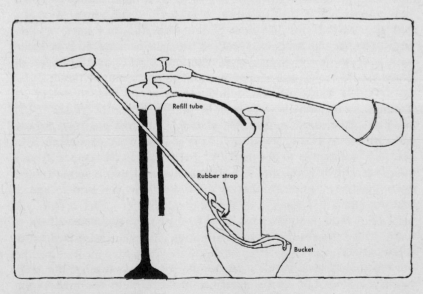

Figure 1-10   Simplified modern flush tank

13

the hole at the bottom of the tank, flushing away waste in the bowl. As the water level in the tank lowers, the tank float (the large floating ball near the top of tank) drops and opens the inlet valve. This allows water from the supply pipe below the tank to enter the tank through the filler tube. At the same time, water goes through the refill tube into the overflow pipe and into toilet bowl to refill it to the proper level. (Bowl is not refilled to proper level by water coming in through flush ball seat, because the ball—or bucket—drops back into position and closes outlet when the tank is empty.)

As the water level in the tank rises the float rises to the surface and in doing so shuts off the inlet valve and stops the flow of water into the tank and into the toilet bowl.

1.16 | If a toilet runs continuously after the tank is filled, the inlet valve is not closed all the way, or it leaks. Take hold of the rod holding the tank float and raise it gently. If the water stops running, adjust the float to this new position by bending the float rod. The tank should fill to about one inch below the top of the overflow pipe. If the water level is higher or lower you can correct it by adjusting float position up or down as required.

If altering the float position does not correct the situation, the float itself probably needs to be replaced. (The float should be about half submerged; if it is more so, it is probably leaking.) Hold the rod in one hand and turn float counterclockwise to remove. If you hear a sound like water sloshing as you shake it, or if it is badly worn, replace it with a new one. The new type of plastic float will not rust or corrode, and should last a lifetime.

1.17 | If water still runs when you raise the float to its highest position (above which water would run down the overflow pipe), flush the toilet a few times while watching how the float arm moves the inlet valve. This is at the top of the pipe to which the water supply pipe is fastened at the bottom of the tank. (See Figs. 1-9 and 1-10.) You will notice how the inlet valve and the arm that moves it up and down can be removed for inspection by removing (*a*) a clip, or (*b*) a few screws, or (*c*) some cotter-type pins. (This will also remove the tank float.) At the base of the valve you will see a washer (Fig. 1-11). It may be held on the end of the stem by a brass screw or a threaded brass ring cap, or it may just snap in. Remove the old one and replace it with a new washer of the same kind. If screws or rings are worn or corroded, replace these as well. There is usually a second washer that fits into the side of the valve. In some models

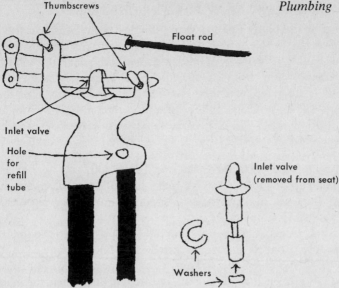

Figure 1-11 Repairing a tank valve

the washer is split; in others, the valve comes apart so you can replace the washer. Be sure you replace it with one exactly like the old one.

If the valve itself appears badly worn, take it down to your hardware dealer and ask about getting a new one. He will frequently recommend that you replace the whole ball-cock assembly. This is good advice. The ball-cock assembly is the float, its arm, the inlet valve, the supply pipe, its washers, and the nut that fastens the whole works through the bottom of the tank to the water supply pipe. A new ball-cock assembly can be installed in minutes, will not leak, and will fill the tank quickly and quietly.

1.18 | **If water runs but tank does not fill,** or if you must jiggle the handle a few times before the tank begins filling, the ball or bucket (Figs. 1-9 and 1-10) is not seating itself properly after flushing. Usually bending or straightening the lift wire on the flush ball, or adjusting the strap or chain holding the ball or bucket (Fig. 1-10), will solve the problem.

In some tanks you will find an adjustable guide that positions the drop of the flush ball. If adjustment is needed, a setscrew can be loosened and the guide moved back and forth until the ball seats properly. The setscrew is then fastened again.

If you cannot properly seat the ball and stop water running by adjusting the guide, inspect the ball and seat. To remove the ball, hold it in one hand and unscrew the lift wire. (If wire is stuck, use pliers.) Clean the seat with steel wool or emery cloth—it should be smooth.

If the ball is in bad shape, replace it with a new one. If the lift wire is badly bent or corroded, replace it. Replacements for lifts, guides, and balls are available in standard sizes at your hardware store.

If adjustments like these do not do the job, you should get one of a number of foolproof flush-ball assemblies now on the market. These units are easily installed. Your plumbing supply dealer or hardware store supplies them.

1.19 | **If flush handle must be held down** to keep the toilet flushing, the flush ball is not being lifted high enough when the handle is tripped. Straighten the linkage wire connecting lift wire and trip arm, then rebend it so flush ball is lifted higher when the handle is turned. This prevents the flush ball from dropping into its seat until tank is completely empty. There's a possibility that the flush ball may leak and be full of water—if so, you'll have to replace the ball.

Another possibility is that the toilet handle is not functioning properly. If it is stuck, the linkage and lift wire cannot return to their normal "closed" position. Jiggle the handle to make sure it is working freely. If not, lubricate the bushing that holds the handle in the tank, or replace the handle. If the handle is loose, hold it in one hand and gently tighten the nut inside.

1.20 | **If there is a leak under a toilet tank,** you need some new rubber washers or gaskets. In tanks that are set on the back of the toilet there are four holes in the bottom: one for water supply, one for letting water into the toilet, and two for the bolts that hold the tank to the toilet.

Locate the leak, turn off the water, and empty the tank by flushing and sponging. First disconnect the water supply nut. Then disassemble as much more of the tank as you have to to get at the faulty washer, and replace it with one of the same shape and dimension.

In tanks that are fastened to the wall and use an elbow bend from tank to toilet, your job is easier. There are only two holes: one at the water supply pipe, the other at the elbow bend. Locate the leak, turn off the water, empty the tank, unfasten the faulty connection with a wrench, and replace the bad washer.

1.21 | **If toilet tank sweats**, you can insulate it. In hot, humid weather all toilet tanks sweat; cold water in the tank condenses water out of the mositure-laden air onto the outside of the tank. An insulating liner will cut down, or may eliminate, sweat. To install such a liner, shut off the water supply, drain the tank, and dry the inside thoroughly. Apply flexible batts of foam synthetic waterproof insulation with waterproof adhesive. You can get these materials at your hardware store. Or you can use a small electric thermostatic immersion heater. These units are designed to hang over the edge of the tank and to bring the water just to room temperature.

FAUCETS

1.22 | **How to repair a leaking faucet.** A dripping faucet is annoying and wastes a lot of water, and the trouble is almost always a worn-out washer down inside the faucet. These are not difficult to replace, but the first time you attempt a repair it will take longer than it will the next time, when you have had some experience. With old faucets it's a good idea to allow time to make an unanticipated trip to the hardware store for replacement parts after you've started work; so avoid making routine repairs when household use of water is likely to be heavy—and try not to choose a time when your hardware store will be closed.

Before repairing the faucet, turn off the water. (See Sec. 1.2.) To save time, assemble tools and equipment before beginning the job. You will need a wrench, screwdriver and pliers, and a supply of faucet washers and screws. (You can buy an assortment of these for about 25 cents.)

Lay a thick pad of newspapers or rags in the basin to prevent possible porcelain damage from dropped tools. This will also keep washers and screws from falling down the drain. Wrap the faucet with tape or cloth so the chrome will not be scratched—tools can damage it easily.

No matter how complicated or concealed its parts may appear, any faucet can be taken apart. Screws that hold the handle in place are often hidden under screw-in or snap-in caps that can be pried off with a screwdriver. Screw-in caps have knurled collars easily grasped with pliers for removal. (See Fig. 1-12.) After removing the handle screw, if handle sticks tightly tap it with a block of wood and rock it back and forth with your hands to free it of serrations

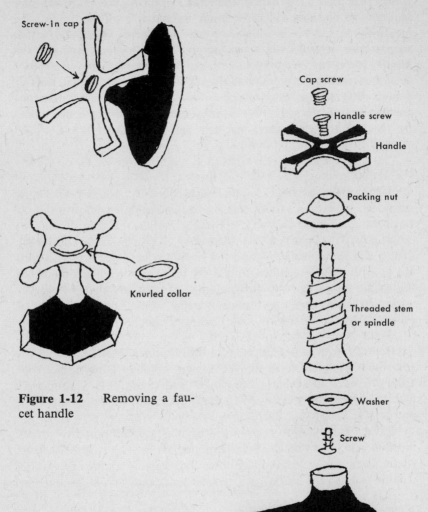

Screw-in cap

Cap screw

Handle screw

Handle

Packing nut

Threaded stem
or spindle

Knurled collar

Washer

Screw

Figure 1-12   Removing a faucet handle

Figure 1-13   Parts of a faucet

on the spindle. Then loosen and remove the packing nut, then the stem. (Fig. 1-13.) When dismantling a faucet, lay out each part in order so you can put them back in the right sequence.

In some faucets it isn't necessary to remove the handle from the spindle to replace a washer. Loosen the packing nut and the handle and stem assembly can be easily removed if you turn it as if you were turning on the water. In repairing shower or bathtub faucets that are recessed into the wall, it may be difficult to reach the packing nut. This is often below the surface of the tile so it can't be reached with the usual wrench. You can get a special socket wrench at the hardware store.

To replace the faulty washer at the bottom of the stem, remove the screw holding it in place. If it is stuck, try applying a drop of kerosene or rust solvent (Liquid Wrench). If the slot is worn or becomes so while you are attempting to remove it, a new slot can be cut with a hacksaw. (See Fig. 1-14.)

Handle a corroded screw with care, or the head may break off. If this should happen, cut away the washer with a sharp knife, or dig it out with a sharp-pointed tool if necessary, and remove the screw with pliers. If every method fails, take the handle assembly with you to the hardware store and ask for help in removing the screw. (It will pay you to make an ally of your hardware dealer.)

If the washer screw has fallen out of the spindle inside the faucet, you can get it out after the spindle has been removed by turning on the water briefly. Hold a rag around the opening to keep the water from spilling over. Always replace worn screws with new ones when you replace a washer. Use only brass screws, never steel. Place the washer on the stem with the rounded side down, or out. Then reassemble the faucet in reverse order from the way you took it apart. Be sure you use the same size and shape of washer—replacing a flat

Figure 1-14 Cutting new slot in washer screw with hacksaw

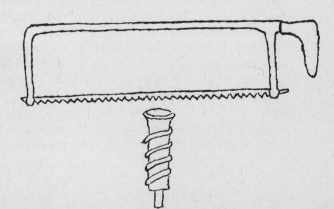

washer with a crowned washer may make the faucet "sing" or be noisy.

The first time you reassemble a faucet it may be difficult to screw on the spindle and packing nut. Don't panic, just persevere. Tighten the packing nut just enough to prevent leakage around the stem—no tighter. If faucet is stiff in turning after you have re-assembled it, loosen the packing nut a bit or put a few drops of oil around the stem.

If you have no new washers and must make a repair, you may be able to reverse the old washer. Or you may make a temporary washer from a piece of leather, rubber, or sheet packing. Leather is better for cold faucets, rubber for hot.

There are new, improved types of washers that require no screws, but merely snap into the spindle hole. These are longer lasting than ordinary washers. To install, simply follow the manufacturer's directions to the letter.

Some new faucets, such as the Moen single-lever faucet, have a new type of dripless valve containing no washers. These are virtually trouble-free. If difficulties do arise, use a nail or small screwdriver to remove holding clip at the rear. (See Fig. 1-15.) You can purchase complete replacement works for about two dollars.

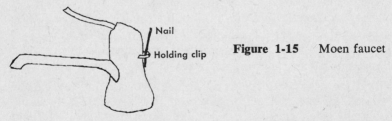

Figure 1-15   Moen faucet

1.23 | If you've replaced washer, and faucet still drips—or if you find it necessary to replace washers at frequent intervals—the seat is defective. The seat is the base inside the faucet body, on which th washer rests when the water is turned off. You can purchase a seat dresser for less than a dollar at the hardware store. To use it, slip faucet-packing nut over the tool's shaft, place tool in faucet, and tighten packing nut on faucet body. Tighten it until the tool's cutter bears down on the faucet seat. As you turn the handle, the cutter grinds down the seat.

If you prefer, you can replace the existing seat with a new snap-in seat, if you are using snap-in washers. A gauge supplied with the washers is used to measure the seat hole. The largest possible section of the gauge that you can insert and turn is the seat size you need. Position the snap-in seat over the seat hole, using a pencil or small stick as a guide. Using a hammer or other blunt-ended tool, press the seat into the hole. If the extra thickness of the seat creates a need for additional height, spacer washers can be placed under the packing nut.

Or, on some faucets you can replace the existing spindle, seat, and valve assembly with a whole new insert. This provides a trouble-free seat and reduces chatter or water hammer if this is a problem. In addition, it eliminates the need of further washer replacement. Ask your hardware dealer about this.

1.24 | **If water leaks around the stem** when you turn on the water, the packing nut probably needs to be tightened. (See Fig. 1-13.) Use a wrench, first protecting the chrome with tape so it doesn't get scratched. If tightening the nut doesn't do the job, remove faucet handle (Sec. 1.22) and packing nut. Inside the packing nut you will find packing (a composition material) or a rubber packing washer—or both. Remove it (if it is stuck dig it out with a screwdriver or awl) and replace it with new packing and/or washers.

Packing and packing washers come in many different varieties and shapes. So, to get the right one for your faucet, it is best to take the old washer and/or packing, the packing nut, and faucet spindle with you to the hardware store. (A temporary repair can sometimes be made by wrapping string around the stem just inside the packing nut, wrapping it in the same direction as the handle turns when you are shutting it off.)

Insert the new packing and/or washer and carefully replace the packing nut on the spindle. Do not twist packing or washer, as the teeth on the spindle may damage it. Tighten the packing nut until the packing and/or washer compresses snugly against the stem.

Some newer faucets have plastic sealing rings, or O-rings, instead of packing. Pry the ring out of its groove and replace it with another of the same size. Sometimes you can merely turn the ring over instead of replacing it.

If a faucet is sticky, the packing nut may be too tight. Loosen it slightly with a wrench, protecting the chrome with tape or cloth to avoid scratching. If this doesn't do the job, try applying a few drops of oil around the stem at the top of the packing nut.

1.25 | **How to repair a sink spray.** If the spray on your kitchen sink does not discharge sufficient water when you press the thumb-control button, the aerator may be clogged. Unscrew it from the end of the faucet. (See Fig. 1-16.) Take it apart and clean all the

Figure 1-16   Swing spout and aerator

screens thoroughly with a toothbrush. Flush the parts out well and reassemble. A clogged aerator will alter pressure inside the faucet and keep the diverter valve (this is what sends water into the spray) from operating. (See Fig. 1-17.)

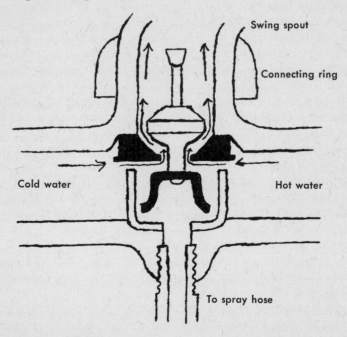

Figure 1-17   Diverter valve

When spray thumb lever is "off," water flows out of swing spout as shown. When lever is "on," water flows out of spray hose—pressure pulls plunger down, cutting off supply to swing spout.

If the aerator is not to blame, another possibility is the spray nozzle. Unscrew it and clean out holes with a brush or toothpick. The single-hole type rarely becomes clogged. A spray that is worn, corroded, or damaged can be replaced with a new one, available through your hardware store, for slightly over two dollars. There are two types of automatic sprays. The most common type sprays only clear water; the de luxe type contains a supply of concentrated detergent, so it sprays either clear water or suds. It is equipped with a nylon brush and is the next best thing to an electric dishwasher. You can replace either type of spray interchangeably.

If nozzle repairs are needed and you can't get the job done locally, you can mail the assembly to the manufacturer for repair. If you do so, you must cap the hose so the faucet can be used during repair. The easiest way to do this is to place a cap-type pencil eraser over the end of the hose and tape it in place.

A kinked hose will also prevent the spray from operating. If hose is broken or otherwise damaged, it must be replaced with a new one of exactly the same size. Occasionally a new hose guide is needed to keep the hose out of the way of drain pipes, disposers, wiring, and so on. If the hose leaves black marks on the sink, it should be replaced. If one type of spray has been attached to a hose design for another kind, the pressure may cause the hose to burst. But hoses now on the market will meet any pressure requirements and they are not expensive.

If aerator, nozzle, and hose are all in good condition but spray does not work properly, remove the faucet's swing spout by unscrewing the connecting ring or nut. (Fig. 1-17.) Lift out the diverter valve by its stem from the faucet body. (In a few models, a bushing must be first removed from the opening.) With diverter valve out and aerator off end of spout (if there is an aerator), replace spout and turn on hot and cold water to wash out any dirt or sludge. Rinse diverter valve thoroughly. Again remove the swing spout and replace the diverter valve. In most cases, the proper position is with the pluck-out stem up.

Finally, you must replace the swing spout in its proper position. This must be done exactly right, or the diverter valve won't function properly. Grasp the base of the spout with one hand and press down as you turn it back and forth with the other hand. Continue rotating while you tighten the connecting ring or nut with your fingers. Make sure spout is in the proper position before tightening with a wrench.

It's extremely unlikely that you will have any difficulty after carrying out these suggestions, but if you should, it is necessary to get a replacement diverter valve. There are several different types of these. Most plumbing supply houses stock all of them.

1.26 | If the shower head has a weak or faulty spray, it needs to be cleaned thoroughly. Examine the shower head and you will see how the spray diverter can be unscrewed from the head, the head from the ball joint, and the ball joint from the water pipe coming out of the wall. (Some shower heads have fewer parts than this.) Turn off the hot and cold water, and take apart all of the shower-head assembly, cleaning each piece thoroughly. Punch the holes (if it's the sieve-type head) clean with a toothpick. Use an old toothbrush and cleansing powder to clean the inside of the shower head.

HOT WATER

1.27 | If there's never enough hot water, the problem is almost always due to one or more of the following conditions:

1. Scale—or mineral deposits—in the tank and the hot-water lines. If your water is hard (has many minerals in it) and either your hot-water tank or hot-water pipes are galvanized steel, then scale can build up over a period of time to clog the outlets in either the tank or the pipes. If your hot water is colored slightly, then you have scale. The only permanent solution to this problem is to replace a galvanized tank with a "glass-lined" hot-water tank (ask your plumbing supply house about this type) and galvanized hot-water pipes with copper pipes. If you're ambitious and your hot-water lines are all exposed on the basement ceiling where you can see them, you can do this job yourself if you learn how to work with copper pipe. (See Sec. 1.39.) If the lines are hidden and the job is complex you should let a plumber do the job.

2. If there's plenty of clear water coming out of the faucet but it isn't hot, the thermostatic controls on your hot-water tank may be set too low, or they are not working. If your hot water is heated by gas, oil, or electricity, either directly or by a coil running from your hot-water tank to the furnace or boiler, have your utility or oil company send someone to adjust your thermostat. (In most cases, they will do so without charge.) Thermostat settings on hot water should never be set above 140° Fahrenheit, or someone may get

scalded. If the thermostat is not to blame, you may have a faulty gas or oil burner, or a broken electric heating element. Your utility man can tell you if this is the case and what it will cost to fix. Let him do it, because this is a tricky job.

3. If readjusting the temperature settings doesn't do the job, you probably have a heater that's too small for your family needs. For four people a 35- to 40-gallon tank should be adequate. Add 5-gallons capacity for each additional person in the house. Look at the number plate on your water heater—the rated capacity is on it and if it's too small, you need a larger tank.

4. If you have hot water produced by a coil in your boiler (only true in hot-water-heated houses), it may be that there is a lot of sludge in your coil. You can "back-flush" this coil by reversing the flow of water and opening a drain valve to wash out the coil. If you can't tell which valve to open and close to do this—just by examining the piping around your boiler—ask your fuel dealer, or get a plumber to come and show you how to do the job. You can also back-flush an ordinary gas or electric automatic hot-water heater in much the same way. Attach a hose to the drain cock at the bottom of the tank to take the sludge to a floor drain or out of doors.

5. The tank may be leaking. (See Sec. 1.31.)

1.28 | **If hot water has flecks or is dirty, or won't suds,** but you are getting enough of it, you simply need some water softening equipment on your cold-water supply to filter out the minerals or other foreign material. Look in your yellow pages for a water softening service, and have them come and inspect your water. They'll do this without charge, and they will install softening equipment at a very reasonable price if you give them a contract to service the equipment. You can rent this equipment from them, but it's cheaper in the long run to purchase it. Water softeners have to be cleaned and re-charged periodically. You can install softening equipment yourself if you follow the manufacturer's directions to the letter, and if you are pretty good at plumbing.

1.29 | **If hot-water faucets belch steam, or are noisy,** (1) the thermostat on your water heater is not functioning properly or is set too high, or (2) your pressure-relief valve is not working, or you don't have one. First get your utility man or your fuel dealer to check your thermostat—see Section 1.27. Then have him check your pressure-temperature-relief valve, which is on one of the pipes coming out of your hot-water tank. (See Fig. 1-18.) If you don't have

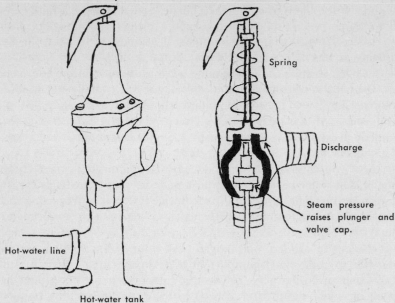

Figure 1-18   Pressure-relief valve

a valve on your tank, get one and install it, or have it installed as shown. Hot-water tanks without pressure-relief valves have been known to blow up and injure people seriously.

If hot-water pipes and faucets are still noisy after checking the thermostat and relief valve, see Section 1.42.

1.30 | **If hot water runs from your cold-water faucets,** there is so much pressure in your hot-water tank that it is forcing hot water back into the cold-water supply line. If your pressure-relief valve is working properly, this condition cannot occur. (See Sec. 1.29.)

1.31 | **If your hot-water tank leaks,** replace it with a "glass-lined" tank. Leaks are due to corrosion and old age (or sometimes irreparable damage) and the tank will never be the same again. Ask your plumbing supply house or your utility man about getting a corrosion-proof tank (ceramic-lined, glass-lined, Monel metal, or copper). As a general rule, don't install a galvanized tank, although there are certain areas in the United States where they may be used successfully.

PIPES

1.32 | How to thaw frozen pipes. If a pipe freezes, start all de-frosting at faucet (no matter where actual freezing begins), leaving faucet open so steam can escape.

Do not use a propane torch, unless you are experienced in such matters. Ordinary household implements will do the job just as well, and more safely. An electric iron is perhaps the most effective. Lash it to the pipe at the faucet end of the frozen section, moving it gradually away as thawing progresses. With copper or brass pipe, the heat will travel at least ten feet. Be sure heat does not touch any of the woodwork. A soldering iron can be used in the same manner if there is not room for the flatiron, but it isn't as effective.

Or you can purchase an inexpensive heating cable, wrap it around the frozen pipe, and plug it in. (The cable can also be used in roof gutters to prevent their becoming plugged with ice.) The thawing process may take hours, so don't be impatient.

If pipe is concealed, you can get at it with a portable hair dryer or a heat lamp. However, when using a heat lamp make sure you keep it far enough from the wall to prevent scorching. If you are using it to thaw an exposed pipe, a piece of sheet metal or aluminum foil behind the pipe to reflect heat will make it more effective.

If you must thaw a frozen pipe without the use of any electrical device, you can use boiling water. Wrap several feet of the pipe with heavy rags and pour boiling water over it. When the pipe thaws, there may be leaks which will have to be repaired. (See Sec. 1.37.)

If the drain is frozen, pour a pound of salt and a quart of boiling water into the drain and give it half an hour to thaw. If this doesn't do the trick, use an ordinary drain cleaner like Sani-Flush. If it is necessary to thaw waste pipes by direct heat, start at the lower end of the pipe so water can run off to sewer or septic tank as it thaws.

1.33 | How to keep pipes from freezing. Water pipes that pass through unheated garages, crawl spaces, or attics should be insulated with felt or insulating tape (Fig. 1-19) wrapped around the pipe (ask your hardware dealer), or with molded pipe coverings of cork, magnesia, or asbestos (ask your plumbing supply house). If necessary, thermostatically controlled heating cables can be wrapped around the pipe and kept plugged in during cold weather. They are available in electrical supply and hardware stores. In an emergency,

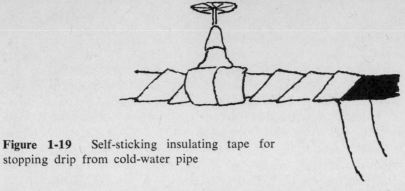

Figure 1-19   Self-sticking insulating tape for stopping drip from cold-water pipe

when a cold snap threatens an undrained plumbing system, you can wrap pipes with layers of newspapers.

If you have seldom-used faucets in unheated rooms, drain them during the winter months. This goes for outside faucets as well. Shut off water at the nearest shutoff valve, which usually has a small plug that can be unscrewed to drain the valve too. (See Sec. 1.2 and Fig. 1-28.) Then open the faucet and drain the pipe—and leave it empty until the weather warms up.

1.34 | **How to drain a plumbing system.** If you are leaving a house or cottage unoccupied during the winter months, or even for a few days during freezing weather when heat may be shut off, you must completely drain the plumbing system to prevent breaks and costly repairs. Shut off the water at the meter and open all faucets, draining branch lines to the level of lowest fixtures. You can drain pipes below the lowest fixtures by opening a valve at the meter. If there is no valve there, there is frequently a union joint that can be opened to drain the lines. In houses on wells, shut off the water on the well side of the pressure tank (Sec. 1.2), and drain the pressure tank through its drain valve. Drain the water-heater tank the same way. (If you don't have a floor drain handy for this water, connect a garden hose to the valve and run the water outside.)

If you have fixtures and lines below the level of the water meter, ask your hardware dealer about a suction pump that you can put on faucets to suck the lines dry.

Flush toilets and sponge out toilet tanks, then pour a quart of kerosene (*not* gasoline) down all sinks, tubs, basins, and toilets (two quarts each) to replace the water sitting in these traps. Drain the washing-machine pump by unscrewing the pumping housing on the bottom of the pump. (See Sec. 3.16.)

If you have a hot-water-heating system, drain it by opening all

28

valves in the system (including the air vents on each radiator or baseboard), and then the drain cock on the boiler. Your fuel supplier can show you where this is if you don't know.

When you turn on the water in the house after the winter, connect opened unions at the meter, shut basement valves, and turn on the water. Turn it on slowly just in case you have left something open.

1.35 | If chronic low water pressure is a problem. If you are on city water, and if your water lines in the house are galvanized, this is almost always due to clogged or corroded pipes. City water supplies almost invariably have enough pressure coming into your house, and the only thing that could slow it up would be pipes that are full of scale. (A temporary drop in pressure is usually caused by a sudden overtaxing of water facilities somewhere outside the house.) If hot-water pressure is lower than cold-water pressure, clogging is almost certainly the cause, because hot water produces scale much faster than cold water. The only solution is to replace your galvanized lines, especially the hot-water lines, with copper tubing. (Putting in a water softener—Sec. 1.28—will prevent additional scale from forming, but it will not bring pressure back up.)

Flexible copper tubing is a very good replacement here because it is flexible enough to be snaked through walls and around corners, eliminating the necessity of soldered connections at every single turn. (See Sec. 1.39.) Old water lines can simply be left in the walls where they are and new tubing run alongside.

If you are on a well, water pressure may often drop way down in dry weather when the water table in the ground drops. At these times your pump may lose its priming, causing the pressure to drop off sharply because the pump is simply sucking air. When this happens turn the pump off and don't use any water for a half-day or so, until the water table around the foot of the well has had a chance to build up again. The best solution to this problem is to go on city water; the second-best solution is to have a professional well-digger come and advise you about digging the well deeper. Both solutions cost money. (If your well pump is not working, see Sec. 1.49.) In some dry areas, pressure in local supply mains sometimes drops off in summer months, but you can remedy this by having a professional put in a pump and pressure tank, just as if you were on a well. Ask your water department about this first, however.

1.36 | If pipes sweat, they need to be insulated with insulating tape or molded material. (See Sec. 1.33.) Water in a pipe that's much colder than the air outside the pipe will make moisture in the air condense in drops on the pipe surface. Don't insulate the pipe until the humidity is low and the pipe dry. (If the insulation gets wet, it may be ineffective.) Your hardware dealer may have a number of suggestions, since new products are constantly being developed for doing the best job of insulating pipes. Figure 1-19 shows one type of insulation.

1.37 | **If you have a leak in a pipe or a fitting,** shut off the water at your meter or pressure tank (Sec. 1.2). Then open the nearest outlet to drain the pipe.

If the leak is small, one of the newest and best ways to seal it is to use a two-part epoxy adhesive that will dry at room temperature. This comes in two tubes; an equal amount is squeezed from each of the tubes, mixed, and applied with a stick to the lead. (Be sure leak is dry.) Glue patch will set fast if you hold an electric iron near it— not touching it—to heat up the pipe and glue. Otherwise you may have to leave the water off for the better part of a day.

Sometimes a leak at a compresson-type fitting in copper lines, at junction of toilet tank and water supply, or at a trap joint, can be corrected by placing a few turns of string around the tubing and tightening the nut on it. When it gets wet the string will expand and seal the leak. If a copper pipe springs a leak at a joint, you may be able to tap old solder around the joint back into the crack with a hammer and small chisel. Heating the joint slightly will help.

Holes in small pipes, and corrosion and cracks in any size pipe, are best repaired with pipe clamps. First cut a gasket of rubber or leather (or flexible plastic if you're not repairing a hot-water pipe) large enough to cover the break. Or you can purchase metal pieces for use as gaskets at the hardware store. Coat both pipe and gasket with iron cement. If pipe is cracked, push iron cement into the crack. Then fit the clamp around pipe and gasket, and tighten the bolts. (Fig. 1-20.)

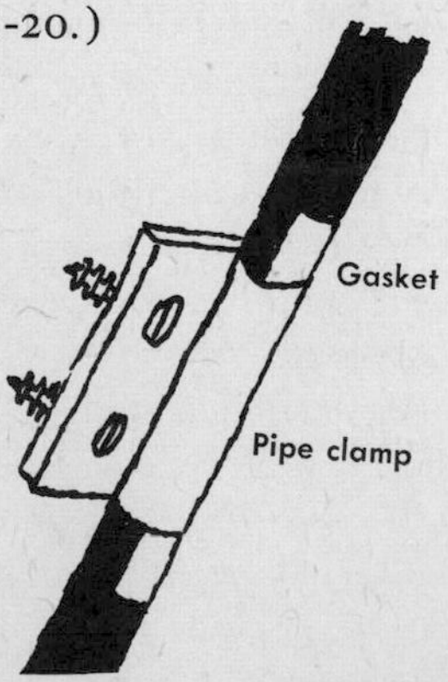

Gasket

Pipe clamp

Figure 1-20   Pipe clamp in use

If the crack is very long, you may have to use two or more clamps spaced an inch or two apart over the gaskets.

Temporary repairs can sometimes be made by wrapping the pipe with electrician's tape (the heavy black kind) or by tying pieces of rubber inner tube around the pipe with string.

If you have brass pipe, you may get leaks at the threads in a joint. The only solution is to open the pipe joint (which may mean opening a whole string of joints to get at the one you want), and then wrap cotton string and pipe-joint compound in the threads before remaking the joint. It's even better to replace the brass pipe with copper tubing. (See Sec. 1-39.)

1.38 | **If a pipe breaks,** turn off the water and drain the line. You can make temporary repairs in ¾-inch or ½-inch-diameter water lines by cutting out a section around the break with a hacksaw and using 1-inch automobile hose with pipe clamps for the ¾-inch line, or garden hose with clamps for the ½-inch line. If your break is in ½-inch waste line from basin, tub, or sink, make a permanent repair by using flexible plastic waste line with pipe clamps to replace the broken section. (Cut it out with a hacksaw. See Sec. 1.40.)

To make a permanent repair to a broken water line, you can solder in a new length of copper (if your waste lines are copper) with couplings. (See next section, 1-39.) If the break is in a short, threaded length, cut through the pipe with a hacksaw, unscrew the cut lengths from their fittings, and replace with two threaded lengths and a union. (See Fig. 1-21.) If you have brass pipe, replace it with copper and don't overtighten threads in the brass fittings. They may break.

Figure 1-21 Replacing broken section of pipe

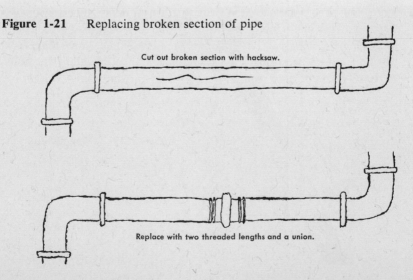

Cut out broken section with hacksaw.

Replace with two threaded lengths and a union.

If your break is inside a wall or inaccessible under a floor, cut out the whole section at the nearest accessible fittings. Remove the fittings and with new fittings bypass the broken section with flexible copper tube worked down through the wall. (It may be necessary to remove a section of the wall to reach fittings that you can work with.)

1.39 | How to install copper pipe. Installing new pipe requires a building permit in most cases, especially in new additions. (See Introduction.)

Copper is the best and easiest pipe to work with. It doesn't corrode, and it will last through the life of the house. The basic technique in copper is soldering: copper pipe is soldered into copper fittings. Figure 1-22 shows you the basic way in which soldering, or "sweating," as the plumbers call it, is done. First you cut the tube or rigid copper pipe (these are the two types of copper pipe used) to the correct length with a hacksaw, cutting squarely across the pipe. The correct length is the distance between fittings, plus the combined depths the pipe can fit into each fitting. Figure 1-23 shows you the various fittings.

With a small file, file off burrs on both the inner and outer sawed edge of the pipe. With emery cloth or steel wool burnish the end of the pipe bright and do the same to the inside of the fitting. Apply paste flux (it's like a salve) to the inside of fitting and to burnished end of pipe. Slide the pipe into fitting. Light up torch and apply to joint. Let the transparent area of the flame between the blue inner

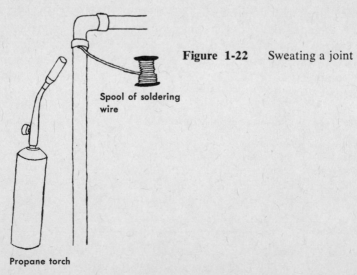

Figure 1-22   Sweating a joint

Spool of soldering wire

Propane torch

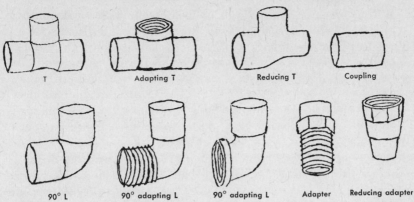

T   Adapting T   Reducing T   Coupling

90° L   90° adapting L   90° adapting L   Adapter   Reducing adapter

Figure 1-23   Sweat fittings

cone and the yellow outer cone concentrate on the joint to be soldered. It may take a minute or two to heat up the join, and the flux will boil before pipe is hot enough. Apply the end of your spool of solid wire solder (without a flux core) to part of the joint where the flame isn't concentrated. When the joint is hot enough, the solder will melt on contact with the joint and be sucked into the joint until you can see a ring of silver all around the joint. Withdraw flame and solder, let cool, and the job is done. You can solder anything from ⅜-inch tube to 3-inch copper waste this way. Practice will improve your skill.

At faucets and drain connections to fixtures, you will use copper fittings threaded at the fixture end for connecting with a wrench, and with "sweat" openings on the other end to connect with copper pipe.

Because copper is so soft and workable, it is possible to work it with compression or flare fitting to eliminate the need for using a torch and "sweating" joints. Figure 1-24 shows you the tools and

Figure 1-24   Flaring and flare fittings

1. With compression nut on copper tube, flaring tool is applied to tube end.

2. Fitting is placed in flared end of tube.

3. Compression nut is screwed into place.

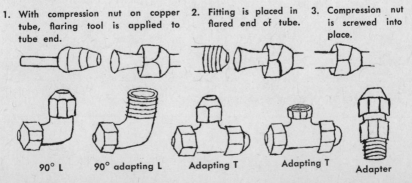

90° L   90° adapting L   Adapting T   Adapting T   Adapter

fittings you use for compression joining. It is not as satisfactory as soldering, because fittings are more expensive and the danger of leakage is much greater.

1.40 | Installing iron, galvanized, and plastic waste and vent pipes. Plastic waste lines, now acceptable in most places, are the easiest to work with. Whatever kind of pipe you use, you will need a building permit. (See Introduction, "The law and your house.")

There are two basic types of plastic pipe: solvent-weld types and pipe-clamp types. In the solvent-weld type, a length of plastic waste or vent is cut with a hacksaw to the length between plastic fittings— plus the depth into both fittings that pipe will go. Then a solvent—a chemical supplied with the pipe and fittings—is wiped on that end of the pipe and the inside of the fitting, and the two are shoved together. (See Fig. 1-25.) In a matter of minutes the joint is fast and the job finished. Other plastic pipes do not react to a solvent and they are used with pipe clamps which cinch down the end of the pipe around the fitting shoved into the pipe. Both types of plastic pipes can be joined to threaded pipe or fittings with adapters.

Galvanized waste and vent installations call for the tools shown in Figure 1-26. These are rather expensive tools and you should not

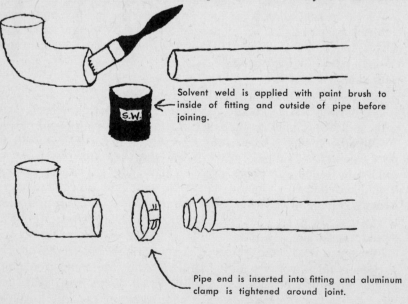

Solvent weld is applied with paint brush to inside of fitting and outside of pipe before joining.

Pipe end is inserted into fitting and aluminum clamp is tightened around joint.

Figure 1-25   Two methods of joining plastic pipe

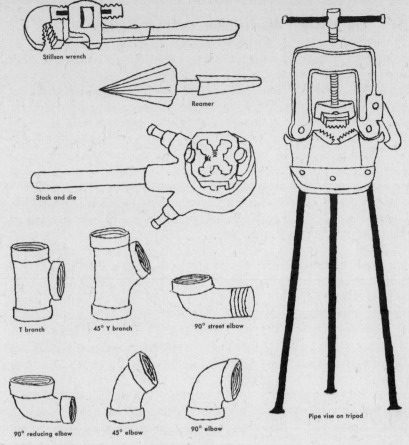

Figure 1-26 Tools and fittings for galvanized pipe

attempt this work unless you have a lot of it to do, and are already a good mechanic and do-it-yourselfer. Galvanized fittings, elbows, tees, and so forth come threaded, but you must cut pipe to the proper length and thread it, in the pipe vise, with pipe stock and dies. Lengths of pipe in galvanized pipe are the distances between face of fittings plus ⅝ to ⅞ inch on either end for the depth that pipe will thread into fitting.

Cast iron waste and vent work is also difficult and should not be attempted unless you are pretty handy already. Most cast iron pipe lengths are five feet. When you need pieces shorter than that, get pipe with a hub, or bell, on each end, so when you cut it you'll have two usable pieces. Figure 1-27 shows the materials you need.

35

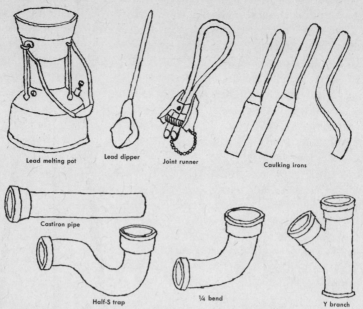

Lead melting pot   Lead dipper   Joint runner   Caulking irons

Cast iron pipe

Half-S trap   ¼ bend   Y branch

Figure 1-27   Tools and fittings for cast iron pipe

To cut service-weight cast iron, score it all around with a hacksaw and tap with hammer until it breaks evenly. Heavy-weight cast iron is first scored with a file, then chiseled around the score with a cold chisel until it breaks.

Cast iron is joined by caulking. A narrow end of cast iron is set into a hub, or bell; then oakum (a fibrous rope of caulking material) is caulked down in the joint with a chisel. Then lead is melted and poured all around the joint. When the lead is cool it is packed tightly into the joint with inside and outside caulking irons (they look like big chisels). For horizontal joints, you must wrap an asbestos joint runner (Fig. 1-27) around the joints to keep molten lead from running out of the joint.

1.41 | **Replacing worn and faulty valves.** In older houses, piping troubles may be concentrated at shutoff valves because they catch and hold sediment and scale in the pipes. Frequently, old valves will not hold—they will leak all the time when shut off. In an old house, even if you don't have a valve problem it is always best to put in new valves when replacing sections of corroded water lines.

When replacing valves, first make a sketch of your water line with all measurements and pipe diameters indicated. From the sketch you'll be able to figure out exactly what parts, and which ones "sweated" or threaded, you'll need. (See Figs. 1-23, 1-24, 1-25.)

If you are simply replacing a valve, cut through the line almost at the valve (after shutting off the water) with a hacksaw, unscrew the valve with the stub of pipe left in it, and screw on the new valve—using a little pipe compound. Then screw in a coupling threaded on one end and "sweated" on the other. Trim the end of the cut pipe to fit into the "sweated" end of the coupling so you can solder the joint. (See Sec. 1-39.)

For infrequently-used shutoff valves, it's best to use gate valves. (See Fig. 1-28.) Gate valves are used where you need a full flow of water—when they are open, the opening is the same size as the pipe. Don't use gate valves where you have to turn them on and off frequently, because they close by wedging metal against metal and will wear out and leak rather quickly.

Where you need a valve that will be turned on and off all the time, use a globe valve. They close on a washer, like a faucet (Sec. 1.22),

Figure 1-28 Valves

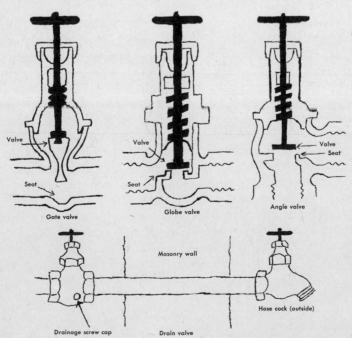

Valve

Seat

Gate valve

Valve

Seat

Globe valve

Valve
Seat

Angle valve

Masonry wall

Drainage screw cap

Drain valve

Hose cock (outside)

and washers can be replaced easily, or the seat ground down for a better fit if necessary. Their disadvantage is that they don't allow a full flow of water.

Where you need a valve on a water line going vertically through the house, use an angle globe valve to eliminate an elbow where a horizontal pipe changes direction to vertical.

For a shutoff valve on an outdoor water connection, use a drainage valve. This permits complete draining of the outdoor section of the pipe so it won't freeze. You simply unscrew the drain cap on the valve to drain it, after opening up the outdoor faucet. Make sure the drainage side is toward the outside of the house.

1-42 | If all your pipes are too noisy. If you hear a thump in a pipe after turning off a faucet, this is caused by "water hammer." In well-designed, up-to-date plumbing systems, water hammer is prevented by air chambers—a 2- or 3-foot extension of the pipe above the top faucet—in each supply line. (Fig. 1-29.) This chamber acts as a cushion to absorb the momentum of the water when the faucet is turned off. If your plumbing system has air chambers and you still have water hammer, the chambers are probably water-logged and need to be drained. If the chamber is above faucet level,

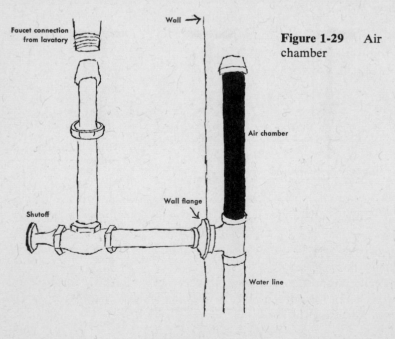

Faucet connection from lavatory

Wall →

Figure 1-29   Air chamber

Air chamber

Wall flange

Shutoff

Water line

shut off the water supply and open the faucets. This will usually drain the chambers.

If you don't have air chambers, you can either open up the walls and install them, or you can install them on lines in the basement. Instead of a short length of pipe for an air chamber, you can use a plastic "water hammer shock absorber." (Ask your plumbing supply dealer about this.)

Another type of pipe noise, usually heard when the faucets are turned on, is a banging of the pipes themselves. This is due to insufficient support at some point along the pipe. Pipes should be solidly anchored with pipe hangers or wood blocks at frequent intervals and where the pipe changes direction. (See Fig. 1-30.) If a pipe sags out of line, water rushing through it sets up vibrations which make it rattle.

Figure 1-30   Pipe strapping and blocking

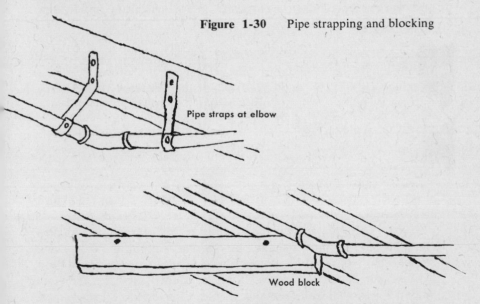

Pipe straps at elbow

Wood block

Whistling, humming pipes are usually too small for the load they carry—or they may be badly clogged with scale. You can muffle some of this type of sound with pipe insulation, but the pipes should actually be replaced.

Chattering in the pipe when a faucet is partly open is caused by a worn faucet washer or the looseness of some other part in the faucet. (See Sec. 1.22.)

If your hot water faucets and pipes make a lot of noise and belch steam, your water is getting too hot and the pressure in your hot-water tank is too high. To correct either condition, see Section 1.29.

PLUMBING ALTERATIONS

1.43 | How to add a new faucet on a pipe. You can easily and quickly install a new faucet for a washing machine or a hose if you have a pipe in a convenient location. You need a wrench and a drill with a ¼-inch bit, and a saddle-type faucet (from the hardware store) that fits over ½-inch or ¾-inch galvanized pipe or copper tubing.

Select a convenient position for the faucet and lightly sandpaper pipe to remove rust and dirt. Take bolts off the strap and slip the unit over the pipe. Pull straps together, insert bolts again, and tighten. (Fig. 1-31.)

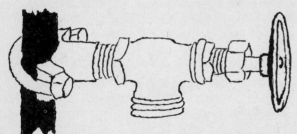

Figure 1-31   A bolted-on faucet

After shutting off the water supply, drill a ¼-inch hole, following directions supplied by the manufacturer. Insert faucet and turn on the water.

1.44 | Installing a new sink spray in a bathroom or kitchen (they are very useful for shampooing or for washing the baby) can be done fairly easily if: (*a*) your present faucets are mounted in a plastic-covered counter like a Formica counter, or (*b*) they are mounted in the flat surface of sink or basin 6 inches to 8 inches apart —from center of faucet to center of faucet. (See Fig. 1-32.) If your present faucets are mounted in one piece like this, it's very likely that there is an attachment for a spray connection on the underside of the unit. Simply turn off the water, unscrew the cap on the spray connection with a wrench, and screw on the spray hose. (You can buy a spray hose and head at almost any big hardware store or plumbing supply house, or from a mail-order house.) If there is no

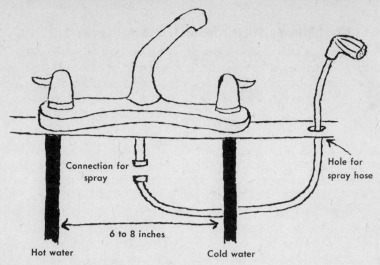

Connection for
spray

Hole for
spray hose

6 to 8 inches

Hot water

Cold water

Figure 1-32   Sink spray connections

counter alongside the sink or basin through which you can drill a
hole to mount the spray head, you can build a shelf beside the basin
with a hole or yoke in it to hold the spray head. Mount the shelf on
brackets glued to the wall with a two-part epoxy adhesive.

If your present faucets do not have provisions for spray, but
are 6 to 8 inches apart, you can replace them with a new faucet unit
with faucets the same distance apart, but with spray provisions. To
connect new faucets, see Sections 1.39 and 1.41.

If your faucets are mounted in a plastic-surfaced wood top, it
makes no difference how far apart they are—you can drill new holes
to accommodate the new faucet. Of course, if you have to do this you
will have to do some repiping below the sink or basin to bring
the water lines up to the right spot. (See Sec. 1.39.) Don't attempt this unless you have had some practice in installing water
lines.

1.45 | Installing a shower head over a tub. The easiest way to
do this is to buy a rig like the one shown in Figure 1-33*a*. These are
fastened to the wall with toggle bolts or expansion screws (see Sec.
6.7) and the hose fastened to the spout by clamping the belled
rubber end of the hose to the faucet mouth. The tub must have a
single spout for both hot and cold for these units. If there are two
faucets 4 inches apart from center to center, you can sometimes get a
unit like that shown in Figure 1-33*b*. Faucets must be removed to
install this unit, which remains exposed outside the wall. The dis-

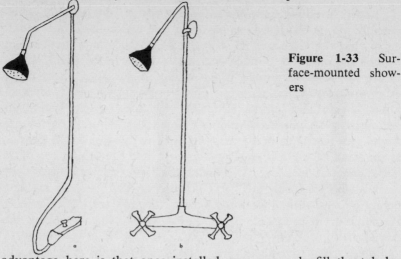

Figure 1-33 Surface-mounted showers

advantage here is that once installed, you can only fill the tub by turning on the shower.

The only other method is to open up the wall behind the tub where the faucets are and do some repiping. Don't attempt this unless you're pretty good at piping. You'll need a shower-type bathtub faucet, a few elbows, a tee, some ½-inch pipe, and a shower head. (See Sec. 1.39.) Most bathtub faucets require water lines to be brought up back of the faucets 6 inches apart, but some newer types bring the water lines together right behind the single control valve on the unit. (Ask your dealer about these various faucets.) Pipe to the shower head runs from the faucet, back of the wall, up to the head, which should be mounted on a board set into the wall. (See Fig. 1-34.) When you've tested out the lines, close up the wall. (See Sec. 6.4.)

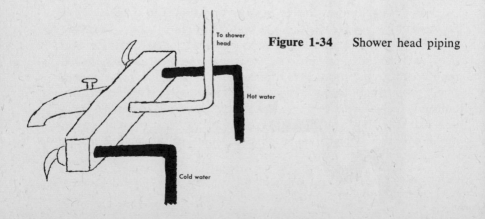

To shower head

Figure 1-34   Shower head piping

Hot water

Cold water

1.46 | Installing new plumbing fixtures. If your bathtub is impossibly old or disfigured, or has claw feet and collects dirt underneath, you can replace it. You may have to make new connections for hot and cold water, drain, and the overflow to the drain. Check to see where your present drain is placed and then check these exact positions against the same positions in a new tub. (Manufacturers furnish this information with their tubs.) Most have their drains from 14 to 16 inches from the wall framing (face of the studs) along the side and from 7 to 9 inches from the wall framing at the head of the tub under the faucets, and the top of the drain is just about at floor level. Drain and overflow connections may have to be rebuilt for a new tub. (See Fig. 1-35.) You'll need a building permit for this work. (See Introduction, "The law and your house.") If your old tub had no overflow, install an overflow pipe from the new drain up to the overflow opening in the new tub. (See Secs. 1.39 and 1.40.) If plastic waste connections are permitted in your town, the easiest way to replumb the drain connection is with plastic. If you have to bring a new drain line in over floor joists, you may want to set the tub on a low platform built of wood to prevent cutting into the joists.

Figure 1-35   Tub drain and positioning

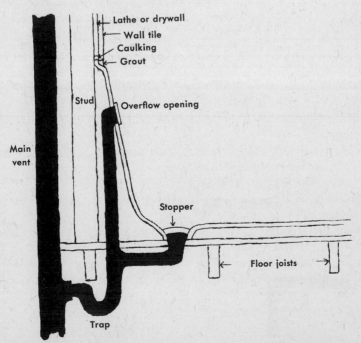

Don't attempt to install a tub until you are sure of every step you'll have to take to install it, and if you haven't had some experience in plumbing, better get a plumber to do the job. When old tub is removed (first unscrew the drain in the tub) be sure tub space is clear and lower walls cut back to studs so flanges of tub can fit against studs. Subfloor must be firm and level so tub cannot rock away from the wall and leave a crack between tub and wall. (See Fig. 1-35.) Most tubs are built to fit against three walls in the end of a 5-foot-wide bathroom. These tubs have one exposed side or apron. If the tub must fit in a corner of a room wider than 6 feet, be sure you get one with an apron, or exposed side, on two sides. If the room is just over 5 feet or 6 feet wide (there are some 6-foot-long tubs), you may want to box in one end of the tub and use a three-wall tub. Follow the manufacturer's instructions carefully in installing the tub.

When the tub is in place, connect the drain and then plaster or patch the wall (Sec. 6.4) down to within ¼ inch of the tub flange. Caulk the remaining distance with putty. Then retile the wall between tile and tub with a strong joint grout or bathtub caulking (buy it at the hardware store).

Before replacing an old basin with a new one, try to get a new one that can be used with the existing positions of hot and cold water supply to the basin. Otherwise you'll have to do some realigning of pipes. If you do have to replumb supply lines, see Section 1.39.

If your old basin was on a pedestal or supported by legs, you can replace it with a wall-hung or counter-style basin. Wall-hung basins are supported by hangers attached, through the plaster, to studs in the wall or to a board recessed into the studs at the right height. (You may already have a hanger there that you can use.)

Basin heights vary from 29 to 36 inches, but 30 inches is the most common.

Counter-style basins are usualy purchased as units already built, with a base cabinet supporting basin and the counter it is set in. They add a lot more storage space to any bathroom.

Basin drain connections are illustrated in Figure 1-36. Water lines are shown in Figure 1-29.

When toilets are cracked or disfigured, or the style is hopelessly old-fashioned, you might as well replace them. Sections 1.11 and 1.12 tell how to remove and reinstall a toilet. Just make sure that your existing waste connection in the floor will meet minimum clear-

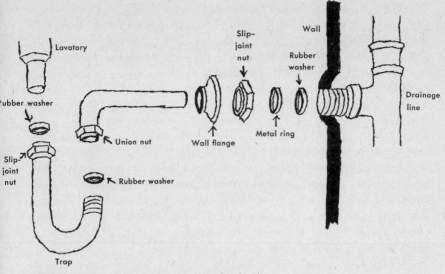

Figure 1-36   Waste connections for basin

ance dimensions from the walls on your new toilet, and that the cold-water supply line to the toilet can reach or be replumbed to reach the new toilet tank.

1.47 | Installing a new dishwasher. A dishwasher should be installed under the counter, and to the left of the sink for the most convenient use by a right-handed person. Reason: You hold a dish with your left hand while scraping it off under the sink faucet; you then put it into the dishrack in the washer with your left hand—no changing of the dish from hand to hand.

If you have no available base cabinet space under a counter near the sink, you can use a model that comes with a counter piece already attached to the top. Simply install this unit as near as you can to the left of the sink.

If you have some base cabinet space under a counter to the left of the sink, take this over for your dishwasher. The dishwasher simply slides into a 24-inch-wide space, and base cabinets or paneling close it in on either side.

To hook up the unit you'll need a 115-volt outlet. This is the same voltage that most outlets in your house have. If you don't have an outlet handy you can install one (Sec. 2.11) or have one installed by an electrician. Then you'll need a hot-water line coming up beside the unit (check manufacturer's directions for the proper positioning) to tie in the hot-water supply—usually with a union. See Section 1.39 for details of installation of lines. You can bring a new hot-water line in to the dishwasher from the line to the sink, or if you have one at a convenient location in the basement, from there straight up through the floor.

You'll need a drain line, 1½-inch size, from the unit to the main waste line. If plastic pipe is allowed in your area—check with your local building department—it's the easiest to use. Otherwise, use copper. Most units have a built-in pump to pump water out after washing and rinsing. If yours has such a pump you can connect the drain of the dishwasher by running a line over to the sink drain, tying into this line with a tee between sink trap and the wall. (See Sec. 1.40.) If your unit will have no pump, but is a gravity drain, you will have to run drain lines down to the waste line in the basement. (This is often the easiest thing to do.)

If you want a basic understanding of how a dishwasher works to help you in installing it, see Section 3.14.

1.48 | What to do if your lawn seeps sewage. This usually means that your tile fields, where the water from your septic tank leaches out through the earth, are clogged with root growth, or the soil immediately around the tile lines has become saturated with solids from the sewage, or the septic tank is full and needs to be pumped out. (See Fig. 1-37.) The first thing to do is to take a look in your tank, if you can easily. If you can't, call up a septic tank service (look in the yellow pages) and they'll inspect your tank for you, and tell you if it needs cleaning. If it doesn't, open up one of

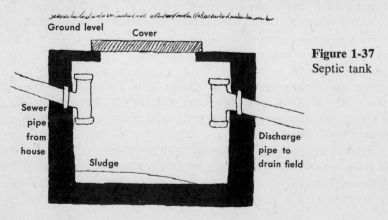

Ground level

Cover

Figure 1-37
Septic tank

Sewer pipe from house

Discharge pipe to drain field

Sludge

the lines in your tile field, right where the lawn is oozing, by digging it open with a shovel. If there is no root growth clogging the line, remove a section of it and inspect the soil immediately under it. If the soil is saturated, it will look muddy and there will be no air space through which water could leach down into the ground. (Tile fields should always be laid in gravel beds.) If the soil looks saturated, you will have to lay a new field, or have an expert lay it for you, placing each line of tile at least ten feet from old lines.

Sometimes tile fields overflow because a truck driven over the field has broken the lines. If this has happened, you will have to rebuild the broken parts of your field, and then stake out the field so it doesn't happen again.

If root growth is clogging the tile field, the best thing to do is to install a new field with pipe that inhibits root growth. Or you can use a chemical, added through the outlet from the septic tank, to kill roots in the field. Ask your plumbing supply dealer about this. (See Fig. 1-38.)

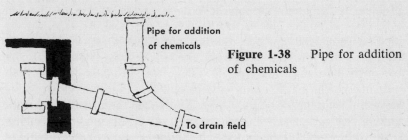

Pipe for addition of chemicals

Figure 1-38 Pipe for addition of chemicals

To drain field

A septic tank, as a rule, should be pumped out regularly every three years or so, as a precautionary measure. This must be done by a professional septic tank cleaner. You can find one by looking in the yellow pages.

Other signs of an over-full septic tank are gas or bubbles on the ground near tank or drainfields, or over vigorous growth of grass or plants above drainfields.

If you notice any of these signs, take immediate action by calling in a septic tank cleaner. After cleaning, the tank is treated with a chemical that reduces solids to liquids.

You may find, if your family has increased or you have added more bathrooms, that your septic tank is inadequate to take care of your needs. (If you add a bathroom, you may be required by local building codes to increase the size of your septic tank.)

Roughly speaking, a tank might be figured to hold about 75 gallons per person per day. For a family of four, capacity should thus be 300 gallons; but since a tank is filled only to the level of the discharge pipe, a tank for a a family of four must hold a minimum of 500 gallons. To be on the safe side, you should have the next larger size.

1.49 | Repairing well pumps. There are three basic types of well pumps. A "shallow well" pump is used on wells where the water comes within 15 feet of ground level. This type of pump has a piston —like the plunger on a hand insect-sprayer—right at the pump that sucks the water out of the well. About the only thing that goes wrong with this pump is that it loses its priming, due to low water. It's easily primed, either by pouring water through the priming valve on the inlet pipe or by shutting off the pump (and the use of water) for a few hours to let groundwater filter into the well again. Then when you start it up again the pump will draw water into the inlet pipe and prime itself. If the pump loses its priming frequently, your problem is the foot valve at the bottom of the inlet pipe. To test this, disconnect the pipe from the pump and pour water down the pipe. It should fill up, because the foot valve when working right will let water into the pipe from the bottom, but won't let water out of the bottom of the pipe. If water runs out of the pipe and the pipe doesn't fill up, you will have to pull up the pipe and check the valve for jamming. If you can't get any water through the pipe, it's probably clogged and will have to be removed to be cleaned with a snake, or replaced. If the motor on the pump doesn't work, you should call in a professional repair man to check it. (Never examine any electrical connections on the motor without first shutting off the power.)

A "deep well" pump runs on the same principle, but the piston is not at the pump—it's located deep in the well inside a pump pipe casing. The motor at the head of the well runs a crankshaft that extends all the way down to the piston. If this pump loses its priming, shut off the motor and the use of water for a while; then pour water in the priming valve at the top of the inlet pipe. If the water does not fill the pipe, the foot valve (see above) is not working right and should be inspected for jamming, clogging of the filter screen, or other damage. You have to pull all the pump works and the crankshaft out of the well to get a look at the foot valve, and this is hard work, so don't attempt it unless you are thoroughly confident of your ability to fix it. Occasionally, the belt and drive connections between motor and the head of the crankshaft need adjusting to make the piston work right.

A jet pump is the third type of well pump. This has no piston, but uses a rotor, or impeller, located right at the motor. The rotor drives a stream of water through a plastic pipe down into the well. At the bottom, this stream does a U-turn at a special intake valve and comes shooting back up another plastic pipe. Water is pulled into the intake valve by the stream of water from the wellhead, so more water goes up than comes back down. If something goes wrong with a jet pump it's easy enough to pull up the plastic pipes, but it isn't easy to tell what is wrong with the valve unless there's an obvious obstruction or a clogged filter. If the motor and rotor won't work, it's best to call in a professional repair man, unless the problem is an obvious one, like a broken piping or electrical connections.

2 ELECTRICITY

2.1 | How electricity works in your house. Figure 2-1 shows the basic way you use electricity. The current comes to the light bulb—or the appliance—along the black, or "hot," wire. After the current runs through the light bulb, lighting it up, it returns to ground along the white, or "ground," wire. For electricity to work, it must have a continuous path to the ground.

Current, or electricity, always takes the path of least resistance, which is usually along the white wire. But when you shorten the path, or make it easier for current to flow somewhere else, you have a "short circuit." If you get a shock, you have shortened the path of least resistance by making your body the path. For instance (don't actually try it): If you are wearing sneakers and standing on a dry floor, touching nothing else with any part of your body, you can grab the bare end of a hot, or live, black wire and nothing will hap-

Figure 2-1   How electricity works

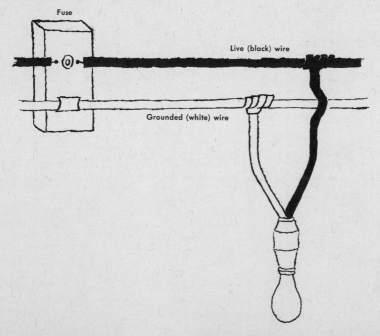

pen. But if the floor and your shoes are wet, you'll get a shock of current going through you to the ground. In the first case, the rubber-soled sneakers will not conduct electricity to the ground—the rubber is an insulator. In the second case, the water around the insulator (the rubber sole) will conduct electricity to the ground.

To protect everyone in your household, particularly children, from electrical shocks, develop safe electrical habits. Never leave lamps without bulbs plugged into the wall. Keep plastic plug-in covers in unused wall outlets.

The power or utility company supplies your house with a lot of current that is divided at the fuse panel, or circuit breaker panel, into a number of circuits, or pairs of black and white wires, that go out through the house in cables to supply current to lights and appliances. Occasionally, a cable will also have a red wire in it. This is sometimes a "hot" wire for another circuit, sometimes a switching-wire for a three-way switch. (See Sec. 2.13.)

Never attempt repairs to the wiring system in your house without first pulling the fuse or throwing off the main switch (at the fuse panel). (See Fig. 2-2.) If you unscrew and remove the face plate from a baseboard outlet, you can see back in the box the black and white wires attached to the outlet. Don't touch these unless you've pulled the fuse or thrown the circuit breaker

Figure 2-2   Entrance panel

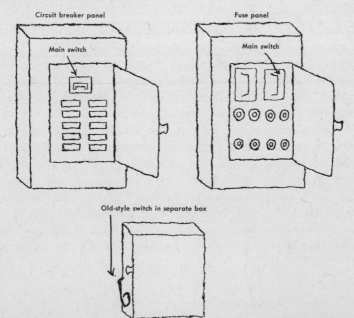

The fuse or circuit breaker is simply a device that makes sure not too much current goes through the black wires to lights and appliances. If too much current should get into the black wire it might heat up, melt the insulation around it, and cause a short circuit, perhaps a fire.

2.2 | What to do if an appliance or light won't work. Obviously, if the appliance or the light won't work on any outlet, it needs to be repaired. (See Secs. 2.5 through 2.7 and Chap. 3.)

Usually, though, if an appliance or light won't work, a fuse has blown or a circuit breaker has tripped because there are too many appliances on the same circuit. (If you know what lights and appliances are on the circuit—see next section—you can quickly tell if the fuse is blown by testing out the other lights and appliances.) Go to your panel and examine it. If a circuit breaker (it looks almost like a light switch) has tripped, it will be in an "off" position— clearly out of line with the toggle switches on all the other breakers. If you have fuses, the little window in a blown fuse will either be all black and burned—unlike the windows in the other fuses—or by looking into the fuse you'll see that the strip of wire or fusible metal that runs across the face of the fuse has broken or melted away. (The advantage of a circuit breaker over a fuse is simply that you don't have to replace it when too many appliances on one circuit throw the breaker. If a fuse is blown, you have to put in a new one. When a circuit breaker trips, you just unplug one of the appliances and flip it back on.)

If you want the convenience of circuit breakers without changing your entire electric service panel, you can buy a new type of screw-in circuit breaker that will replace your fuse in the old fuse panel. When a circuit is overloaded, a little button pops up out of the center of the screw-in circuit breaker, or mini-breaker. Just push this little button in to get your circuit back in working order.

When replacing a fuse, be sure you have one of the same size— usually 10, 15, or 20 amperes (an ampere is a measure of the amount of electric current)—to replace it. You'll see the amp number on the face of the fuse. Throw the main switch at the side of the panel before unscrewing the fuse. If you can't do this for some reason, very carefully unscrew the old fuse with just the tips of your fingers touching the top edges or face of the fuse. Screw the new fuse in just as carefully, touching nothing else in the panel box.

Don't plug the appliance that blew the fuse back in without first removing some of the other appliances from the circuit. (If it is still overloaded, it will just blow the fuse again.) If you're sure the circuit is *not* overloaded (see Sec. 2.3) and the appliance blows a fuse again anyway, you have a short in it somewhere—even if you looked before and found nothing. If the appliance won't work at all (but did before the fuse blew), you had a short that burned out a connection. In either case, see Section 2.5.

If an appliance will work on some outlets but not on its own, and no fuse blew, it may be that the outlet is faulty. (See Sec. 2.8.) Or if the nonworking outlet is a switched outlet, the switch may be to blame. You probably can't tell by looking if a switch is faulty, but if everything else seems all right, get a new switch and install it as in Section 2.8.

2.3 | How many things you can have on one circuit. To find out which lights, appliances, and receptacles (plug-in outlets) are on what circuit is more or less a matter of making a simple test and tabulating the results on a rough floor plan of the house. Get a plug-in bulb socket at your hardware store (this lets you plug a bulb into a receptacle) or an extension cord with a bulb socket on the end of it. Then remove one fuse or throw one circuit breaker. Now go through the whole house turning on lights, plugging in your light bulb in every open receptacle, and trying all the appliances. Every outlet, light, and appliance that doesn't work is on the circuit whose fuse you've pulled. Make a list of that circuit's load. Then go back, replace that fuse and pull the next one, and repeat the process. When you're through you'll know what each circuit carries.

You can figure out the total load on each circuit by adding up the watts indicated for each item in the table below. Each circuit can carry as many watts as its volts multiplied by its amps. All general purpose circuits are 120 volts—so you multiply this number by the amp number on the fuse. A 15-amp fuse can control 1,800 watts; a 20-amp fuse, 2,400.

When you add up watts, there's no point in adding a toaster's wattage and an iron's wattage on a kitchen circuit, because in most households the two appliances are never on at the same time. Just figure the maximum wattage that could be used all at once on each circuit. If you have some overloaded circuits, the only simple solution is to move some appliances and lights to another circuit. If all your circuits are overloaded, you will have to get an electrical contractor to install adequate wiring. (See next section.)

Here are the average wattages of major appliances. These are almost always on separate circuits—one for each appliance—so the circuits seldom give trouble unless the appliances themselves are shorted.

	watts
Automatic washer	700
Built-in bathroom heater	1,000–1,500
Dishwasher-waste disposer	1,500
Waste disposer (alone)	500
Dishwasher (alone)	500
Electric clothes dryer	4,500
High-speed electric clothes dryer	9,000
Electric range	8,000–16,000
Electric water heater	2,000–4,000
Electric water heater (quick-recovery type)	up to 9,000
Home freezer	350
Motor for fuel-fired heating plant	800
Room air conditioner—3,000 B.t.u.'s	750
Room air conditioner—9,000 B.t.u.'s	1,200
Water pump	700

(Obviously, some of these appliances require too much wattage to be supplied by a 120-volt circuit. A separate heavy-duty, 220-volt circuit is required for each dryer, range, and so forth.)

Here are typical wattages of lights and small appliances:

	watts
Ceiling or wall light (each bulb)	40–150
Floor lamp	150–300
Fluorescent tube	15–40
Ultra-violet lamp	385

(Check individual light bulbs for exact wattages.)

Baker (portable)	800–1,000
Bottle warmer	95
Broiler-rotisserie	1,320–1,650
Clock	2
Coffee-maker or percolator	440–1,000
Corn popper	1,350

	watts
Deep-fat fryer	1,350
Electric blanket	200
Electric fan (portable)	100
Electric roaster	1,650
Food blender	230–250
Hair dryer	250–400
Hand iron (steam or dry)	1,000
Heating pad	60
Ice-cream freezer	115
Ironer	1,650
Knife sharpener	100
Mixer	100
Portable heater	1,000
Radio	100
Record changer	75
Refrigerator	150
Sandwich grill	660–800
Sewing machine	75
Shaver	12
Skillet	1,100
Television set	300
Toaster (modern automatic)	up to 1,150
Vacuum cleaner	125
Ventilating fan (built-in)	140
Waffle iron	up to 1,100
Waxer-polisher	350

2.4 | How to tell if your house is inadequately wired. The first signs of inadequate wiring are the signs of poor performance. You have inadequate wiring if any of the following things happen all the time:

- Lights dim or flicker when appliances go on
- Appliances are slow to start
- Fuses blow or circuit breakers trip too often

- Radio fades or is scratchy when appliances go on
- Television picture shrinks
- Outlets and switches are few and far between
- Extension cords are in common use

Even if these things don't happen to you now, they may happen when you add more appliances and more people to your household. It's simple to check your electrical service entry to find out whether your wiring is adequate for any eventuality. You should have 100-amp service for today's use of electricity.

Check the main switch and fuse or breaker at your panel in the basement. The outside service from the telephone pole comes through this switch or breaker to supply the house. (See Fig. 2-2.) Close examination of the main switch fuses or breakers (but don't touch them) will show you what size your service entrance is. Two fuses, each marked 60 amps, means your service is 60 amps—not 120 amps. There are two simply to serve two rows of breakers or fuses—each main fuse feeds a "bus" bar that supplies a row of fuses.

If you decide to have an electrician look over your wiring system, have him look at the wiring itself as well as the service panel. If you change the service you may have to change some of the old wiring too. If you don't want to do this, you'll have to make sure fuses or breakers are sized right in the new service panel so they don't overload old circuits. Ask your electrician for his recommendations.

2.5 | Simple repairs to cords and plugs. If a plug slips out of a receptacle, bend the prongs out slightly—away from each other—to make the plug stay in place in the outlet.

If a lamp cord breaks, pull out plug, then cut off the frayed ends and remove about 2 inches of the outer sheath or braid. Then cut the ends of the wires so they are staggered. (See Fig. 2-3.) Strip the insulation from the end ¾ inch of each wire. (Use a paring knife and cut all around the insulation down to the wire, but don't cut the wire itself. Then simply pull off the insulation.) Now twist wires together as shown in Figure 2-3, and wrap with black electrician's tape. The plastic kind is better than "friction tape." (Get it at the hardware store.) Put a few turns of tape around each splice as shown, then around both wires together.

If any cord is frayed, tape the wires separately with electrician's tape, then tape them together. Cords frequently get frayed at plugs. Figure 2-4 shows you how to rewire plugs and cords. On the business end of conventional plugs you'll see two screws, called terminal screws. Unscrew these and remove the frayed cord from the plug. Then cut the cord (with wire-cutting pliers) right behind the frayed parts. Stick the wire back in the plug from underneath, then remove

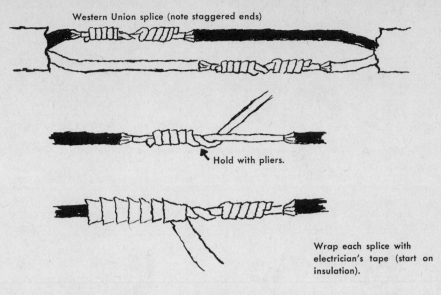

Western Union splice (note staggered ends)

Hold with pliers.

Wrap each splice with electrician's tape (start on insulation).

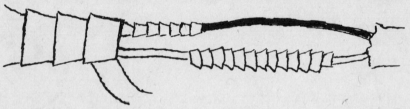

Then wrap both splices together.

Figure 2-3   Western Union splice

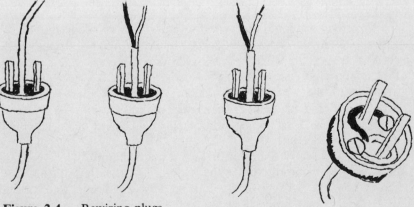

Figure 2-4   Rewiring plugs

about 1½ inches of the outer sheath or braid. Strip about half an inch of insulation from the end of each wire, and wrap the bare ends around the terminal screws. Then tighten the terminal screws. Be sure wires are only bare at the terminal screws—they must be insulated in the rest of the plug.

For cords that get a lot of rough wear, an "underwriter's knot" (Fig. 2-5) in the two insulated wires will keep them in the plug. After you have tied the knot you can strip the insulation from the free ends of the wires.

Figure 2-5   Underwriter's knot

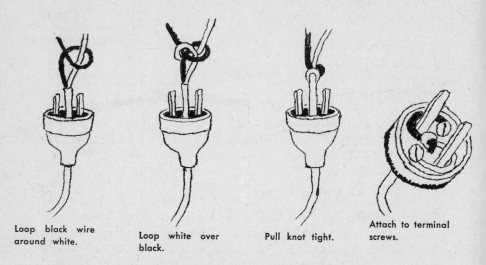

Loop black wire around white.

Loop white over black.

Pull knot tight.

Attach to terminal screws.

Your hardware dealer carries several kinds of plugs that work without terminal screws and don't require insulation stripping. A cord is simply cut clean and shoved into the plug, where prongs lock it into place, puncture the insulation, and make electrical connection with the wires. Have your hardware dealer show you these. They are often much handier than using the old plug.

Special problems in repairing appliance cords and plugs are discussed in Section 3.3.

2.6 | Making or fixing table and stand-up lamps. The electrical parts of a lamp are the bulb, the socket, and the cord. Figure 2-6 shows how the socket works. The cord is wired into the bottom of the socket and fastened to the two terminal screws in the same

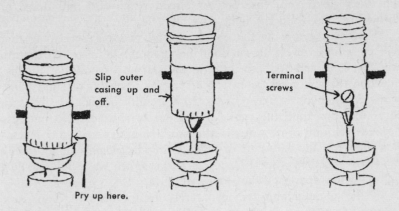

Figure 2-6   How a socket works

way it is fastened to a plug. Naturally, before attempting any repairs to a lamp, you must unplug it.

If a lamp won't go on and you've tested the bulb and the baseboard receptacle (by plugging another lamp into it) and found them both working, and the cord is in good condition, you have a bad socket that must be replaced. First, unplug it. Then carefully examine how the lamp is put together. Then disassemble it piece by piece, starting with the shade (usually held in place with a round nut at the top). Remove the socket and the socket seat (if there is one) which holds it to the lamp base. Take the socket apart by inserting the end of a small screwdriver into the flange of the base of the socket where it says "Press"; then slip the two parts of the socket apart. Slip the casing off the top part of the socket to get at the terminal screws that hold the wires. Remove the cord from the socket and wire it into a new socket just as it was wired into the old one. Take the old socket and seat to the hardware store if there is any question about the kind of replacement you need.

You can make any lamp a three-way lamp by replacing the old socket with a new three-way socket and using a three-way bulb. And you can convert vases, jugs, and other suitable bases into lamps by taking the base to the hardware store and asking your dealer to supply you with a socket, socket seat, and wire loop to support the shade.

2.7 | Installing a new fixture. If you want to replace an old ceiling fixture or wall-bracket lamp with a new one, the first thing to do is to turn off the power at the old fixture. Turn the light on and then go to your fuse box or circuit panel and pull fuses, or throw breakers, until the light goes off. (See Sec. 2.2.)

Now start removing the old fixture by undoing everything that will come unscrewed. It will soon be apparent how the old fixture was installed, and you can lower it away from its position. Finally, unfasten the splice of the two fixture wires to the black and white wires coiled back in the outlet box. Carefully unfold the wires in the outlet box until they are hanging out of the box. Do not fuss around with any other wires in the box. Do not remove any insulation. Unscrew the wire nuts or unwind the electrician's tape holding the wires together. (See Fig. 2-7.) If the splice was soldered, just pull the wires apart and the solder will give.

If the manufacturer provided directions for installing your new fixture, follow them carefully. Twist the white fixture wire and the two white wires in the box together, as in Figure 2-7. Then do the black wires the same way. Splice the fixture wires to the wires in the box with wire nuts. When you are ready to screw the new fixture into position, coil the wires and their splices back in the box, as in Figure 2-7.

If your outlet box does not have the right kind of metal bracket for fastening the new fixture, you can get one at the hardware store.

Figure 2-7   How to wire an outlet box

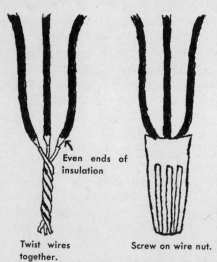

Twist wires
together.

Even ends of
insulation

Screw on wire nut.

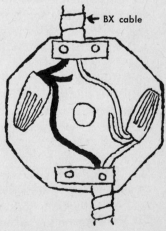

BX cable

Lay away splices to fit fixture outlet.

The bracket is usually a strip of metal with a threaded hole in the center to take a threaded connector on the new fixture. The bracket is fastened to the outlet box with screws at either end.

Fluorescent fixtures can be used in place of any incandescent fixture. If they require any special mounting, they will come with the necessary hardware, or your dealer can supply it.

2.8 | Replacing old switches and receptacles. Broken and non-functioning switches and receptacles should be replaced. They can be dangerous even when they no longer work.

Before attempting to replace a switch or receptacle, be sure the power is off. (Sec. 2.2.) If you can't locate the fuse or circuit breaker, pull the main switch and shut off all the power. (Obviously, you must be working in daylight.) Remove the cover plate, then the screws that hold the receptacle in the outlet box. Pull the receptacle (or switch) out of the box and disconnect the black and white wires. (Observe carefully how they are connected, so you can wire them back in exactly the same way.) If removing the wire is difficult, and there is plenty of it coiled in the outlet box, you can simply cut the wires free from the old receptacle with wire-cutting pliers. Then strip the insulation—about ¾ inch from the ends of wires—and fasten wires to the new receptacle or switch by coiling them around screw terminals and tightening screws.

(Many new switches and receptacles come with "pressure-lock" connections or terminals. In these, the wire is stripped of its insulation and simply shoved into the receptacle, where it is held fast. This is easier than fastening to a screw terminal. Ask your hardware dealer.)

When you are replacing a switch, be sure to check the number of wires that go into the switch. A switch may have two, three, or four wires connected to it, depending on whether it is a single pole, three-way or single pole with through splice for the ground wire. (See Sec. 2.13.) If you aren't sure, draw a diagram showing number and colors of wires, and take it to your hardware dealer so he can supply you with a suitable replacement.

2.9 | What to do if the doorbell doesn't work. First of all, check the button itself. Remove the screws holding the button to the door casing and then, while the bell wires are still connected to the back of the button mechanism, touch a screwdriver across the two terminals on the back. This shorts the button, or completes the circuit, and should cause the bell to ring. (Don't be afraid to hold the button when you do this—the bell has only a 12-volt current, which you can't feel.) If the bell rings, you merely need a new button. Take the old one to the hardware store and get a replacment.

If the bell won't ring when you connect the two wires with a screwdriver, check the connections at the transformer. (Before you do, turn off the power at the main switch, as this is 110-volt current.) The transformer is usualy mounted on or near the fuse panel. (See Fig. 2-8.) Tighten the terminal screws on the transformer and be sure the 110-volt connections to the transformer are tight. Check the fuse on the circuit that handles the doorbell transformer, too, to see if it has blown, or is seated too tightly in the fuse box. Check the length of the bell wire lines for breaks—a break is unlikely, but if it does occur, repair it as you would a lamp cord. (See Sec. 2.5.)

Figure 2-8   Doorbell button and transformer connections

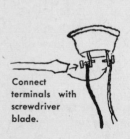

Connect terminals with screwdriver blade.

Doorbell button (dismounted but still connected)

Tighten terminal screws.

Doorbell transformer (mounted on fuse box)

If everything seems all right and the bell still won't work, you probably have transformer trouble. You can obtain a replacement— it must be just like the old one—at the hardware store. Shut off the power before you remove the old transformer, and take careful note of what steps you take—you'll merely reverse them in installing the new transformer.

In very old houses, doorbells often work off dry cells instead of transformers. You can test the dry cells with a small bulb in a lamp socket that has terminals you connect with copper wires to the dry cell terminals. If a dry cell doesn't make the bulb glow, it needs to be replaced.

2.10 | How to install surface-mounted outlet strips. Practically every kitchen, garage, and workshop could use more electric outlets. The easiest way to get them is to install a surface-mounted outlet strip that gives you a number of outlets where you had only one before. Outlet strips can be either plastic or steel. The steel kind is a raceway in which wires are placed. The steel back of the raceway is first fastened to the wall and then the wires, with outlets already attached, are placed in the raceway and the cover is snapped in place. Openings in the cover occur wherever there is an outlet on the wires. Plastic outlet strips come with the wires molded in the plastic strip, which is simply nailed to the wall or baseboard.

You can merely plug the outlet strip into an existing outlet, but if you are using the steel kind it is better to mount it permanently with a box extension that you can get at your electrical supply store. (See Fig. 2-9.) To do so, first shut off the power at the existing outlet. (See Sec. 2.2.) Remove the old receptacle and fasten the box

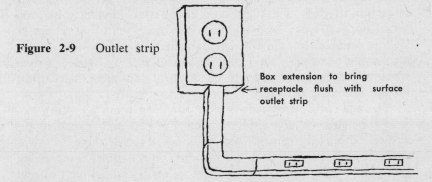

Figure 2-9   Outlet strip

Box extension to bring receptacle flush with surface outlet strip

extension to the wall. With your outlet strip in position, running right up to the box extension, reconnect the white wires to the receptacle—adding to the terminal screws the white wire from the outlet strip. Do the same with the black wires. Then fasten the receptacle to the box extension and put the cover plate on.

Surface-mounted outlet strips are also available with switches to be mounted on the wall.

2.11 | Installing a new outlet. You should get an electrical permit for this work. (See Introduction, "The law and your house.")

The easiest way to do the job is to use a small steel channel, called a raceway, like those used for the steel outlet strips described in the preceding section, that runs from an existing outlet to the new position. You can get them, with the wires and the surface-mounted outlet, from your electrical supply store or mail-order house. A box extension like that shown in Figure 2-9 is used on the existing outlet to connect your new wires to an existing circuit. The back of the raceway is fastened to the baseboard or the wall, the wires for the new outlet are placed in it, and the cover is snapped on. At the new outlet location, a backing plate is fastened to the wall, the new receptacle with the wires fastened to the terminal screws is mounted, and the cover plate is fastened in place.

If you want a new outlet built into the wall, the job is more difficult, but it can be done by anyone willing to take enough time and work carefully. You can get all the materials you'll need at your electrical supply or hardware store.

First of all, check the present wiring in your house. It represents, in almost all cases, what is acceptable to the local electrical code and your fire insurance company. If your present wiring is BX (armored) cable—see Figure 2-7—you should use BX for your new outlet box. If there is any question about what kind of cable you should use, call your local building department and ask. Types of cable in common use are BX, or armored, cable; thin-wall conduit; nonmetallic sheathed cable; and knob-and-tube (a wiring system where porcelain knobs support conductors, and tubes carry them through framing members.)

You must also specify the type of wire you want. Two-wire No. 14 is the most common for new lighting outlets and baseboard receptacles. It's easier to work with than No. 12, and thinner. "Two-wire" means there are only two conductors in the cable. Some wiring systems are "three-wire"—so that both 120-volt and 240-volt current can be drawn off the same cable (or so that three-way switches—Section 2.13—can be used), but these are not common. If you have three-wire circuits, you can still use a two-wire extension for your new outlet. Just use the black and white wires in your present cable to hook up your new outlet cable. (See below.)

Start work at a present outlet box or a junction box—a box where two or more cables are spliced together. First turn off the power by throwing the main switch (Sec. 2.2) or by pulling the fuse (or throwing the circuit breaker) on the circuit you're going to tap into. Then remove the cover plate and the receptacle from the box. Note that the black wire to your new outlet will be attached at the same point where the present black wires are attached. If it's a junction box, you'll splice the new black wires to those already spliced. If you mix up these connections and splice white to black, dangerous short circuits will result.

Now cut your cable to length, leaving about two feet to spare. Use a hacksaw on first one side, then the other, of the BX cable, being careful not to cut into the insulated wires, to remove an 8-inch length of the armor from each end for insertion into the box. Figures 2-7 and 2-10 show how to fasten the cable to the box and how to run it behind the baseboard. Remove the section of baseboard carefully by cutting it with a saber saw or keyhole saw—even better, remove it entirely along full length of wall. (You can't run cable horizontally through the wall itself because there's a stud every 16 inches. But by chopping a little plaster behind the baseboard, you can fit the cable in neatly.)

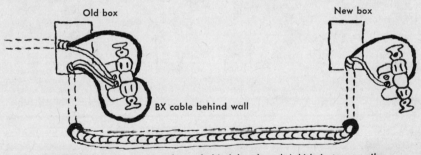

Old box   New box

BX cable behind wall

BX cable in groove in plaster behind baseboard (which is temporarily removed)

Figure 2-10   Running cable behind baseboard

If you are running your cable exposed along a cellar or attic ceiling, attach it to the framing with big wiring staples so it won't sag and get in the way.

If the cable must run from one floor to the next or from floor to ceiling, you can fish the cable up through a stud space in the wall. To do so you'll have to chop a few holes in the plaster so you can drop a string down to pull the wire up. Just bend the end of your wire around the string. Patch up the holes later, as in Section 6.4.

The easiest way to mount a new outlet, and the easiest outlet box to use, is shown in Figure 2-11. There are a number of different boxes and brackets on the market. The secret in using any of them is to cut the hole in your wall to exact size, so the metal clips you insert with the box can pull against the back of the wall—while the

Figure 2-11   Setting a box in the wall

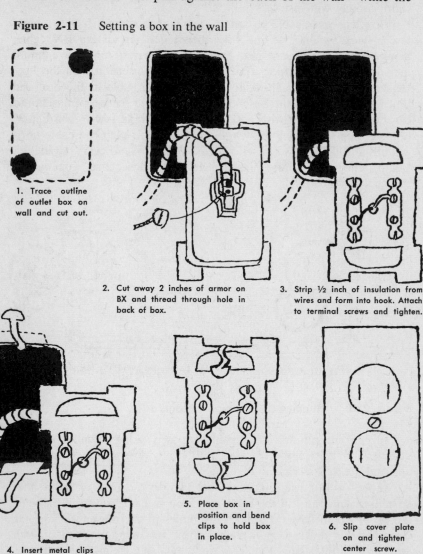

1. Trace outline of outlet box on wall and cut out.

2. Cut away 2 inches of armor on BX and thread through hole in back of box.

3. Strip ½ inch of insulation from wires and form into hook. Attach to terminal screws and tighten.

4. Insert metal clips in wall and bend teeth back inside opening.

5. Place box in position and bend clips to hold box in place.

6. Slip cover plate on and tighten center screw.

box pushes against the front—to hold it in place. In plaster walls, do your cutting with a cold chisel and hammer. Otherwise, drill two holes in corners as shown, and cut with a keyhole saw. If your new outlet is right beside a stud, you can cut your hole in the wall a little larger, and screw the box to the stud.

Be sure all your wire connections are tight, and if they are splices, be sure they are insulated.

After all connections are made, patch plaster if necessary (Sec. 6.4), and replace baseboard.

2.12 | **How to install outdoor lights and outlets.** All outdoor electrical light fixtures in the garden, plug-in receptacles on the patio, and cable strung overhead or run underground must be weatherproof and waterproof. Your electrical supply dealer carries the special equipment needed for outdoor use.

The best way to wire for lights out on the lawn or in the garden is with neoprene insulated cable. Use cable with an extra ground wire in it—3 wires in all—and use grounded outlets. You lay this in a trench about two feet deep and cover cable with a layer of boards for protection before you back-fill. Where the cable comes out of the ground it must be housed in rigid pipe or conduit of galvanized metal (See Sec. 1.40 for working with pipe.) Conduit must start in the bottom of the trench, run up the foundation wall and into the house (on the house side), or up to the light on the light side. Cable is snaked through the protective conduit. A hole big enough for the conduit must be drilled through siding and wood sill behind it at the top of the foundation wall. The conduit can terminate inside the house and the cable is connected with a junction box in the basement. After running in the cable and connecting it, caulk around the conduit to close up the hole and make it watertight.

Outdoor outlets are mounted and wired as in Section 2.11, but the receptacle and its cover plate are especially made for outdoor use. Do not install a regular inside receptacle out of doors.

(See Sec. 13.9 also.)

2.13 | **Putting in a switched outlet.** If you have a light fixture that operates by a pull chain, you can install a new wall-switched fixture in its place if you want to. Or you can convert a single-switch fixture to a double-switch fixture (you could have a switch at the head of the stairs and another at the foot, both operating the same hall light). Figures 2-12 and 2-13 show how the two basic types of switches work.

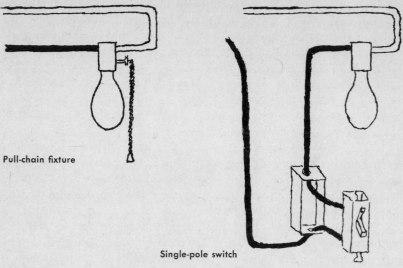

Pull-chain fixture

Single-pole switch

Figure 2-12   Pull chain and single-pole switch

Figure 2-13   Three-way switch

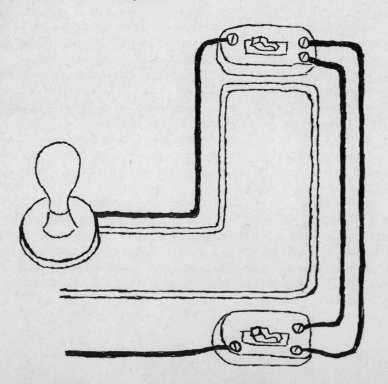

When a single-pole switch is "on," the electric current can run from the black wire on the bottom of the switch to the black wire on the top, causing the fixture to light. When it's "off," no current can flow. On a three-way switch (used for fixtures controlled by two separate switches), when you flip the toggle you change the path of the electric current, making it go from one to another of the two black wires (or a black and red wire) on the bottom of the switch. (Study Fig. 2-13.) When the light is on, flipping either switch will cause it to go off; when it's off, flipping either switch will make it go on.

Before you start any work at wiring new switches, be sure the power to the fixture is off. (See Sec. 2.2.) Then disconnect the old fixture to get at the cable in the outlet box. Install a new outlet box for your new switch (Sec. 2.11), and run a new two-wire No. 14 cable, behind the wall and over the ceiling, from the new outlet box for the switch up to the fixture on the ceiling. (Obviously, you will have to patch some plaster after the job is done. See Sec. 6.4.) Now, at the fixture outlet box, splice the black wires from the fuse box (old cable) and the black wire from the switch together with a wire nut. (See Fig. 2-7.) Next, fasten the white wire from the switch to the "hot," or black, side of the fixture (this may be a terminal screw, but it's usually a short black wire). In this case, the white wire from the switch is "hot"—it is carrying the current to the fixture. (Actually, the white and black wires are alike inside—that is, they are both insulated copper conductors—but they're colored differently to indicate that one wire carries current to the fixture, and that the other wire carries it back to ground.)

Next, fasten the "ground" side of the fixture (usually a white wire) to the remaining white wire (in the old cable running to the fuse box) which will carry the current from the fixture to ground. Finally, fasten the black and white wires (new cable) at the switch to either side of the switch, and mount it in the new outlet box. Turn the power back on, and the job is done.

Installing three-way switches at the top and bottom of the stairs is more complicated, but it is basically a matter of installing a three-way switch in the old switch outlet box and running a three-wire cable from that box down to the new switch outlet box and three-way switch. Figure 2-13 is a schematic diagram of how a three-way switch controls a light. (See Sec. 2.11 for installing cable and outlet boxes.)

This job will involve some carpentry and considerable plaster patching, so unless you're ambitious, you should probably get a professional to do it.

2.14 | How remote-control wiring works. Remote-control wiring is used to let you have switch control of any or all of your lights from a number of places around the house. The more controls you have, the more expensive the job. A professional should do this work, because it is complicated. In a remote-control system a hot wire leads from the fuse or breaker panel to all light fixture outlets that are to be controlled by remote-control wiring. But instead of the hot wires connecting to the light fixtures, they connect to a relay, which serves as a switch, at the light fixture. The relay is operated by small bell wire circuits that run to the low-voltage switches that you operate to turn lights on or off. The bell wire circuits can be run along the baseboard like telephone wire.

2.15 | Installing electric snow-melting cable in walks, driveways, and gutters. Your electrical dealer, or your hardware store, or a mail-order house carries insulated resistance heating cable which can be installed in concerte or bituminous driveways and walks, almost like reinforcing steel, to melt snow automatically. You can't install it in an existing driveway surface—you must pour a new surface. The cable should be rated at 220 to 240 volts and must be connected to 240-volt service at your service panel. (Again, this is a job for an electrician.) When you flip a switch in the house after a snowfall, the snow melts off the walk or driveway as the surface warms up.

The same principle can be employed to melt ice dams in your gutter, except that lower voltage resistance heating cable is used. You merely staple the cable loosely to the roof at the eaves, and plug it into any available outdoor 120-volt receptacle.

③ APPLIANCES

3.1 | The right approach to appliance repairs. Most people could have done a good many of the appliance repairs they paid someone else to do. Not all, but many of them.

Obviously, any appliance that won't work must be repaired, and any appliance that has given anyone even a mild shock should not be used again until it has been repaired. If an appliance suddenly stops working, a fuse may have blown. (See Sec. 2.2.) If an appliance heats slowly or operates at slow speed all the time, the circuit may be overloaded—see Section 2.3—or, if you are using an extension cord it may be too long. The appliance can't work properly if it isn't getting enough electricity.

Before you can repair any electric appliance, you must have a basic understanding of how electricity works. (If you haven't, read Secs. 2.1, 2.5, and 2.6.) The wires of an appliance cord are fastened to its wall plug and its appliance-end plug (or directly to terminal screws), just as a light cord is fastened to its wall plug and its socket. (See Figs. 2-4 and 2-6.)

To protect children in your household from electrical shocks, make it a habit never to leave a small appliance plugged in when not in use. This is particularly true of those with appliance-end plugs, for that plug may become disconnected from the appliance and is "hot" if the wall plug is in an outlet. Keep plug-in covers in unused outlets, and teach young children not to touch small electrical appliances or outlets.

There are four basic rules to follow in repairing any appliance (after first checking to see if a blown fuse, overloaded circuit, or over-long extension cord is causing the trouble).

1. If it doesn't work at all, check the cord for a break (Sec. 3.3) and check the outlet. Plug a table lamp in the same outlet—if it doesn't light up, the outlet is faulty.

2. Read the manufacturer's manual of instruction (if you have lost it, you can write the manufacturer for another one for your

particular model, provided it isn't too old), and read the name-plate. Every appliance has a nameplate either stamped on it or affixed to it, specifying type of current (AC or DC), frequency of current, voltage, wattage or amperage, horsepower (for motor-driven appliances), manufacturer's name and address, and model number. You'll need this information to obtain replacement parts. If you have a warranty, read it to see if its terms apply.

3. Unplug and examine the appliance carefully before you do anything. Most appliances, except some new ones with sealed elements, are designed to be opened for repairs without damage—usually by removing screws or by taking off a snap-on panel. You will usually find that you start dismantling on a part not exposed to view, such as the bottom of a toaster or the back of a washing machine. Careful observation of how the appliance works will let you do all kinds of repairs you thought you couldn't do.

4. Work in a careful, orderly fashion with the proper tools (see Fig. 3-1) and lay out parts in sequence as you remove them. When you replace parts, be sure every piece is exactly as it was originally.

Figure 3-1   Basic tools for appliance repairs

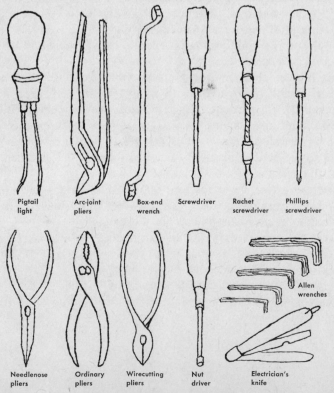

Pigtail   Arc-joint   Box-end   Screwdriver   Rachet   Phillips
light   pliers   wrench   screwdriver   screwdriver

Needlenose   Ordinary   Wirecutting   Nut   Electrician's
pliers   pliers   pliers   driver   knife

3.2 | Small appliance repair. Any patient, intelligent person can fix a small appliance—if it can be fixed. But you must be willing to sit down and figure out the appliance as you take it apart. If a new part is needed, you must order it from the manufacturer—never use a makeshift part.

Where you are prevented from dismantling an appliance by a shaft with some large part on the outer end, or an arm with a control knob on the end, you'll often find a setscrew holding the part to the shaft. Remove the setscrew and pull off the knob, so the shaft can be slipped through the hole in the appliance casing.

The best way to handle tight screws is to use the largest screwdriver that will fill the slot. You can remove tight screws by applying penetrating oil and allowing time for it to work its way in. Then tighten the screw slightly before you attempt to loosen it—or, if there is no risk of damaging other parts, strike the screw a sharp blow by holding the screwdriver in the slot and hitting the handle with a hammer. Or use a brace with a screwdriver bit in it—see Figure 7-5.

When examining the electrical connections inside an appliance, make sure there are no possible electrical contact points (metal to metal) between terminal screws and the appliance casing, or between bare wires and casing. They must be separated either by an air space, or by the insulation of the wire at points where the wire goes through the appliance casing. Be sure every electrical connection is tight, and that no wild strands of wire from the cord protrude around the terminal screw. Trim off stray strands, and try to have the insulation on the wire butt right up against the screw. When refastening the cord to the appliance, make one complete right-hand turn (clockwise) of the wire under the terminal screw head and cross the free end of the wire over the starting point. It's often easiest to strip a little more wire than you actually need so that you can hold the end of the wire as you tighten the screw. After it's tight, snip off the surplus wire close to the screw. Never splice wires together inside an appliance. All electrical connections that you make—if not to a terminal screw —should be made with porcelain wire nuts. (See Fig. 2-8.)

3.3 | Repairing cords and plugs. More often than not, when an appliance won't work the fault lies in the cord. This is especially true of vacuum cleaners, but rough use in pulling any appliance cord from the plug can put it out of commission. (Read Sec. 2.5.)

The best way to check an appliance cord for breaks, if there is an appliance-end plug on the cord, is with the test lamp shown in

Figure 3-1. This is a regular light bulb in a socket with "pigtail leads" —the wires for the socket are hanging out. You can get one at a hardware or electrical supply store for less than a dollar. It's usually molded in plastic, with the wires permanently attached.

Plug the cord in and then put the prongs of the test lamp in the ends of the flat plug on the appliance end of the cord. If it works, the cord is all right; if it doesn't work, check the outlet itself.

Sometimes a break in a cord will allow the test lamp to go on and off intermittently. By flexing the cord with your fingers at different points along the cord, while it's plugged in with the test lamp, you can determine the exact point of the break. Then you can resplice the cord as in Figure 2-3. The outer sheath of the cord is easily removed with a knife. Be careful not to cut the fine wire strands as you strip the insulation from the individual wires. If you cut many, you will reduce the current-carrying capacity of the wire. If the broken cord is an iron or toaster cord, wrap some asbestos paper (from the hardware store) around the splices and tape it in place. Asbestos is not to keep hot wires from burning anything, but to keep the iron or toaster from burning through the insulation around the wires if it should happen to touch the cord.

If there is more than one break, or the cord seems in bad shape generally, you should replace it. Take it to the hardware store and get a replacement of the same type.

When you are rewiring a plug on a cord, particularly one that gets rough treatment, like the vacuum cleaner plug, use an underwriter's knot (Fig. 2-5) to take the strain off the terminal screws.

Cords frayed at the appliance-end plugs of toasters, irons, and other appliances are repaired in roughly the same way as at the wall-plug end. First unplug the cord from the wall, then take apart the appliance-end plug by unscrewing the small screw that holds the two sides of the flat plug together. You will see inside how the bare ends of cord wires wrap around terminal screws. Just cut the cord behind the frayed part and refasten the wires to terminals screws as in Section 2.5.

If there is no flat plug on the appliance end—that is, if the cord is fastened directly to terminals within the appliance—and if the break is at the terminals, you can refasten the cord this way. Remove some of the outer sheath or braid of the cord by unraveling with an awl. Begin at the end and unravel the cord back about 2 inches, and then trim the ragged ends of the outer sheath with scissors. Now strip the wires back clean to about ½ inch from the sheath and twist the strands tightly so they hold together well. If you are connecting the cord to a heating appliance terminal, do not use electrician's tape, because the heat may melt it. Instead, bind the insulation and the ends of the sheath of each wire with asbestos string. Then fasten your wire ends to the terminal screws as in Section 3.2.

3.4 | Toasters. If bread gets stuck in the toaster, turn the toaster upside down and shake it out. Never use a fork to remove toast, as this can injure the heating wires inside and might give you a shock if the toaster is connected. Remove crumbs regularly by taking off the crumb tray under the toaster.

If toast burns or doesn't toast much on either side, first check the "dark-light" control if there is one—someone may have accidentally pushed it to the wrong position.

Before beginning any repairs on your toaster, read Sections 3.1 and 3.2. If the toaster won't work at all, the first thing to check is the cord and plug—see Section 3.3.

Next remove the crumb tray and carefully study the interior for obvious breaks or loose connections. If your bread toasts unevenly or just on one side, a heating element may be broken. Dangling wires can usually be spotted easily by examining the bread slots from above and below with a flashlight. If you find such a break, order a new element from the manufacturer, specifying model number and position of the element. Heating elements should never be patched, nor should they be unwound to make slack for reconnecting to a terminal.

The basic parts of most pop-up toasters, aside from the heating elements, are (1) a thermostat made of a blade that bends as it heats up and flips, (2) a switch that controls (3) a clock-timer. The blade bends proportionately to the increase in heat. The switch is a spring-loaded lever on the clock. As the toaster temperature rises, the blade moves toward the lever, strikes it, and moves the lever to increase the speed of the clock, which finally trips the carriage and makes the toast pop up. (Essentially the same system, without the timer, provides the automatic control in coffee-makers, irons, and most portable cooking appliances. See Fig. 3-2.) The blade thermostat, called a bimetallic strip, can usually be adjusted up and down the scale—to make the appliance heat up more or less—by turning a small regulating screw on the thermostat. But any thermostat that lets your appliance get too hot, or prevents it from getting hot enough, must

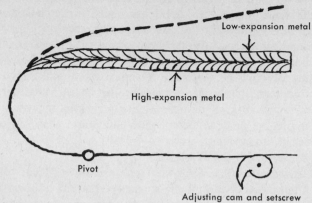

Figure 3-2   Bimetallic strip

be replaced with a similar unit from the manufacturer if it cannot be adjusted by turning the setscrew. Before you remove a thermostat, be absolutely sure your problem isn't a cord that's too long, or an overloaded circuit.

In many toaster models you can see the thermostat, switch, and timer after removing only the crumb tray—they are just above it. To see how they operate, expose the bottom of the toaster, elevate it three or four inches with wooden blocks under the corners, and place a small mirror below the mechanism. Then aim a flashlight about in line with your vision and you will be able to see how it works—or should work. When you have studied the controls you can see what needs adjusting and how to adjust it.

If you find you must take the toaster apart to get at the mechanism, it isn't terribly difficult. The usual toaster case has three sections held in place by the base, which is screwed on. The knobs are removed first, then the bottom screws, then the base, and finally, the case will come apart. In some toasters the bread-slot wires will drop out when the outer shell is removed. To be on the safe side, remove the shell with the toaster right side up. Then if you have to remove guide wires, you can lift them out one or two at a time.

Sometimes you can put the toaster through its cycle with the shell removed so you can observe the actual operation.

3.5 | Coffee-makers. A good coffee-maker should stay in working order for years. But if you have trouble with one, read Sections 3.2 through 3.3 before tackling any repair. If coffee is too weak or too strong, be sure the control button is properly set. Most electric coffee-makers are built with heating elements sealed in the base, and elements virtually never fail. They may melt the built-in fuse—which all nonautomatic coffee-makers have—if they are plugged in and empty. Usually the fuse is in the bottom of the base, looking like a small round plug with a slot in it. You can remove it with a screwdriver and replace it with a new one the same way. But before you replace it, try tightening it, because it may simply have loosened.

An automatic coffee-maker has a blade-type thermostat and switch-lever control (Fig. 3-2) in its base that may go out of order in time. This control is somewhat like a toaster's. (See Sec. 3.4.) Look on the bottom of the unit and you usually will find inscribed, *Do Not Immerse in Water.* If there is such a warning, there will be two or three screws on the bottom of the unit; by removing them you can take the bottom off the unit to see what might be the trouble. If you see a loose or broken connection in there, you've probably found your problem. If the connections look all right, and if the water in the pot heats up at all, you can probably fix the unit simply by adjusting the blade-type thermostat with its setscrew. If everything in the unit looks all right, but nothing happens, the heating element probably has failed. This is a repair job for a professional.

If the unit is the immersible type that you can put into dishwater, you should not try to open it up, but should send it back to the manufacturer.

3.6 | Irons. A good iron will rarely give you trouble, but if it should, first read Sections 3.1 through 3.3. Most iron troubles come from breaks in cords or plugs—so check this first if your iron doesn't work. If the iron heats up but the control isn't accurate, or if the cord is not at fault and the iron doesn't heat up, you will have to take the iron apart to examine the works and check the connections between heating elements and thermostat. (Only rarely is the thermostat or heating element itself at fault.) The heat control knob on an automatic iron is connected to a thermostat in the soleplate of the iron. When the soleplate gets hot enough the blade-type thermostat (Fig. 3-2) and its switch lever shut off the electricity and then let it come back on when the iron cools. The control knob simply moves the thermostat and the switch lever farther apart, so that more or less heat can be brought to the soleplate before the unit shuts off.

To dismantle an iron, usually you start by removing the control knob, which is held in place by a setscrew. Place parts down in the order of removal and examine the unit closely as you take it apart. After the control knob, you usually take out cover screws and remove the cover and handle as a unit.

Inside the unit you will find that the thermostat and control switch have electrical contact points that close or open the circuit the electricity takes to heat the unit up. You can often solve your problem by cleaning and smoothing these contact points with an automotive ignition file. (Ask your garage man for one.) Slip it between contacts and slide it back and forth. Stop filing as soon as the contacts look smooth and clean.

Heating elements that don't look absolutely perfect and with solid connections should be replaced. Write the manufacturer for a new one. Don't try to patch heating elements. A completely sealed element cannot be repaired, but you are seldom faced with this problem. If you are, you may be able to return the iron to the manufacturer for a credit toward a new iron.

If nothing else is at fault, the thermostat itself may need adjusting. In this case, see Section 3.4 and Figure 3-2.

3.7 | Portable electric cooking appliances. There is a portable cooking appliance for practically every purpose—broiling, frying, stewing, grilling, roasting, waffle-making—and over the years they have become extremely dependable and trouble-free. If you have a really old one and it doesn't work, it's not worth repairing. Many new appliances have completely sealed units that are immersible for washing, which means they cannot be taken apart for repairs. (But you can, of course, check the cord, plug, and outlet.)

However, if the unit can be dismantled for inspection, read Sections 3.1 through 3.3 before you do anything.

Most portable cooking appliances have blade-type themostats and switch levers (see Sec. 3.4 and Fig. 3-2), just like those on a toaster. To get at this mechanism you must take the unit apart. Most troubles lie in loose connections at the thermostat and switch. Close examination here will show you where the break lies. (In certain new appliances, there is a thermostat called a "probe tube," which assures greater accuracy of heat control than the blade-type thermostat. This thermostat is a small tube filled with liquid silicone that expands during the heating process and pushes a piston out. The piston breaks open an electrical contact to shut the current off. As the unit cools a spring action pushes the contacts back together again and the unit starts heating up. If this type of thermostat is not working right, you'll have to have a professional repair it.)

Before dismantling a roaster, broiler, or rotisserie to get at the thermostat and switch lever—incidentally, these appliances also have a clock timer, like a toaster—check the heating elements. These are exposed and can usually be spotted without any dismantling. The heating elements are open coils wound around porcelain bushing and spools. There may be side, top, and bottom elements. If you have a broken element or a broken connection of an element, you will have to order a new one from the manufacturer—or through your local dealer. Specify make, model, serial number of the appliance, any numbers you find on the element, and the position of the element in the unit. When you are ready to install a new heating-element coil, first stretch it out, by pulling on the ends only, to the same length—or slightly less—as the old coil. This keeps the coil even so there will be no hot spots that might cause an early failure of the new element. In broilers and rotisseries, the elements are frequently fastened permanently to liners that are fastened into the unit. In this case, the whole liner or the whole unit must be returned to the manufacturer if it is necessary to replace a heating element.

In a waffle iron, the most common source of trouble is in the wire running between the top and bottom sections of the unit. This asbestos-insulated flexible wire may get too much flexing in time and simply break from fatigue. These "hinge wires" may be concealed in the hinges of the waffle iron, or they may be armored with a steel spring around them for protection. If you have to replace these wires, be sure to replace *both* of them with exact replacements from your hardware store or the manufacturer. Allow an extra length of this wire when you replace it so that the grids will not be "hinge-bound."

3.8 | Motor troubles and repairs. Before trying to fix any small motor, or trying to find out what is wrong with it, read Sections 3.1 and 3.2. One of the most frequent causes of trouble is not the motor itself, but an over-long extension cord that is too light for the motor. Ordinary lamp cord is not big enough. Be sure the cord is a heavy-duty one designed for the motor.

If radio and TV reception is jumbled when a motor is running, the circuit is overloaded—see Section 2.3—or the motor is not grounded properly. The latter is true especially of motors mounted on rubber to minimize vibration. To ground the motor, simply run a wire attached to the motor housing to the frame of the appliance.

Another basic cause of poor motor performance is a slipping motor pulley. If there is a belt connecting the motor to the appliance mechanism, check it for slipping. If it is slipping, you may smell burning rubber and probably will find that the motor-mounting bolts have worked loose. Tighten the bolts while the belt is drawn fairly taut—with the electricity off, of course. If the belt is damaged in any way, get a new one at the hardware store.

Problems in the motor itself rarely occur. Most electric appliance motors have built-in lifetime lubrication and rarely need to be oiled. (If you think your motor needs oil, check the motor casing carefully to see if any oiling instructions are included on casing or nameplate.) Occasionally, vibration will work screws loose or cause short circuits, and usually you can spot and repair these yourself. If you suspect something like this, check all connections around the motor for loose screws and look for scorched insulation or burned spots on the metal casing that would indicate a short circuit. Check points where wires go through the motor housing to be sure no bare wires are rubbing against the metal. If insulation on a wire doesn't look sound, wrap it carefully with electrician's tape.

If none of these things is the apparent source of trouble, and the appliance is a large one, call a repairman. It's not safe or wise to tinker beyond a certain point with a major appliance.

If the appliance is a small, portable one with a motor that won't work after you have checked all the above, check the *commutator*. (See Fig. 3-3.) A commutator is part of a *universal* motor, often used

Figure 3-3   Universal motor (removed from casing of food mixer or other small appliance)

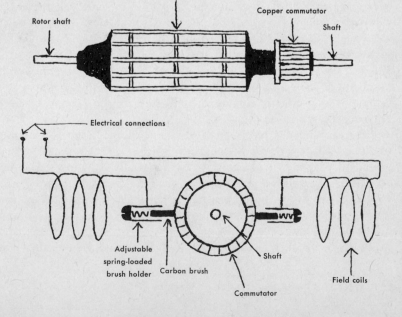

in small appliances. The commutator is always at one end of the motor shaft, just inside the housing. It's usually cylindrical and made of a number of copper segments. If these segments are not bright and coppery, but dark, pitted, and dirty, you've found your trouble. To shine them up, use a strip of fine sandpaper pulled taut over the end of a small stick which will fit through the holes in the motor housing. (Don't use emery paper, because this is an electrical conductor and can cause short circuits.) If the motor will run at all, turn it on and hold the sandpaper down against the commutator as it revolves. This will shine up the copper. Hold the sandpaper on it lightly, just long enough to shine it—don't wear it down. When it's shiny the motor should run properly.

Another possible source of trouble is the carbon brushes that rub against the commutator. Sometimes these wear down and need to be replaced. You can do this yourself if you are handy at dismantling and assembling, but otherwise don't attempt it.

If you've tried everything mentioned and still can't get the motor working, the best thing to do is take it out and replace it with a new one of the same kind. You can obtain one from the manufacturer or have your dealer order it for you.

3.9 | Mixers and blenders. Internal problems in mixers and blenders are rare. Before making any repairs read Sections 3.1 through 3.3. First of all, look for breaks in the cord, and check the outlet.

If the cord isn't to blame it's possible that the bearings need to be lubricated. Use oil sparingly, and follow directions if you have them.

It's also possible that there is a loose connection in the switch. To look at this you'll have to remove the casing—an easy job on a mixer but a little harder on a blender. Blenders often come apart by first removing the stud at the top of the unit that drives the chopper in the glass container. Unscrew the stud with a wrench. Then lift off the cover plate and unscrew the nut that holds the rest of the casing in place. Check for any loose connections and correct them.

If the blender motor runs without the blender glass on it, but won't run when the glass is in place, the chopping blade is frozen shut in its housing in the base of the glass. Use penetrating oil and a screwdriver to loosen the shaft. Then lubricate it and run it for a few minutes to loosen it up well. To remove oil, run the blender with water and detergent. It should be dried with a towel each time it is washed, not left to dry by itself—this is usually what causes the trouble.

If the gears on mixers or blenders are noisy or seem stripped, get a professional to repair them. This is very tricky work and usually involves getting a new set of gears from the manufacturer.

If you have motor trouble with a mixer or blender, see Section 3.8.

3.10 | Vacuum cleaners and electric fans. A vacuum cleaner is essentially an electric fan, and the commonest problems are breaks in cords and clogged dirt in hoses. If your vacuum doesn't work, read Sections 3.1. through 3.3. Examine the cord carefully and repair any breaks as in Section 3.3. Be sure to use an underwriter's knot (Fig. 2-5) when rewiring a vacuum cleaner plug.

If the vacuum doesn't run at all, and you've checked the cord, the trouble probably is a loose connection in the switch or a broken switch. (Foot-operated switches are especially likely to wear out.) This repair will involved dismantling the vacuum.

If the motor is running poorly, read Section 3.8. If you have an upright vacuum with revolving brushes, and the motor runs but the brushes don't revolve (or go too slowly), you need a new belt from motor pulley to roller pulley. You can get one the right size at your hardware store.

If the vacuum runs but isn't picking up dirt as it should, check the hose for clogged dirt (you can shake it out or run a thin stick through it) and be sure the bag inside isn't too full. Check the hose for air leaks. (If there's a worn-out spot, it leaks.) If you find one, the only solution is to buy a new hose. In upright vacuums with revolving brushes, you may have a problem in picking up dirt if the nozzle and the brushes are not set right. To clean a rug most effectively the nozzle should be in the highest position at which there's an obvious suction working on the rug. To set it, raise the nozzle to its highest position, turn on the motor, and lower the nozzle slowly until you hear the motor accelerate noticeably. This position will save wear on the rug and do a better job of cleaning than if the nozzle is shoved down hard into the rug. Also, be sure the bristles in the brush are at the right level for cleaning. To check this, lay a straightedge across the nozzle. The bristles should just touch the straightedge at all points. If they're too long or short, adjust the bristle roller. Check the ends of the roller to see how they are mounted, and you'll see how it can be adjusted. When bristles are worn too short to let adjustment bring them to the right level, get a new roller from the manufacturer.

If a vacuum vibrates excessively or is too noisy, the chances are that a blower blade is broken. (This is also true of electric fans.) The big drum-type fan in the back of the vacuum is called the blower. In some vacuums the blower can be lifted out with the motor when the motor-mounting bolts are removed. In others you can remove a cover plate to look at the blower. If you have a broken blade, you'll have to get a new blower from the manufacturer. Sometimes it's difficult to remove a broken blower for replacement. If it's stuck tight to the shaft, use kerosene or penetrating oil to loosen it, and then hammer a wooden dowel against the end of the shaft. (If you hammer directly on the shaft, you may damage it.)

If there is nothing obviously wrong with the blower but the vacuum (or fan) still vibrates too much, check the blades for symmetry. To do this, pick a guide point on the cage around the blades and measure with a ruler from a guide point to a blade. Then slowly rotate the fan so you can check the distance on each blade. If they are out of line, bend them gently into the proper position. This should greatly reduce the vibration.

3.11 | Major appliance repair. Before doing anything about repairing a major appliance—a range, refrigerator, dishwasher, garbage disposer, washing machine, or clothes dryer—read Section 3.1. Then read your instruction manual. (Always save your manuals on major appliances. They carry valuable information for the right operation and maintenance of the unit. They also spell out the warranty the manufacturer puts on the unit, and you may need this warranty if something goes wrong with the appliance. If you lose your manual, you can get another by writing the manufacturer, but you probably can't enforce the warranty.)

If a new appliance is not working right, make sure it has been installed exactly according to the manufacturer's directions by checking the instruction manual or recalling the serviceman who installed it if you didn't do so yourself. Never try to install or repair a major appliance unless you have confidence in your ability to tackle the job, and don't try it if you are absentminded or disinterested in the job—you may hurt yourself and the appliance. If you call a professional serviceman, be sure to get one authorized to install and repair the make of appliance you have.

If the appliance smokes, smells, sparks, pops, flashes, or makes a grinding noise, shut the power off immediately (at the fuse box) and unplug the appliance (if it unplugs). *Be sure the power is off before you even touch the machine.*

Assemble the tools you'll need before starting any repairs. (See Fig. 3-1.) Don't start at all unless you have at least two hours you can devote to the problem.

3.12 | Ranges and ovens. If your electric oven doesn't work, check the automatic clock and timing device if there is one. If the timing device knob has not been turned back to "manual" from previous use on "automatic," the oven will not heat if you are not using the timer.

If something is wrong with your electric range or oven, read Sections, 3.1, 3.2, and 3.11. (Note: The following instructions can be applied, in general, to built-in ovens and surface-cooking units as well as to the conventional range.)

Don't attempt any repairs to an electric range or oven without first turning off the power—and unless you know a good bit about electricity, don't attempt it at all. A range is wired directly to the fuse panel—it is not plugged into the wall. So pull the fuses or throw the circuit breakers that control the range. (If you don't know how, see Sec. 2.2.) A range is always on 220- or 240-volt service, so if you have fuses, they'll be the big cartridge or tubular fuses. If you have breakers they'll be double breakers—two breakers on which the switches are tied together with a small bar.

If the entire unit seems faulty, pull the range out from the wall (after turning off the electricity) and you'll usually find a wiring diagram on the back, showing how the range is wired. Even if you can't understand the diagram, check for loose connections in back of the range. The big cable from the wall, bringing the current from the entrance panel, is fastened to terminal screws behind a plate on the back. Simply remove the screw holding the plate to check the terminals.

If the only failure is a surface burner, remove the burner (usually you just unplug them) and check the connections at the burner to see if they are solid. If you find nothing wrong here, pull the range out from the wall and remove the back so you can check the wiring at the switch control of the burner. If nothing is amiss here either, you have a burned-out element that must be replaced with a new one just like it. Order one from the manufacturer or have your dealer do it for you.

If one or both of the heating elements in your oven (there is one on top, one on the bottom) are faulty, first check the connections at the plugs. The elements usually unplug easily. Next check the connections at the switch in back of the back panel on the range. (You'll have to pull the range out from the wall and remove the back.) If nothing is wrong here either, the faulty element is probably burned out and will have to be replaced with a new one from the manufacturer.

If both heating elements are working but the oven is too hot or too cold, the thermostat is not doing its job. This requires the services of a professional repairman, for the instrument is too delicate for an amateur to tinker with. If it is faulty it usually must be replaced but sometimes can be adjusted. Oven thermostats are usually liquid-type thermostats (see Sec. 3.7) that are sealed tube-and-bulb units. As the temperature rises, the liquid expands and presses against a diaphragm in a switch at the temperature dial. When temperature gets too high the switch shuts off electricity to the oven. The thermostat is usually located near the oven roof. (Meat probe thermostats operate in the same way. They are inserted in the meat and when the selected temperature is reached, the liquid pressure on the diaphragm at the dial switches off the electricity.)

Gas ranges are much simpler than electric ranges, and almost invariably your gas utility man will fix or adjust them for almost nothing. The principal parts of a gas burner are the mixer head with its air shutter and an opening for the gas orifice, the mixer tube, and the burner head where the flame appears. The gas orifice usually has a set of hoods sized for different types of gas—natural gas, liquefied petroleum gas, and manufactured gas. (See Fig. 3-4.) The orifice

Figure 3-4   Gas burners

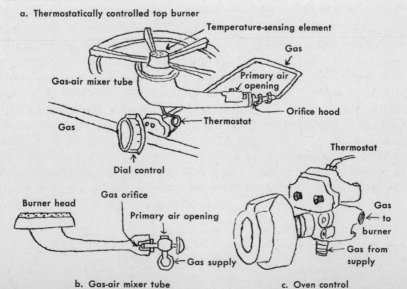

a. Thermostatically controlled top burner

Temperature-sensing element

Gas

Gas-air mixer tube

Primary air opening

Orifice hood

Gas

Thermostat

Dial control

Thermostat

Burner head

Gas orifice

Primary air opening

Gas
to
burner

Gas from
supply

Gas supply

b. Gas-air mixer tube

c. Oven control

hood assures the proper flow of gas. If your range isn't working properly, you may have the wrong orifice hood. If you can't tell by looking, you can get your gas or utility man to check for you. In gas ovens, the burner is located beneath the oven floor, which can be removed to check the orifice hood.

Gas ovens have a bulb-type thermostat that moves a small bellows that expands and contracts against a gas valve. The bellows works against a spring, which may lose its tension over the years. If it does, and the thermostat is not acting right, have your utility man adjust it. He will remove the thermostat dial and adjust the screws behind it. These screws adjust the pilot light in the oven, and the height of the flame which comes on either too low or too high if the thermostat is not set quite right. You should not attempt to adjust these screws yourself—you might start a fire if the adjustment was clumsy. This is delicate work and takes the skill of an experienced serviceman.

If you have an electronic oven (it cooks food at room temperature) don't try to repair it if something goes wrong, unless you are handy and self-confident and have a good understanding of electronics. This type of unit is very simple to operate. There is just one control: a timer. What happens in the unit is that the 240-volt current from the entrance panel is changed by a transformer in the oven into a 5,000-volt current, which then activates a magnetron tube. There is a special control that heats up the magnetron tube before the high voltage is applied to it. Then the tube turns the current into high-frequency microwave energy, which cooks the meat as heat does in a conventional oven. The timer, the magnetron tube, or the special control might be at fault if the oven stops working. It's best to call a professional in any case.

3.13 | Refrigerators and freezers are two of the most dependable and long-lasting appliances in the house. If cared for properly they will last for many years without any major repair.

If unpleasant odors develop, your refrigerator needs to be defrosted. One disadvantage of automatic-defrost refrigerators is that odors may develop if the interior is not cleaned often enough. To minimize odors, always cover strong-smelling foods when you store them.

If your refrigerator sweats or drips too much in hot weather, the temperature control may be set too cold. The condensation is caused by too great a difference in temperature inside and out.

The two most common problems in a refrigerator or freezer are fuse-blowing and failure of the unit to run enough to keep cold. (A refrigerator or freezer does not run continuously, but shuts on and off as needed to maintain temperature.) If a fuse blows, the cause is almost always a cord that has been damaged (see Sec. 3.3) or an overloaded circuit (see Secs. 2.2 and 2.3). If the refrigerator doesn't run enough to keep cold, there are three most likely reasons:

1. The unit may need to be defrosted. Never let the deposit get more than ½-inch thick at the most. You can defrost a refrigerator quickly by placing pans of hot water in the open unit after shutting it off. If there is too much frost in a freezer, do not use hot water because it might build up too much pressure in the evaporator coils. (The pressure is different in a freezer because it is designed to operate at a much lower temperature than a refrigerator. Use regular tap water to wash down the frost—with the current off, of course.)

2. Too little air may be reaching the back of the unit to cool off the coils, or there may be a big accumulation of dirt and dust on the coils. Move the refrigerator or freezer away from the wall a little, and clean the coils with a stiff brush and the vacuum cleaner.

3. Warm, room-temperature air may be leaking in through the door seal. Check the seal by holding a dollar bill in the door opening, then closing the door on the dollar. If you can pull it out, too much warm air is getting into the refrigerator. You can usually make the door tight by adjusting the latch on the door. Careful inspection of the latch will show you how to do this. Then check to see if the refrigerator is level. If it's not, the hinges may in time warp and break the door seal open slightly. It may be that the gasket around the door needs replacing. This can usually be done simply by pulling out the old one and replacing it with a new one from the manufacturer. (To order this or other parts, specify model and serial number.) You can also use certain types of foam plastic weatherstripping tape to improve a loose seal—ask your hardware dealer.

If these suggestions do not solve your problem, the difficulty lies within the works. Read Sections 3.1 and 3.11 before you tackle anything. Repairs are seldom needed and you shouldn't attempt them unless (1) you can readily spot a break in an electrical connection or (2) you're well acquainted with refrigeration systems and are handy at tricky machinery repairs.

The principal parts of a refrigeration system are these: (1) the compressor and its motor—usually sealed units that must be replaced if anything goes wrong with them; (2) the condenser coils, and sometimes a small fan to blow air over them; (3) the evaporator coils in the refrigerator or freezer box; and (4) the bulb-type thermostat (see Sec. 3.12 and Fig. 3-5). Briefly, here is how these elements work: Freon gas coming from the evaporator coils with any heat it picked up in the refrigerator is compressed by the compressor. In this process the gas gets very hot and gives off heat. It is cooled down to a liquid as it runs through the condenser coils where it is still under pressure. Then when it reaches the first of the evaporator coils again it can suddenly expand (through an expansion valve) into a gas. And to expand into a gas it must absorb heat (this is a physical law) so it gets very cold and keeps the refrigerator cold. The thermostat starts and stops this whole operation.

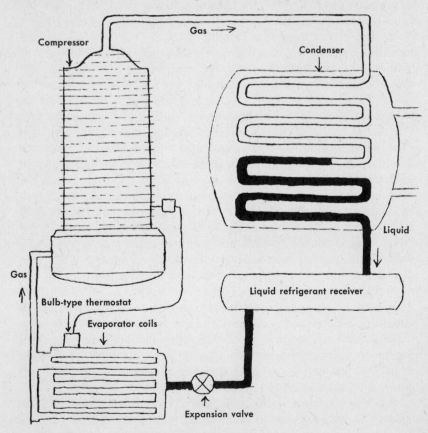

Figure 3-5   A typical refrigeration cycle

3.14 | Dishwashers. You can't begin to repair a dishwasher unless you understand how it operates. The basic operation in most models is that hot water comes streaming up through a whirling impeller in the bottom of the unit. This impeller is driven by the shaft of a motor right under the floor of the unit, and is connected to an elaborate set of mechanical controls. Briefly, here is the way the machine works: (1) When the unit is turned on, the small timer motor operating the mechanical controls (actually cams that turn switches on and off) is put into operation. (2) The first cam to hit a switch turns on a solenoid valve to let hot water in. (A solenoid is a coil of wire that acts like a magnetized plunger when electric current goes through it. It's usually spring-mounted and when current hits it, it works against the spring to open or close a valve.) (3) The next cam (sometimes it's the same one) switches on a preheater that heats up the hot water even further. (4) The next cam throws the impeller motor on, which whirls water all around the box of the dishwasher. (5) The next cam shuts off the impeller motor and opens the drain solenoid valve so water can run out. (6) The next cam closes the drain and opens the inlet solenoid valve again (for the "rinse" operation). Then steps (4) and (5) are repeated. Next, (6) a cam actuates the preheater and starts a hot-air stream, which dries the dishes. (7) The final cam shuts the machine off. There is a great deal of variation among different dishwashers, however, so your model may not follow these steps exactly. Read your manual of instructions for specific information on your model.

Obviously, if you are going to repair such a complicated mechanism, you must be carefully organized and competent at mechanical things. (Read Secs. 3.1 and 3.2.) If you doubt your ability to repair the trouble, call a professional.

Here are the most common problems and their solutions:

• *Slow drying.* Either your hot-water supply is not hot enough (see Sec. 1.27) or your preheater elements are burnt out or disconnected.

• *Leaking water.* A minor adjustment of the hinges and latch on the door of the unit may stop the leak. But if the gasket has deteriorated too far you should get a replacement from the manufacturer.

• *Blows a fuse when it's turned on.* This almost always indicates a short circuit ahead of the control mechanism. Inspect the wiring up to and into the control point on the unit. (See Sec. 2.2.) You should have a separate 15-amp circuit for the dishwasher alone, or a

20-amp circuit if the dishwasher and garbage disposer are connected to the same circuit. (See Secs. 2.3 and 2.4.) If the fuse is blown after the machine has just started, you probably have a broken connection in the control.

• *Blows a fuse after groaning.* This usually means that the impeller is jammed. You can check by opening the unit and trying to move the impeller by hand. If it's jammed you can see what is jamming it. If it isn't jammed, you probably have trouble in the motor that drives the impeller, A faulty motor should be replaced and the seal around the impeller shaft should be checked for leaks that might have let water corrode the motor.

• *Water won't come into the washer.* In this case, the solenoid valve that controls the intake is probably broken and must be replaced. If it's jammed or the electrical connections are loose, these troubles may be fixed on the spot.

• *Water won't drain out or won't stay in the dishwasher.* Here, the solenoid drain valve is at fault.

3.15 | Garbage disposers. If you have a septic tank and are considering installing a disposer, check with your local building inspector to make sure your tank is large enough. Ordinarily, 100 to 200 extra gallons of capacity (above the minimum requirement) are needed for a disposer, but this figure varies.

Briefly, here is how a garbage disposer works: The disposer hangs from the sink drain by its upper casing, which is the storage chamber for garbage. The lower part of the disposer contains the shredder and the motor that drives it. The shredder has two parts: a stationary set of cutting teeth and a rotating impeller. When the machine is running, the impeller drives the garbage against the stationary cutting teeth as they turn. (See your instruction manual for specific details about your disposer.)

A good stream of cold water should always be running when the machine is in action, and the disposer should not be packed too full before it is turned on. Do not put big bones, glass, china, metal, string, plastic, shells, or filter-tip cigarettes into the disposer. Do not use drain-cleaning chemicals or you may eventually corrode the disposer. Follow the manufacturer's instructions for operating.

If your disposer suddenly stops, turn it off and turn the water off. Shut off the power at the entrance panel—see Section 2.2. (A disposer is usually wired directly to the fuse box, like a range.) Turn the impeller back a bit, and look in with a flashlight so you can see and remove obvious jams. When the motor has been off at least five minutes and you think you've cleared the jam, turn the power on and push the reset button on the side of the lower casing. (You may have to tap the reset button with a wood block to push it in.) It should now run.

If there is no jamming, but the disposer shreds too slowly—and you have had it for some time—you may need a new stationary shredder. The teeth sometimes become too dull to do a good job. You can replace the shredder with a new one from the manufacturer.

If the disposer blows a fuse when it's turned on, the motor has probably been damaged by water coming in through a leaking seal, or the controls have been short-circuited. Before you attempt any repairs, read Sections 3.1 and 3.11 and study your instruction manual carefully. If you lack confidence, don't try doing it yourself—call in a professional. However, if you want to do it, first shut off the power at the entrance panel, then block up the disposer so that when you unbolt it it won't fall to the floor and be damaged. If you find parts that need to be replaced, be sure you get the right size from the manufacturer. If something is wrong with the motor, see Section 3.8.

3.16 | Automatic washing machines. A washing machine has a control for its cycles very much like that described in Section 3.14 (Dishwashers). It has solenoid valves for water intake and drain, a motor for the action of the machine, a pump, and a filter.

When you have trouble with your washing machine, you should always refer to your instruction manual. (If you've lost it, you can get a new one from the manufacturer by writing them and telling them your model number.) Most washing machine troubles are caused by overloading, insufficient hot water, use of too much or not enough soap, water that is too hard, or a filter clogged with lint. If the machine stops during the spin-dry cycle, it's often because the clothes need to be repositioned evenly around the tub. (The machine is probably overloaded, too.) If it continues to stop, take out part of the load. If your machine is excessively noisy, you are probably overloading it and causing excess vibration. (This may eventually damage the spring-suspension of the tub and cause it to slam against the frame of the washer.) Another possible cause is that the machine isn't perfectly level.

If your problem isn't due to any of these causes, read Section 3.11 before you do anything. If the washer will not run at all, check the fuse panel (see Sec. 2.2). If a fuse has not blown, turn the timer switch through all its positions and listen carefully. If you can hear clicking, you know that electricity is getting to the solenoid valves that let water in and out, so a failure in the motor is probably the trouble. This is a job for a professional unless you are experienced with motors. (If you are, see Sec. 3.8.)

If the washer drains too slowly (this can make it skip the spray-rinse cycle), there are three possibilities you can check: (1) The drain hose may be clogged. Unplug the machine, move it out from the wall, and take the back off—it is usually held in place with sheet-metal screws. The drain hose is usually secured by small metal clamps easily loosened with wide-jawed pliers. Put a pan under the washing machine and disconnect the drain hose to check for clogging. (2) The pump may be jammed. (The drain hose is connected to the pump.) The bottom part of the pump is held in place with a number of screws or bolts in a flange around the outside. Remove the bottom of the pump (after bailing out the machine), being careful not to damage the gasket between the two parts of the pump. If there is any foreign object clogging the impeller of the pump, you'll see it. (3) The drain solenoid valve may be jammed or have an electrical break. Do not attempt this repair yourself unless you are an experienced mechanic.

If water won't enter the tub, won't stop flowing into the tub, or will only stop when you turn the machine off, the inlet solenoid is at fault. A professional is usually needed for this repair—see above.

If the washer leaks, run it through part of its cycle while you have the back off. Carefully observe the way the machine works; watch it with a flashlight, after placing a mirror on the floor under the mechanism. This will show you the exact location of a leak. If the leak seems to be under the pump, remove the bottom of the pump (see above) and inspect it for pinholes. If there are only a few, you may be able to solder them. If there are quite a number you should replace the part with a new one from the manufacturer.

If the washer's dial must be turned manually to make the washer complete its cycle, the clock that runs the control is not working. If the machine fails to shut off after one complete cycle, or repeats parts of its cycle, both the clock and control may be at fault. Usually they must be replaced, and unless you are thoroughly experienced it is best to have a professional do the job.

3.17 | Clothes dryers. If your dryer is too noisy, it is probably not exactly level. If it dries too slowly, the lint screen is probably clogged. (Look down below or behind the lint screen—depending on its position—for lint clogs, too.) The screen should be cleaned before or after every drying cycle.

If anything goes wrong with your dryer, you should always consult the instruction manual that came with it. (If you lose it, you can get another from the manufacturer.) Also, see Sections 3.1 and 3.11 before making any repairs. Clothes dryers are relatively simple appliances. (See Fig. 3-6.) They have a rotating cylinder, a heater—either gas or electric—a blower, a motor to drive the blower and the cylinder, and a thermal cutoff control that shuts off the heat, but not

Figure 3-6   Typical clothes dryers

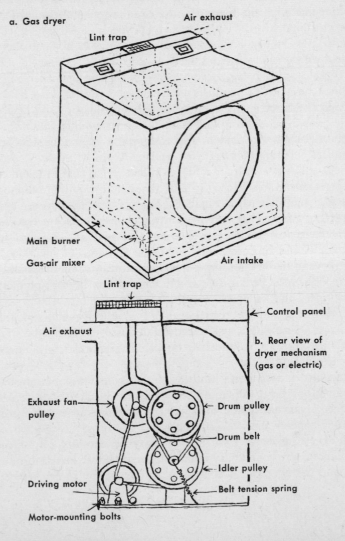

a. Gas dryer

Air exhaust

Lint trap

Main burner

Gas-air mixer

Air intake

Lint trap

Air exhaust

Control panel

b. Rear view of dryer mechanism (gas or electric)

Exhaust fan pulley

Drum pulley

Drum belt

Idler pulley

Driving motor

Belt tension spring

Motor-mounting bolts

the cylinder, if the temperature gets too high. (The thermal cutoff is a thermostatic control in back of the dryer near the main control.) When the dryer cools down, the thermal cutoff lets the heating coils go back on again if the dryer cycle is not complete. A clogged lint screen can keep the thermal cutoff from working properly, or cause it to shut off the heater entirely. There is also a heat fuse, like a small cartridge fuse, on the casing around the cylinder. This fuse will blow and shut the heater off if the thermal control is not working.

If nothing happens when you turn on the dryer, first check the power supply. (See Sec. 2.2.) If this isn't the solution, you probably have some burned-out connections at your timer control. Unplug the machine, take the back off, and examine all the connections and wiring at the control. (The power should be shut off first, of course.) If you find any bad connections, repair them, or replace the whole control with a new one from the manufacturer, if necessary.

If the dryer runs but there is no heat, unplug the dryer and check the heat fuse first. Sometimes you can spot fuse trouble by looking through the holes in the cylinder with a flashlight at the fuse (it's a small glass-cylinder fuse with wire inside that will appear broken if the fuse has blown) and at the electrical connections on the fuse. Or, in an electric dryer that has been used for some time, a heating element may have burned out. A break in a heating element can usually be seen through the holes in the cylinder. If you find one, order a new element from the manufacturer. (If you want to install it yourself, read Sec. 3.7, but if you don't want to tackle the job, call in a repairman.) If fuse and heating element are all right, remove the back of the dryer and look for loose electrical connections. Also, look to see if the belt tension between motor and cylinder looks loose. If the belt is loose, a belt switch will shut off the heater automatically. (Otherwise, clothes might scorch.)

If the dryer motor runs but the cylinder doesn't turn, the belt is at fault. Check the tension and tighten bolts holding the motor in position if they seem loose. If the belt is worn out, get a new one from the manufacturer.

If the dryer scorches clothes, the thermal cutoff control is not operating properly and should be looked at by a qualified repairman.

Gas dryers are much like electric dryers except that instead of heating elements they have burners and thermostatic controls, somewhat like a gas oven. (See Sec. 3.12.) If a gas dryer runs too hot or too cool, get your utility man to check it for you. He usually can spot and correct trouble at a very nominal fee.

4 HEATING

4.1 | **If your house is too cold, check the thermostat first.** This may sound obvious, but there is a lot you can do with a thermostat besides just turning the dial. If your heating system is running too intermittently, it may be that the thermostat isn't working properly. Thermostats for gas- and oil-burning central heating systems are always low voltage, 12 to 24 volts, and can be cleaned without shutting off the power. If you have electric heating in which thermostats usually operate at full voltage—120 to 240 volts—you can get a dangerous shock if you tinker with them while the power is on. So be sure you shut off power on electric heating circuits before you do anything. (See Sec. 2.2.)

To check the thermostat, take the cover off and move the control up and down. Blow out any accumulation of lint and dust—this alone can keep the thermostat from working. Unless you have a brand-new thermostat, clean the contact points by sliding a piece of paper between them when they are closed. Don't use an abrasive, like emery cloth or sandpaper. In new, improved thermostats, contacts are made by mercury in a sealed capsule so dust and moisture can't get at them.

The next thing to do is to make certain there are no heat-producers like radios, television sets, or lamps near your thermostat, because they will keep it from functioning properly.

If the thermostat is in a spot that is warmer than the rest of the house (near a heat register or a fireplace, for instance), naturally it will turn off the heat when the rest of the house is cold. In this case it needs to be relocated by a professional. (Your fuel dealer can often do the job or recommend someone who can.) The thermostat should be in a location where conditions are typical of the whole house. Most often this will be in the living room. It should be on an inside wall (outside walls are cold) three to five feet from the floor, in a spot where people and furniture can't bump into it. Of course, it shouldn't be on an inside wall that has an unheated room on the other side. It shouldn't be in direct sun or behind doors, drapes, or anything else that might cut down air circulation. It shouldn't be near a heat register or fireplace. If you have electric heating, and the thermostat is built into the baseboard, you may have to get an electric heating contractor to install a new wall-mounted thermostat that bypasses the one on the baseboard.

Since most thermostats are slow to respond to sudden changes in outdoor temperatures, it is often advisable to install an outdoor thermostat that senses changes in temperature, wind, and sun and causes the indoor thermostat to adjust its setting accordingly. They are especially helpful in houses of light construction or in those with large glass areas. If you think you need one, ask your fuel dealer.

4.2 | If a warm-air system doesn't deliver enough heat. If a warm-air furnace suddenly stops producing heat and you've checked the thermostat, here are the most likely causes:

1. Someone may have flipped the "oil burner emergency switch" that every oil heating system has. If you don't know where yours is, ask your fuel dealer to show you. If it is in a location where children can reach it, tape it permanently in the "on" position.

2. The filters in the furnace may be clogged with dirt—which causes the furnace to overheat and shut off. The filters are just behind the removable panel on the furnace. If there are two panels, try both. Surface dirt on a filter can be removed with a vacuum cleaner, but if dirt has penetrated the filters you must get new ones from your dealer.

3. The "reset" button on the burner relay, or the one on the stack temperature control, may have turned the current off. The first button is located just outside the firebox of your furnace;,the second is on the smoke flue just a few feet from the furnace. Both buttons are usually red and marked "push to reset" or "twist to reset." Try it to see if your heat comes back on. If heat does come back on, turn your thermostat down until you've had your fuel dealer look at the situation; the reset button popped off because things got too hot.

4. On a gas burner the gas pilot may have gone out, in which case the whole burner shuts off. You can check the pilot through the removable access door on the burner housing. Directions on the housing tell how to relight the pilot. You have to turn off the gas first for a full minute—turn it off at the burner. Then turn it on to the position marked "pilot," and hold in the small red button near the turn-off dial for about half a minute until the pilot will stay lit when

you take away the match. Then you can turn the gas-burner dial to full "on." Have your utility man check the pilot.

5. The fuel tank may be empty—even if the gauge doesn't say so. (Of course, if you are under regular contract with your fuel dealer and he fills the tank automatically before it is empty, this isn't likely.) The gauge may be stuck. Remove the cap and check oil with a thin stick. There should be at least 3 inches to maintain the proper flow of fuel to the burner. If the gauge doesn't work properly, your fuel dealer can fix it.

If your furnace delivers some heat but not enough, and you've checked the points mentioned above as well as the thermostat, it may be that your ducts pass through some unheated area, like an open crawl space (or an unused room). If they are uninsulated, the warm air inside loses its heat to the cold air in the crawl space—so very little of it is left by the time it gets to the rooms you want to heat. Check out your ducts to see where they run, or have your fuel dealer do so, and you'll easily find the trouble spots if there are any. Then you can insulate the ducts with rock wool or glass fiber batts. Both products come in easily applied sheets that are sealed with tape as you wrap them around the ducts. (Note: Uninsulated ducts in a closed basement are not usually a problem, because warmed air from around the duct rises, and will eventually get upstairs one way or another.)

If the upstairs of your house is warm but the downstairs isn't, too much heat is rising up the staircase—warm air always rises. One of the simplest ways to keep more of it downstairs is to install a screen or a folding door either at the top of the stairs or at the bottom. (This is best if you have a closed staircase.) You should also have dampers installed in the main ducts at the first-floor level—this is far more effective than trying to close the register upstairs, because closing the registers still leaves the upper length of the main duct full of hot air. Ask your fuel dealer or a heating contractor about putting in dampers—it isn't something you should try to do yourself.

If your house is warm in some rooms but not in others, and it isn't due to the reasons mentioned above or to a poorly located thermostat, perhaps your registers are badly placed. (Also, make sure they aren't blocked with furniture or drapes.) Warm-air registers should all be at the perimeter of the house. You can either relocate registers, which involves a lot of duct work and expense, or you can "balance" your system. This way you can have the temperature 72° in the living room, 68° in the bedrooms, and 80° in the bathroom —if you want to. Here's how to go about it: Choose a typical cool day when the temperature is not over 40°. Place a thermometer near the center of each room, a few feet from the door, with the room door in its normal position. (If it is normally closed, leave it that way.) Open all dampers and registers and leave the thermostat at one setting for several hours. Then check the temperatures in all rooms. For rooms that are too warm, start shutting down registers and dampers. Close them halfway and give thermometers about an hour to register the new temperatures. Cold rooms should get warmer, warm rooms cooler. Continue adjustments until you have the room temperatures you want.

Another way you can get more even heat distribution is to have your fuel dealer adjust your furnace to provide continuous air circulation (CAC) if it doesn't already. If your furnace fires too infrequently, rooms farthest from the furnace may get cold before the furnace goes on again. It is reasonably simple for your fuel dealer to adjust your furnace to provide CAC. Then the furnace will cycle on and off more often, and the fan will continuously send air out and pull it back to the hot firebox—maintaining a steady flow of warm air around the house. The operating costs of CAC are less than the hotter but less even operation of noncontinuous air circulation.

In any case, the best way to make sure of getting the best results from your warm-air heating system is to have your fuel dealer check it over periodically. Many dealers have regular maintenance contracts which are well worth considering, because if anything goes wrong it is taken care of under the contract—you're not suddenly hit with a big bill you didn't expect. If anything does go wrong with your furnace, you should call your dealer whether you have a contract or not. If you are a regular customer, his service charge will probably be low. He can make most repairs easily, often in just a few minutes, so you should not attempt them yourself—if you do, you may end up spending far more in the long run.

4.3 | If a radiator (hot-water) system isn't producing enough heat—and you've checked the thermostat, as in Section 4.1—first of all, check the oil burner emergency switch and the fuel tank, as in Section 4.2. Then make sure the radiators are working properly.

All radiators have an air valve at the top to let air out of the system so the hot water, or steam, can enter and circulate freely. (Hot water enters through a valve in the bottom, but air pressure in the radiator will keep it from getting in.) Most air valves are automatic, but some must be "bled" manually to let the air out. In an automatic valve, the hot water or steam trying to enter the radiator gives the air enough of a push to open the valve. (When the hot water or steam hits the valve, a thermostatic control closes it.) But if the valve is stuck the radiator is air-bound and no hot water or steam can enter.

If you have automatic valves and the boiler is working but a radiator is not hot, shut off the radiator at the shutoff valve near the floor and unscrew the air valve by hand. If air rushes out, replace the valve and turn on the radiator. If it heats up some now, the valve is clogged. To unclog it, remove it (after shutting off the radiator, of course) and boil it in washing soda for half an hour, or soak it in carbon tetrachloride. If you have manual valves, all radiators should be bled of air at the beginning of the heating season, and whenever a radiator fails to heat up. Open the valve until water runs out, then close it immediately. It's a good idea to replace manual valves with automatic ones so your heating system will function more efficiently and you'll be spared the trouble of bleeding them manually. If you don't know whether you have manual or automatic valves, your fuel dealer can tell you.

If there is no rush of air when you remove the air valve, the radiator and the supply line are probably clogged with trapped water. The supply line from the boiler must pitch slightly from the radiator back to the boiler. Check it with a carpenter's level. If it doesn't, slip wedges under all four legs of the radiator so the supply line does pitch. (The radiator itself must be level.) If you can't get the proper pitch this way, you'll have to have a professional do some pipe fitting.

Radiators that are dirty can't throw all the heat they should, so clean their fins regularly with a vacuum cleaner. If your radiators are painted with aluminum or other metal paint, you can make them supply about 15 per cent more heat by painting them with a flat alkyd oil paint in a pale or pastel color. First remove the scaling and peeling paint. Leave the back of the radiators bare or paint them with metallic paint that will reflect the heat back into the room. Or you can place a reflector of aluminum foil or metal against the wall behind the radiator. You can mount your reflectors in frames to improve their appearance.

If all radiators are in good working condition, but some parts of the house are warm while others aren't, you can adjust the radiators to make some of them heat before others. That is, you can balance the system, as in Section 4.2. Those radiators farthest from the boiler are generally the last to heat up and their adjustable valves should be set for the widest opening, those nearest the boiler with smaller openings. If a big radiator near the thermostat heats up too fast, causing the thermostat to shut off the boiler before other radiators are hot, the unit must be replaced with a smaller radiator before you can balance the system. You can balance the system somewhat by partially shutting off the radiator shutoff valve. On a hot-water system, if you have balancing valves on the other end of radiators, you can do a better balancing job just by turning the valve a bit at a time. A balancing valve is opened and closed with a screwdriver in the slotted top of the valve. In a steam system, you should balance radiators by adjusting automatic air valves. If you have manual valves for bleeding air in a steam system, replace them with automatic valves.

If (in an older house or a very large one) radiators farthest from the boiler are not hot enough, and you can't correct the situation by balancing the system, it may be that the hot water or steam can't reach the radiators before losing most of their heat in the pipes. If they pass through unheated areas, they should be insulated to prevent heat loss (see Sec. 1.33). Or you may need a new circulating pump at the boiler. Any plumbing and heating contractor or your fuel dealer can tell you if you need one, and can install one. In a large house, the only good way to get even or controlled heat in all parts of the house with a hot-water system is by zoning. Zoning, in effect, gives you two or more hot-water circulation systems, all running off the same boiler, but each system serves just one part of the house and is controlled by a thermostat in that part of the house. If you don't have zoning, it will cost a fair amount of money to put it in, but it won't cost you anything to talk to your plumbing and heating contractor about it. If you aren't sure whether you have zoning or not, take a look at your boiler and see if you have more than one circulating pump in the piping around the boiler. Or ask your fuel man to tell you.

Like a warm-air furnace, a hot-water system should be checked over periodically by your fuel dealer, even if it seems to be working properly. Or you can get a maintenance contract with your dealer (see Sec. 4.2). If any adjustments to your boiler are needed, you should call your dealer or maintenance man—don't try to do the work yourself. A hot-water system will not work right unless the water is at the right level. All radiators should be full, and the expansion tank half full. The black arrow on the boiler gauge should rest over the red arrow that shows what the level should be. If the black arrow falls below the red arrow, a valve should automatically replenish the system. If it doesn't, the valve needs checking. Your maintenance man can make these adjustments in a matter of minutes. In very cold weather he can also increase pressure in your system to raise water temperatures and increase the heat delivered to the radiators.

4.4 | If your electric heating system isn't functioning properly the only thing to do is to call a qualified electrical contractor. Tinkering with such a system can be very dangerous.

It's possible that your house is not sufficiently insulated to allow electric heat to work well. In this case you will need the services of an insulating contractor.

4.5 | If your heating system is too noisy you can almost always make it quieter. Check your long runs of ducts for reverberation. They can be stiffened with wood bracing, or light sheet-metal ducts can be replaced with rigid glass-fiber ducts that won't transmit noise. Another cause of noise is a loose fan-motor mounting. (You can also remount it on rubber antivibration mountings.) If this doesn't cut down the noise, have your fuel dealer or maintenance man check the belt tension, fan speed, blower centering in cabinet opening, fan bearings, end play in shaft, thrust collar adjustment, oil or grease cups, and the inner casing of the furnace. (Occasionally this gets loose.) Don't try to repair any of these parts yourself—a heating system is too expensive and complicated to tinker with.

If you have a hot-water system and are bothered by water hammer, it is usually due to a water trap in your lines. They should slant back to the boiler, but in older houses, where there has been a lot of settling, they sometimes don't in spots. Check your mains and return lines with a carpenter's level to see if they slant back. If they don't, prop them up to get the right slant by putting wedges under all four radiator legs. If you can't get the slant this way, you'll have to have them refitted by a professional.

A roaring noise in the firebox of either furnace or boiler is usually due to the design of the firebox and flue. The only way to correct this is to have the firebox and flue opening rebuilt. Your fuel dealer can tell you whether this is feasible and how much it would cost.

4.6 | If you have dirt and odors in a warm-air heating system, first of all check your filters. (See Sec. 4.2.) Filters should be inspected and cleaned every few months. Dirt streaks can also be the result of too much fan speed, dirt on the blower fan, air leaks around the registers, or dirt in the registers. Registers should connect fairly tightly with the duct leading to them, or the rush of warm air can pull dirt particles at the floor into the air stream and up onto the walls. If there is a big leak around the base of the register you can glue a piece of felt around it to seal it off. Clean registers thoroughly at least once a month. Do not sweep dirt into the return, or cold air, register—this does not lead to the firebox, but. back to the fan and then again out to the warm-air registers.

If you detect any odors in your heating system, have your fuel dealer check the burner and the firebox immediately. If the burner is not operating properly, it will need expert adjustment and if the firebox is leaking, it will have to be recemented or rebuilt.

4.7 | If the air is too dry you can humidify it. The simplest type of humidifier for a warm-air system is a special type of pan of water in the furnace, right in the warm-air stream. Water in the pan is automatically controlled by a float valve that allows more water to come in as water evaporates into the air stream. In hard-water areas, the float and valve have to be checked every month to be sure they're not blocked with mineral deposit. More dependable and better humidification is possible with a "spray"- or "plate"-type humidifier. These are both automatic pieces of equipment mounted like the one above, in the warm-air stream in the furnace. But they are far more efficient, can be set for any amount of moisture, and can be governed by a humidistat—which is somewhat like a thermostat and sends down a signal for more water when the air gets too dry. These units also should be checked every month for hard-water mineral deposits. Your fuel dealer can tell you about all three types of humidifiers and what they cost to install.

If you have a hot-water system, about the easiest way to get more moisture into the air is to put a cloth wick over the radiator and supply it with water. To do this, take two long and narrow pans filled with water, and wire them like saddle bags across the radiator; then drape a piece of cloth over the radiator with its ends on either side in the pans. (There are special galvanized radiator pans made for this purpose.) This is unsightly, but a radiator enclosure will hide the wick and pans. This will throw far more moisture into the air in a short time than just a pan of water sitting on the radiator. Another alternative is to have a heating dealer install an independent vaporizing type of humidifier.

4.8 │ How to cut fuel costs. The best way to keep heat bills down is to keep the heat in the house. If you don't have storm sash on your house, you may lose more heat to the outside through your windows than through all the rest of the house put together. Close-fitting storm sash may pay for itself in fuel saved in two heating seasons for most houses. (In big old houses, they pay for themselves in one heating season if you put them up yourself.) Section 8.29 tells how to install storm sash.

The next biggest heat loss you may have is the leakage of cold outside air into the house through cracks around doors and windows. (A stiff wind can change the air in a house with a few good cracks once an hour—this makes your heating system heat up the house all over again every hour.) All windows and doors should be thoroughly weatherstripped. (See Secs. 8.1, 8.2, and 8.14.) All joints where siding meets the window frame (Sec. 12.2) and joints at the foundation (Sec. 10.2) should be caulked tight.

Next, if your house is not insulated, you should consult a building or insulation contractor about insulating it. If your ceiling is uninsulated, this is the first area to tackle, because more heat goes up through a ceiling than out through a solid wall. You can take up attic floor boards to put down ceiling insulation. It can be blown in the ceiling because this space is well ventilated—this is also the easiest method. An insulation contractor can do a good job of this for a reasonable price. You should not insulate uninsulated walls in modern houses by blowing insulation into them. Reason: There may be no vapor barrier in the wall (see Sec. 12.7) and moisture migrating through the wall in winter, when it pushes out through walls (because air inside is more moist than that outside), will condense in the insulation and make it wet, unless the wall is ventilated well enough to evaporate the moisture. In old houses with no sheathing in the wall, the wall is ventilated quite well through the joints in shingles and clapboards, and insulation can be blown in these walls with very good results. If your floors are cold and you have a crawl space, the floors should be insulated with 4-inch batt-type insulation or aluminum insulation. This is an accordion type of insulation that when unfolded and stapled into a floor joist space provides several layers of aluminum foil with air spaces between each layer. Ask your dealer how to install this so layers stay apart.

Here are a few additional fuel-saving tips:

1. If you have a fireplace, make sure the damper in the chimney is closed when you don't have a fire in the fireplace. An open damper is the same thing as an open window. The same is true of an open garage door in an attached garage.

2. Don't turn your thermostat back much more than 10 degrees at night—it's cheaper to keep the house warm all night than to heat it up all the way again in the morning.

3. If you have heating ducts or hot-water pipes (either for heating or hot-water supply) in unheated areas, make sure they are insulated to reduce heat loss. (See Secs. 4.2 and 4.3.)

4. If you have leaky hot-water faucets, fix them—they're pouring fuel (or electricity) down the drain. (See Secs. 1.22 through 1.24.)

5. If you have a warm-air system, have your dealer set it for continuous air circulation—this is cheaper than intermittent operation. (See Sec. 4.2.)

6. If you have a hot-water system, have your dealer turn the aquastat down in the summer. The aquastat sets the temperature of the water in the system, and the thermostat sets the air temperature in the room. In summer you only need hot water at the faucets, so your system can be turned down perhaps 20 degrees. Of course, this will save fuel.

4.9 | Remodeling your heating system. If your heating system is beyond salvage call in a few fuel dealers or heating contractors for bids on various heating systems that could replace it. If you are going to use warm-air heat, specify that you want perimeter heat at the floor. This puts the registers at the ouside wall where you need the heat to supplant that lost to the outside walls. If the perimeter of your rooms is warm enough, then the whole house will be. Your thermostat should be on an inside wall. When the furnace goes on, the coldest part of the room—the outside wall—will heat up first. (See Sec. 4.1.)

If you now have hot-water heat you can often use the old risers and returns for a new hot-water system, so you don't have to do a lot of chopping and tearing open of walls. You'll want to replace old radiators with new baseboard radiation units. This is just like the perimeter heat mentioned above, except that it is radiant heat instead of being convected by an air stream. Baseboard radiation units are unobtrusive and save floor space that radiators used to take up.

If you live in a hot climate and are considering adding air conditioning, you may want to consider a combination heating and air conditioning system. (Read Sec. 5.4.)

In any case, it will pay you to scrap your old furnace or boiler. Today's new units are much better and more efficient.

5 COOLING

5.1 | How to cool your house without air conditioning. On the hottest day in summer, it can still be cool under a shade tree. Your house can be reasonably cool too, even without an air conditioner.

Here's how to make it cool. First make sure that the top of your house is adequately ventilated, just like the top of a tree. Attics without ventilation, under dark shingle roofs, can be very hot in summer and serve as a radiator to heat up the whole house. An attic can heat up to more than 140 degrees, and unless the attic is ventilated its heat will dissipate down through the ceiling into the house, well into the cool night. The hot ceilings then radiate heat to everything within the rooms.

A deep blanket of insulation in the attic floor is the first necessity for cutting down this heat flow, but it is no cure-all for the build-up of heat in the attic. (Insulation delays the penetration of heat, but doesn't stop it altogether.) You must provide a way for the heat to get out—that is, vent the attic. If you don't have openings in the soffit (See Fig. 11-10), try to provide for some and put in gable-end louvers or open your attic windows.

An even better way to vent the attic, especially if you are not planning to install an attic fan, is to install a special metal venting strip along the roof ridge as in Figure 5-1. This strip, available at most lumber dealers, takes advantage of the fact that hot air rises —in this case, right up out of the house. You can install it yourself by cutting back shingles and sheathing 1 to 2 inches on either side of the roof ridge and nailing it in place. Or you can have a carpenter put it in. Once installed, it is barely discernible from the ground. Even with a ridge vent, you still need gable-end openings or soffit vents to provide a steady flow of air to the ridge vent.

If venting alone isn't enough, you should install an attic fan. There are several ways of using such a fan: (1) You can place the fan in one gable opening so it will exhaust air drawn in under the soffit or in through the other gable. In this case, the fan is primarily draw-

106

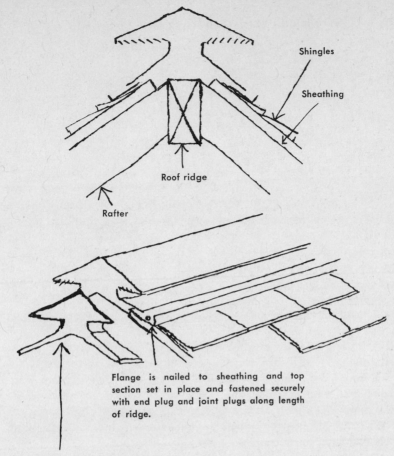

Shingles

Sheathing

Roof ridge

Rafter

Flange is nailed to sheathing and top
section set in place and fastened securely
with end plug and joint plugs along length
of ridge.

Figure 5-1   Ridge vent

ing hot air out of the attic. (2) You can install the fan in a gable
opening as before, but make it primarily remove hot air from the
living area of the house by closing all other attic louvers and windows
and providing a central ceiling vent from the house. (Or you can
leave the attic door open if you prefer.) (3) If there are a number of
louvers in the attic, it may be simpler to install the fan in a suction
box over the ceiling vent—see Figure 5-2—than to close up all the
openings. In this case, the fan is mounted in the suction box and
draws hot air from below into the attic, where it escapes through
louvers and the ridge vent, if there is one.

Attic fans can lower attic temperatures as much as 30 degrees,
which can lower room temperatures below as much as 10 degrees.

107

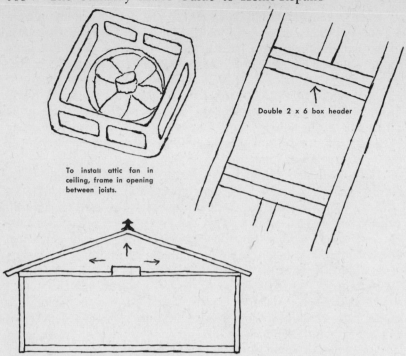

To install attic fan in ceiling, frame in opening between joists.

Double 2 x 6 box header

Figure 5-2   Fan in suction box

If you have an air conditioner, an attic fan can help it do a better job of cooling.

You should also eliminate as much as possible of the heat you produce in the house. Installing ventilating fans through the wall in kitchen and bath is a good way of dispelling the heat generated by cooking and hot showers. Most through-the-wall fans come with instructions for cutting through the wall and mounting the fan. The outside of the unit has fold-up metal louvers that protect from the rain and prevent cold air from pouring into the house in winter. For more information on cutting an opening in an outside wall, see Section 8.31; also, see Section 2.11 for wiring in a new outlet.

In addition, individual rooms can be ventilated with fans that are mounted in the window. These are very useful if there is an open window on the opposite side of the room. They can pull the breeze right through. But be sure they aren't pulling in air from the sunny side of the house.

Finally, you should cut down on sun and hot air coming in from outside by protecting the sunny side of the house from the direct rays of the sun. Planting shade trees or using shading devices, like patio roofs, will help. A wide overhang will greatly increase shade too. (See Sec. 11.10.) It's best to use adjustable venetian blinds or louvered shutters on the *outside* of the windows if possible. This will keep the sun from building up heat on the window itself, and at the same time let the breezes go right through. The trouble with using awnings over windows is that they often let a hot pocket of air build up just outside the window.

Light-colored roofs and walls reflect the sun's rays and cut down on much of the heat the house would otherwise absorb.

5.2 | Cooling with an air conditioner. If you have an air conditioner but it isn't cooling enough, it's probably your fault—not the air conditioner's. No machine can possibly overcome the full effect of a hot sun, so do everything you can to cut down on hot air coming in from outside. (See the last two paragraphs of preceding section.)

Make certain that the filter on the air conditioner is clean. (All conditioners have a filter to remove dust from the air before it is cooled and dehumidified and pushed into the room. As it becomes blocked with dust, the cooling operation is slowed down. In a central air conditioning system, the filter can become blocked in only a few weeks.) Filters are easily accessible behind the snap-on cover of the air conditioner. If you have the disposable type of filter, replace it when it is dirty. If you have a "renewable" or "lifetime" type, remove it and clean it. The vacuum cleaner does the best job on glass fiber filters. Aluminum mesh or plastic foam filters (most new filters are either of these kinds, and last three to five years) are washable in soap and water. After washing, the aluminum mesh type must be recoated with a filter oil.

If you have both an air conditioner and attic fan, make sure the attic fan is not drawing cooled air from the living area of the house.

If hot pockets of air develop in some spots, you can improve circulation by placing a small electric fan near the ceiling, aimed in the direction of the air conditioner, and running it at low speed. With a little experimenting you'll find it can break up stagnant pockets of hot air near the ceiling and make the whole room cooler.

If your air conditioner won't work at all, the trouble is usually not in the machine but in your electric wiring. It may be that your wiring and fuses can't handle the starting load or the running load. If this is the case, you should use slow-blow fuses or delayed-action circuit breakers, and have the air conditioner on a separate circuit. (See Chap. 2.) If the problem doesn't lie in your wiring, but in the unit itself, take it to a reputable repairman or the dealer you purchased it from. Don't try to repair a faulty unit yourself. Sealed motors, compressors, and refrigeration cycles need a professional for repair. See Section 3.13 for a description of a refrigeration cycle, which, basically, is the same in an air conditioner as in a refrigerator.

5.3 | **How to maintain your air conditioner year-round.** Like any fine piece of carefully engineered mechanism, an air conditioner needs periodic attention. All room units should be thoroughly cleaned at the end of the cooling season, whether you are going to store them or leave them in the wall or window. Clean with the vacuum cleaner nozzle wherever you can reach without hitting anything. (Of course, the plug should be pulled out first.) Use a small brush for hard-to-reach parts. Remove all dust and debris from the motor, frame, compressor, and coils. Remove and clean the filter (see Sec. 5.2), or replace it if it is the disposable type. Check for worn belts, bent fan blades, and loose bolts. Oil the motor—unless it is sealed—according to the manufacturer's directions. In addition, inspect the outdoor end of the machine. The space between window sill and the overhanging cabinet of the conditioner, sheltered as it is from rain and snow, can collect birds, leaves, and insects.

Every so often it's a good idea to have the dealer from whom you purchased the unit—or some other qualified maintenance man— make a routine check of your air conditioner. Or you can get a service contract from your dealer. They are not expensive and provide you with excellent service. If there's trouble with your unit, you may encounter considerable costs (even if the unit was guaranteed) unless you have a service contract.

5.4 | **Can you put central air conditioning in your house?** The answer is almost always Yes, at a reasonable price, if you choose the right system for your house. (But in some older houses, it is often easier and less expensive to install a number of room units than to tear up walls and ceilings to install the ductwork for a central unit. (See Sec. 5.7.) Get opinions and estimates from a number of reputable air conditioning dealers. Before you can install any kind of air conditioning equipment, you may have to put in a new electrical service entrance to give you enough power—see Chapter 2. If this is the case, your dealer will tell you.

If you now have ductwork for warm-air heating, a cooling system may be able to use the same ductwork. This costs less than having a completely separate cooling system, for even filters and furnace blower do double duty for cooling. The cooling coil is located in the furnace plenum (where ducts connect to furnace), and from it small copper refrigeration pipes connect to a weatherproof refrigeration section—called the condenser—set in the yard, garage, or carport. But your ducts and blower have to be big enough to handle cooling or you can't add it on this way.

If your ducts aren't big enough (your dealer will tell you) or if you have hot-water or steam heat, you'll need a separate air conditioning system. The best system to use is a split system where the compressor and condenser are set outside the house. In addition to functioning better this way, this keeps the noise of the compressor and condenser fan outside the house. The cheapest kind of separate system uses a self-contained unit like a big room air conditioner equipped with insulated glass fiber ducts to distribute the cooled, cleaned, dehumidified air. They are insulated because these units are usually installed in attics and you don't want the hot attic air to cut down on cooling. In a long, rambling ranch house, two such units can be installed, one serving the living area, the other the bedrooms. In a two-story house, one unit is usually installed in the attic, the other in the basement.

In a separate air conditioning system, outlet registers for cold air should be at the ceiling because cold air drops. Return registers, to let warmed-up air get recooled, should be across the room at the ceiling also, because warm air rises.

If you want the quietest unit possible and are in a position to install a heating and cooling system all in one (and your house is on a gas main), you should get one of the new gas-fired units that have no compressor, motor, or valves to cause noise or vibration. The only moving part is the blower, and both heating and cooling use one fuel—gas. Another combination heating and cooling system you may want to look into, if you live where winters are mild, is the heat pump. These units are essentially reversible air conditioners. They can make indoor air cool by pumping the heat out of it and releasing this heat outdoors. When you turn a switch you reverse a cycle so the machine runs backward, taking hot air from outside and bringing it in. This system cannot handle the heavy heating loads of northern winters.

5.5 | How to select a wall or window air conditioner. Keep in mind, first of all, that you get just what you pay for. There are scarcely ever any real bargains, though once in a while you can find one off-season when a dealer is selling out last year's models.

Second, make sure you have enough wiring—or can put it in—to handle an air conditioner. Some units can be plugged into almost any outlet in the house. But most require a separate circuit—115 or 230 volts. In some cases, you might have to install a new electrical service panel. You can't run an air conditioner on an overloaded circuit, or on one with insufficient voltage. Check your wiring with your dealer or the local power company. For a better understanding of wiring, see Chapter 2.

Third, don't take anybody's word for how quiet an air conditioner is. The simplest way to check for noise is to turn the unit to "High Cooling" and put your ear right against the cold air grill, which will be inside the room. Compare all units you are considering. If there are two similar models, the heavier one will usually be quieter.

Fourth, make sure the unit you buy is just large enough for your needs. If it is too small it may frost up too heavily and burn out. If it is too large it will run intermittently and fail to remove enough moisture from the air, and the atmosphere will be clammy. If you can't get exactly the size air conditioner you need, get the next smaller size rather than the next larger, because an undersized unit will run continuously and remove more moisture than an oversized one running intermittently. Even if the temperature gets a little higher, you'll be more comfortable.

The size, rating, or capacity (they all mean the same in this case) of an air conditioner is a measure of how much heat it will remove in one hour of operation. The measure used is a British thermal unit (BTU). The higher the number of BTU's, the greater the cooling power of the unit. A good dealer or salesman will figure out the BTU rating your unit should have by working out the heat losses through windows, walls, and floors, and taking into consideration the direction the room faces, amount of roof overhang, and so forth. If he asks only how large the room is, he doesn't know enough. Most dealers use special tables or forms, which take all factors into account, to figure out the BTU you need. If you want to figure out capacity for yourself, get the NEMA "Cooling Load Estimate Form" from your dealer or send a stamped, self-addressed envelope to NEMA, Department ICN, 155 East 44 Street, New York, N. Y., 10017.

5.6 | Installing a room unit is not difficult if you take your time and follow the manufacturer's directions implicitly. Most window units are designed for double-hung windows up to 48 inches wide, and come with do-it-yourself installation kits. A unit with adjustable panels that slide out from each side to fill the window frame is handiest if you plan to remove the unit in the fall.

A window unit should be installed as far away from doors and other windows as possible. This is to prevent drafts from carrying away cool air before it can cool the room. Try to place the unit in a shady spot. If it must be in the sun, protect it with a ventilated awning.

Before installing the unit be sure to check the level of the sill. To work right the unit must be exactly level. If the sill isn't level, shim up the unit with thin pieces of wood. Then check the level both from front to back and from side to side with a carpenter's level.

Installing a through-the-wall unit involves cutting a hole in the wall and putting in a wall sleeve, outside bracing, and supports. The air conditioner is then inserted into the sleeve and bolted into position. (If you want to do this job yourself, read Sec. 8.31.) An advantage of through-the-wall units is that they don't take up valuable window space, and can be placed where you want them—on the shady side of the room, even if there are no windows there.

⑥ WALLS AND CEILINGS

MINOR REPAIRS AND CLEANING

6.1 | **Cleaning walls, woodwork, and ceilings.** Most wall and woodwork paints are washable, some more than others. Use a household cleanser with trisodium phosphate in it. (You can tell by reading the label.) If you prefer, you can buy trisodium phosphate at the hardware store and mix your own solution of 1 or 2 tablespoons to a gallon of lukewarm water. This cleanser will remove grease and dirt from painted plaster, drywall, or woodwork, without leaving a soapy film. To prevent streaking, wash only a small area at a time and begin at baseboard level, working upward with a circular motion. Rinse at once with clear water before the wash water can dry. If your walls are drywall (they'll resound like a drum rather than a hard rock when you rap them with your knuckle) be extremely sparing with water, because the drywall surface may absorb water and swell slightly, making a noticeable spot in the wall.

If your ceiling has become dark through age, dust, or smoke from kitchen or fireplace, there's not much you can do about cleaning it. You can get the dirt off, but the surface will always look streaked. The only solution is to repaint it.

The method of cleaning wallpaper depends on the type of paper. Washable (plastic-surfaced) paper can be cleaned with ordinary mild soap and cold water. Keep your cloth or sponge as dry as possible and do only a small area at a time, working from bottom to top to avoid drip marks. Nonwashable papers can be cleaned with special puttylike cleaners. It's a good idea to clean a hidden corner first, to make sure the cleaner doesn't remove color as well as dirt. Rework the cleaner frequently so that a fresh surface is always exposed. All crumbs and dirt from the cleaner should be wiped away after cleaning. Fabric-covered walls can usually be washed like washable wallpaper, but try out a small section first. Grass cloth and

114

rice paper are not washable but can usually be cleaned with regular wallpaper cleaner.

Grease, oil, or crayon stains on wallpaper can be removed by covering them with a ¼-inch-thick layer of a paste made of powdered chalk (at your hardware store) or regular flour mixed with carbon tetrachloride or clear liquid spot remover. Let the paste dry, then remove it with a soft brush. (This same method can be used to remove water stains from washable wallpaper.) If you are removing a spot from badly soiled paper, clean around the spot with wallpaper cleaner first—or you will have a dirty ring around it.

Ink stains can be removed with a commercial ink remover or with a weak solution of chlorine bleach, immediately followed by cold water. If you are able to treat the ink spot while still wet, blot up the excess and apply absorbent powder to the spot. Brush it off when it begins to absorb the ink and repeat the process as many times as necessary.

If a stain will not come out by any method, you can cover it with a new piece of the same wallpaper. First seal the old stain with a coat of shellac—which will be covered by the new patch—so the grease or color cannot come through. Then patch the stain, as described in the next section.

6.2 | How to repair torn wallpaper. If corners or seams of wallpaper pull loose while the paper is still in good repair, you can stick them back with ordinary library paste slightly thinned with water. If paper should separate from the wall and form a bulge, cut a slit with a sharp knife along a line of the design and apply paste with a small brush. Press the paper in place and hold a clean white blotter against it until the paper sticks. With washable plastic-surfaced paper, Scotch tape can be used to hold the wallpaper down until it sticks.

If a piece of regular (nonwashable) wallpaper is torn off and you must patch it, tear the edges of the patch gently to make them blend in more smoothly—being sure, of course, that the pattern matches. If plastic-surface wallpaper must be patched, cut out the bad spot in a perfect rectangle (use a square and a razor blade) and replace it with a new piece of exactly the same dimension (of course, the pattern must match exactly). There should be no overlap at the joints. (See Fig. 6-1.) A good way to do this is to lay one piece of wallpaper over the tear and cut both out at once—then you have an exact fit for your patch.

1. Cut out damaged spot in shape of perfect rectangle, using square and razor blade. Where possible, follow design lines.

2. Replace with another piece of exactly same size, matching design carefully.

Figure 6-1   Patching wallpaper

6.3 | Patching cracks and small holes in plaster walls and ceilings is not difficult, and sooner or later every plaster wall needs such repairs. Cracking occurs when the framework shrinks or settles, and in a new house a few cracks may appear until settling has ended —which may take several months. Do not attempt repairs until new cracks have stopped appearing.

The easiest material to work with in filling small cracks, nail holes, and the like is spackling compound, a white powder that is mixed with water to make a thick paste. It hardens less rapidly than painter's patching plaster (plaster of Paris), so it's a better choice for the amateur.

Caution: When working with spackle or other plaster compounds, do not pour leftover mix down the sink, for it will harden and block the drain.

The first step in patching is to clean away any loose plaster. Hairline cracks should be widened sufficiently to accept the spackle. (An excellent tool for this is a beer-can opener.) The crack should be "undercut"—that is, made wider underneath than on the surface, so plaster can lock itself in.

Prepare your spackle in an old dish or pan to thick puttylike consistency, according to the package directions. Wet down the crack or hole with a wet paint brush. This prevents old plaster from drawing too much moisture from the spackle so it cannot "set" or cure right. Force the spackle into the crack with a putty knife or your finger. (See Fig. 6-2.) (You may find it easier to apply and smooth spackle with your hand.) When thoroughly dry, sand off rough spots, blending in edges with a circular sanding motion. It may

Figure 6-2   Tools for patching

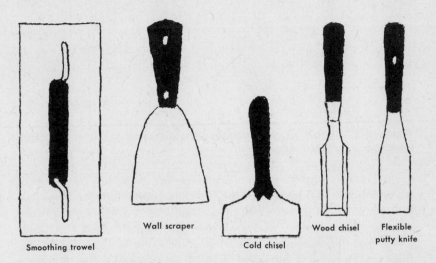

Smoothing trowel

Wall scraper

Cold chisel

Wood chisel

Flexible putty knife

be necessary to apply a second coat of spackle to even out the surface completely. Spackle shrinks when drying, so if your crack is large let the patch bulge from the wall slightly, and when dry, sand it even with the rest of the wall.

Textured surfaces can be matched when patching by stippling with the tip of a paint brush when the patch is still wet. If the surface is sand-finished, a little fine sand or texture additive (from the paint store) can be added to a skin, or topping coat, of spackle.

Large and persistent cracks are usually due to expansion and contraction—from summer to winter—of the framework behind the wall, or to the woodwork and trim working away from the wall in the dry winter and resealing cracks when it expands with higher humidity in the summer. If the cracks appear seasonally at corners and where walls and ceilings meet, your best bet is to cover them with wood moldings, rather than trying to patch them. Drill the moldings with a fine drill for nailing holes and then nail them to just one surface so they can move with that surface—riding back and forth over the crack. (See Fig. 6-3.)

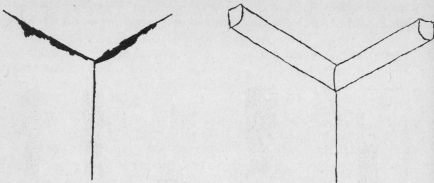

Figure 6-3   Using quarter-round corner molding to cover persistent crack between wall and ceiling

If it is necessary to patch a persistent crack, drywall joint cement is the best material to use. It acts like a glue, tending to bond a crack together so that it doesn't open up as readily as it would with ordinary spackle. Your lumber dealer carries joint cement (for very wide joints, you will also need paper joint tape) and the mixing instructions on the bag are very clear. First clean out and widen the crack if it is very narrow—see above—then apply joint cement in two coats. The first coat should fill the crack only to about half the depth and should not be smoothed off—the second coat will adhere better to a rough surface. Let the first coat dry six hours before applying the second coat, and let the second coat dry overnight before sanding smooth.

New plastic and fiber patching materials, which are considerably stronger than joint cement and will prove much better for persistent cracks, are just now coming on the market. Ask your hardware dealer about them. If he carries any, he can give you complete instructions as to their use.

6.4 | How to patch larger holes or bulges. If the hole or bulge is less than 16 inches at it widest, it's easiest to repair it with painter's patching plaster (plaster of Paris). If it's larger, it's easiest to patch with a piece of drywall.

Holes and bulges are usually caused by moisture. Before making any repairs to the wall, check to see if there are any leaks; if so, repair them. (See Secs. 8.2, 8.15, and 11.1.) Then remove all loose plaster or drywall, and if there is a bulge remove all the bulge area with a hammer and cold chisel. (If you don't, it will probably remove itself before long by simply falling out of the wall or ceiling.)

If there is a surface beneath the plaster you have chipped away against which you can patch—wood lath, wire lath, or gypsum lath—and your patch is less than 16 inches, you're all set to patch with plaster of Paris. When using this material follow instructions on the bag, and mix only what you can use within ten minutes—it will harden in this time. (You can slow its set somewhat by adding a little vinegar to the mix.) Pour some of the powder into a clean galvanized bucket, add water until your consistency is like heavy cream, and stir. You'll feel it thicken and start to set as you stir. When it can stand up in a tip, like whipped cream, apply it to the patch with a trowel. Work fast, filling only one part of the patch at a time. Smooth with trowel and wet brush. If plaster sets up too fast, you can trim it down with a surform (it's like a wood rasp with handles—see Fig. 16-1) and an old saw blade. When leftover plaster sets hard in the bucket, knock it out by hitting the bucket with a hammer. Mix another batch to complete the patch. The next day you can sand it smooth.

If the hole is wide open, with no surface behind it on which to plaster, or if the lath is damaged and must be removed, you can provide a backing of a board, a piece of drywall, or a wire screen. Hold it tight against the back of the hole by a string held in place by wooden blocks. (See Fig. 6-4.) String and blocks can be removed within a

Figure 6-4   Holding backing screen in place with wood block

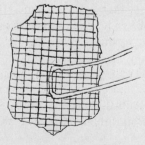 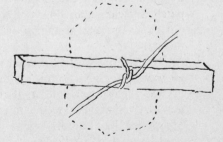

1. Place wire screen behind hole and thread string through openings. Hold string taut while patching plaster is applied with flexible knife.

2. When hole is completely plastered, tie string tightly around wooden block bridging ends of hole. Leave in place until plaster sets.

half hour after plaster of Paris has set. Or, you can cut a piece of expanded wire mesh slightly larger than the hole and force it in against
the hole's edge. This will make a fairly rigid backing against which
you can plaster. (Fig. 6-5.) On top of the mesh use plaster of
Paris or some perlite ready-mixed plaster (from the hardware or
mason supply store).

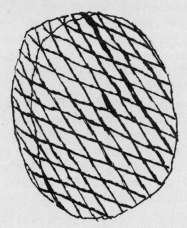

Figure 6-5   Using expanded
wire mesh as backing for
plaster

If the hole or bulge is bigger than 16 inches, use a piece of drywall that you can nail to the studs. Cut the drywall just smaller than
the holes and nail it through the lath, if there is any, to the studs in
the wall. Then treat the joints with joint cement, as in Section 6.3.
If drywall is not thick enough to rest against lath or framing and
come out to the surface of the surrounding wall, fatten out the
studs or the lath over the studs with pieces of wood. You can cut
the drywall for the patch most easily by using an old keyhole saw—
this is a saw with a thin blade about 12 to 18 inches long. If your
patch is rectangular, however, you can cut it by cutting through just
the paper surface of the drywall with a knife, and breaking along
the cut.

If an entire wall or panel has been damaged, it's best to remove
all the plaster or drywall, including the baseboard, and put up new
drywall, as in Section 6.34. If depth is not important you can apply
new drywall right over the new surface, without removing anything
except the baseboard.

Plaster that has been applied directly over masonry (a chimney,
for example) will inevitably crack, soften, and fall away from con-

densation. If you have such a situation, it can only be remedied by furring out an inch or so and applying drywall or paneling. (See Fig. 6-14.)

6.5 | Repairing holes and cracks in woodwork and cabinets. Most holes, dents, and cracks in a wood surface can be repaired easily with putty or plastic wood, and painted when dry. If your wood is stained, add some matching stain to the plastic wood. If nailheads are showing in your woodwork or cabinets, counterset them with a nail set (which looks like a steel pin with a long tapered point) and fill holes with putty or plastic wood. Don't use spackle on wood, because when it dries it may fall out. (You can use joint cement, however.)

Cracks in cabinets may consistently pull away from patches, especially if they are structural cracks caused by the weight of a door, or a door closing against an obstruction. In this case, you should reinforce the door by gluing a strip of solid wood behind it, using a two-part epoxy adhesive (available at the hardware store). Cracks may be filled with the same material, compressing the two sides of the crack to get a good bond. (If you can't do this, use two applications of the adhesive.)

6.6 | Cleaning and replacing wall tiles. If ceramic, metal, or plastic tiles become loose and fall off the wall, they were either improperly applied in the first place—or you have a leak somewhere. In the latter case, locate the leak and repair it (see Secs. 8.2 and 8.15) before proceeding. (Water from a shower bath is not a leak. But if this is loosening the tile, or the general bathroom moisture is loosening it, you should remove all tile and retile as in Sec. 6.25.)

If just one or two tiles are loose, usually from a failure of a mortar or adhesive bond just behind those tiles, pry them loose carefully with a chisel, being sure not to damage adjacent tiles. Break the loose tiles if necessary to get them out. If tile was set in a bed of adhesive, chip away the old adhesive, let the wall dry thoroughly, and then place new tiles in a good thick bed of new tile adhesive. (Use the one recommended by the tile manufacturer—ask your hardware dealer.) If you can't get a regular adhesive, use a two-part epoxy—it can do almost any job. When the adhesive has set a day, grout the tile as in Section 6.25.

If tile was set in a bed of cement mortar, chip away enough old mortar so you can get a thick bed for new mortar without having the new tiles set out too far. Buy a bag of mortar mix from your hardware dealer to make your patch. Wet the hole to be patched, apply mortar, set the tile in, and grout the joint as in Section 6.25.

If glazed white ceramic tiles develop a network of fine lines (old ones usually do) there is no cure except replacement. If ceramic or quarry tile is stained with old mortar that won't come off, clean it with sulfamic acid or dilute muriatic acid. If the grout between ceramic tiles becomes soiled, it can usualy be cleaned by wiping with Chlorox.

Cracks which develop between tile walls and kitchen or bathroom fixtures can be filled with bathtub caulking. (See Sec. 1.4.)

6.7 | Hanging pictures and other objects on the wall. If you are hanging a heavy picture or shelf, it is safest to choose a spot where the wall is strongest. This means nailing brackets or picture hangers into a stud, for in between the studs there is only a thin surface of plaster or drywall.

Studs are most frequently spaced 16 inches apart, although in some houses the intervals may be as great as 24 inches. (Measurements are center of stud to center of stud.) To locate a stud, check the baseboard for any visible nailheads. If you find one, tap the wall lightly above that point with a hammer or your knuckles. If it sounds hollow, there is no stud; a solid, thudding sound means you are over a stud. In drywall surfaces, you may find a joint in the wall where two panels meet. This is usually at the center of a stud. You can find the next stud by measuring 16 inches along the wall. Or ask your hardware dealer about a "stud finder" (a small tool).

You can also try measuring from a corner inside two exterior walls. Mark off 17 inches from the corner and you should find a stud. In measuring along the wall for studs, do not include the extra studs for doors and windows—these are in addition to the standard 16-inch spacing.

If the location of studs is inconvenient for hanging pictures or other objects, you can still fasten them securely and safely to the plaster or drywall, provided the weight is not too great. To do so you must use the proper fastener—one made to expand and grip the back of the wall surface. The most widely used of these are toggle bolts and expansion (Molly) anchors.

Both toggle bolts and expansion anchors are especially made for use in stud wall construction. Toggle bolts are particularly good on soft, crumbly materials. The object to be attached is threaded on the bolt before it is inserted into the wall, and the toggle screwed on the end of the bolt. The wings of the toggle bolt spring open when it is inserted in the hole in the wall (drilled to the proper size) and are drawn up tight when the bolt is screwed down. (See Fig. 6-6.) If the bolt is withdrawn from the hole later, the wings will fall off inside. Expansion anchors have a sleeve which remains in the wall to allow for removing and replacing the bolt—so it is not necessary to fasten the shelf or other object on the anchor before screwing it into the wall. Expansion anchors will work only if they are correctly sized for the wall thickness.

Other fasteners that expand and grip the wall are plastic anchors, fiber plugs, and lead plugs. Plastic anchors come in groups attached to a plastic base and are broken off for use as needed. To insert, a hole the same diameter as the shank of the fastener is drilled in the wall. The anchor is then placed in the hole and a wood screw inserted into it, which makes it expand behind the wall. Fiber plugs and lead plugs work in approximately the same fashion.

It is also possible to hang an object weighing up to ten pounds on the wall without drilling any holes, by using adhesive anchors. These are flat perforated steel plates with a nail or bolt attached. A strong epoxy adhesive is applied to the hanger, which is then pressed into place on the wall.

Figure 6-6 Wall anchors

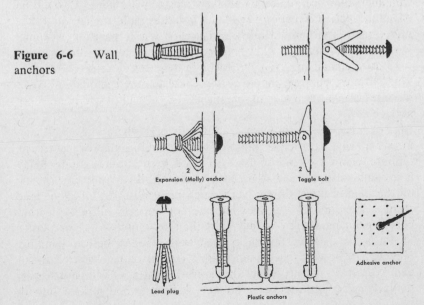

Expansion (Molly) anchor   Toggle bolt

Lead plug   Plastic anchors   Adhesive anchor

PAINTING

6.8 | Choosing the right paint. With reasonable care, even a complete novice can turn out a professional-looking paint job. But there are so many interior paints to choose from today that you may easily become confused when you arrive at the paint store— unless you have some idea of the kind (as well as the color) of paint you want.

For most purposes (not, however, for kitchens or bathrooms) the amateur can get best results with latex paints that have a water base. (Brushes and spots are cleaned with water, too.) They are easiest of all interior paints to apply, and come in a wide range of ready-mixed colors. Your dealer may also have a color-dispensing machine which mixes paint to the exact shade you select. Latex paints are tough, durable, and dry quickly, so that the second coat may be applied in a few hours. Spots and dirt can be easily cleaned off latex paint without changing the surface. What is more, latex paint may be applied directly over fresh plaster without priming or sealing. If you have patched your walls or ceilings with plaster of Paris (painter's patching plaster), you must either prime the wall with shellac or use a latex paint. New plaster will "burn" through an oil paint applied directly over it and you'll be able to see the patch. Latex paint is virtually dripless, even when you're painting a ceiling. If you have a choice of what paint to buy, by all means choose latex.

Latex paints are even available in textured finishes containing sand silicates, pumice, and so forth. These textured paints will cover hairline cracks, dents, and blemishes in a wall so they are not noticeable.

For kitchens, bathrooms, and woodwork where oils, dirt, and moisture may accumulate and frequent scrubbing may be necessary, oil base enamels should be used. (The oil base in many paints today is a combination of modified linseed oil and alkyd resin, a synthetic oil that makes a fast-drying, very tough paint film. An all-alkyd base paint is exceptionally durable. The back of the can will tell you what base a paint has.) New plaster (less than six months old) or plaster of Paris patches should be primed with shellac before painting. Shellac can be cut 50 per cent with wood alcohol to stretch it out and keep it flat so no brush marks are left on the wall. For a particularly good job, especially on new walls or woodwork, a smooth undercoat of flat paint, recommended by the manufacturer, should be applied before the enamel. The flat paint has an open surface that the enamel can cling to easily to give you an even one-tone finish.

Semigloss or eggshell enamels are preferable to gloss because they don't glare or show up irregularities in the wall the way glossy paints will. Good semigloss enamel (sometimes called trim paint or woodwork paint) will flow evenly, not leave lap or brush marks, and is easy to apply by brush and roller. These paints are very washable and resist marring and yellowing. If the paint gets too thick, it can be thinned with turpentine or benzene (brushes are cleaned in the same thing). Usually, though, the paint is mixed to the right consistency when you buy it.

A new type of paint on the market now combines the best qualities of both latex and alkyd paints. These new paints are odorless, very scrubbable when dry, and wet splashes and brushes can be cleaned with water. (When they are dry, turpentine or paint thinner must be used.) These paints can be used in kitchen or bath, but since most have a flat finish their open-type surface can collect more dirt— so will require more scrubbing—than a semigloss enamel.

If you are going to paint radiators, use a flat paint. Don't use aluminum paint because it tends to seal heat in rather than to let heat out. (Ideally, and for the highest efficiency, a radiator should be black.) So paint only the visible parts of the radiator, leaving the back of the radiator open metal that can throw off more heat. The best way to prepare a radiator for painting is to use a wire brush to remove old, scaling paint. Just remove what will come off and paint over the rest.

It's always a good idea to tell your paint dealer just exactly what you are going to paint so he can help you select just the right paint for your job. New special-purpose paints are always coming on the market, and your dealer will know all about them.

6.9 | How much paint will you need? The amount of paint required will depend on the condition of the surface—more paint is needed for unpainted plaster or wallboard than for previously painted walls. If you are painting a dark color over a light wall in good condition, one coat may suffice (unless you are using enamel). However, if you are painting a light color over a dark one, you will need two or more coats, as on a new wall. Remember that two or more thin coats will look better than one thick one—which may drip, dry slowly, and stay tacky.

Here is a rough guide for determining the quantity of paint needed for each coat. Measure (in feet) the height of the wall and multiply by the distance around the room. From this, subtract one half the area of door and window space. (To get this figure, multiply the width of each opening by its height, and add them all together.) The result will give you the approximate square footage.

When you tell your paint dealer the square footage and the condition of the walls, he can tell you how many gallons to buy. Most paints cover between 400 and 600 square feet per gallon, so dividing your square footage by 500 will give you a rough indication. If the walls are particularly rough or textured, as much as 20 per cent more paint per coat may be required. When in doubt, buy an extra can and return it later if you didn't have to open it.

6.10 | Preparing the surface for paint is an important part of the job if you hope to get a professional-looking finish. This work is often neglected by amateurs, never by professionals. All walls and ceilings should be washed before painting (see Sec. 6.1) unless you are absolutely certain there is no dirt or grease present. At the very least, dust them thoroughly. Kitchen and bathroom walls should *always* be washed, no matter how clean they look.

It's not too likely, but if calcimine or whitewash was used before (you can tell by rubbing your hand over the wall—if paint dust comes off easily on your hand, it's calcimine or whitewash), it must be completely removed by washing. Soak the surface with warm water applied with a sponge. Then scrape off the coating with a calcimine scraper—you can get one at the hardware store. If whitewash does not come off easily, brush on the following mixture: one pound of alum (from the hardware store), one pound of gelatine size dissolved in one gallon of hot water, and two gallons of mixed wallpaper paste, all stirred together. This will make the whitewash curl up and drop off. Walls with a very glossy surface must be rubbed with fine sandpaper or steel wool before painting.

If the wall is new plaster—or a patch is new plaster—prime it with shellac cut 50 per cent with wood alcohol, if you are going to use an oil paint. If you are using latex, you don't need a primer. Drywall requires no priming for any type of paint.

All holes and cracks in plaster or drywall must be patched and smoothed before painting. (See Secs. 6.3 and 6.4.) All loose and peeling paint must be removed by scraper and wire brush from the surface. Be sure wood trim is securely nailed to the wall. If it is not, fasten with finishing nails, sink nails, and fill holes as in Section 6.5. Toe moldings should be securely attached by driving nails diagonally into the subfloor, not into the baseboard or finish flooring. Fill cracks between walls and baseboards or door trim with spackle or joint cement.

If there is old, uneven, or many-layered wallpaper on the surface to be painted, remove it as in Section 6.15. If there is just one layer of paper and it is in good condition, with butted joints (joints that do not overlap), you can paint right over it. If it has lapped joints, you can cut them out with a razor blade and smooth with joint cement as in Section 6.3. If there are just a few bad spots, treat them the same way.

It is not practical to try to paint over a very old plaster wall that has been repapered several times. Taking off the paper is tedious and time-consuming. And by the time you have removed all the paper, you will have so many holes in the plaster that the repair job will be practically insurmountable. The wallpaper may be serving to hold the wall surface together in a very old house, anyway. Your best bet is to remove only the loose paper and what other will strip off easily, smooth the surface as best you can, and apply a heavily textured, canvasbacked wallpaper or wall cloth. (See Secs. 6.17 and 6.18.) As an alternative, you can install new drywall (Sec. 6.32) or wood paneling (Secs. 6.19 through 6.22).

Woodwork with a very glossy surface must be rubbed with fine sandpaper or steel wool to dull the surface. If woodwork has been waxed, remove the wax with turpentine or a thinner used for oil-base paint. (This will also remove clinging oil, grease, or furniture polish.) Remove any loose or peeling paint with a scraper, and smooth with sandpaper. If woodwork is in very bad condition, you may have to remove the old finish entirely. (See Secs. 6.23 and 6.24.)

If you want a very fine paint job on new woodwork or cabinets, use a liquid or paste wood filler to fill the open grain in the wood. Your hardware dealer can help you select the right type for the type of wood you are finishing. (See Sec. 6.22.) Wood filler is wiped across the wood with a rag, let dry for 20 minutes, and the excess then wiped off.

New wood should also be primed before painting (whether or not you use a filler). There are special priming paints on the market that seal the wood and form a good bond between the wood and the final paint coat. Or you can use the same oil paint for a primer that you are using for a finish coat. If you do this, thin out the paint for priming by adding about 10 per cent (by volume) more linseed oil. This makes the paint penetrate deeper into the wood. Be sure the prime coat is thoroughly dry before you apply the finish coat.

Before you actually start to paint, protect the edges of adjacent surfaces (floors and woodwork not to be painted the same color) with masking tape (it's sold in rolls at the hardware store). Masking glass panes in doors and windows will simplify your cleanup job, but you may prefer to skip this and scrape paint away with a razor blade when dry. Floors should be completely covered with dropcloths (you can use sheets of plastic) or several layers of newspapers.

Remove as much hardware as possible from doors and windows. It is much easier to replace knobs and handles than to clean the paint off—in fact, you usually can't get it all off anyway. Remove plates from switches and outlets, and lower light fixtures if possible, so you can paint under their edges. (See Chap. 2 for how to do this.)

6.11 | Good tools are essential for good results, and will shorten your working time. Large areas of ceiling and wall are easier to cover with a roller than a brush, and the technique is easy to learn. Rollers are usually dipped in a pan of paint to fill. (After the first few strokes you'll know how much paint you need in the roller.) Some rollers have a perforated hollow core that is filled with paint, but this type is rare and only good for special uses—it is not recommended for ordinary paint jobs. Some rollers accommodate a long extension handle for painting ceilings without ladders. Rollers for inside use are usually covered with mohair over a fiber core. When buying a roller, make sure the roll may be easily removed and changed. It's easiest to buy a new roller (just the roller, not the handle) for each paint job and throw the roller away afterward. (See Fig. 6-7.) But a roller can be carefully cleaned with the proper solvent (turpentine or thinner for oil-thinned paints, lukewarm water and soap for water-thinned

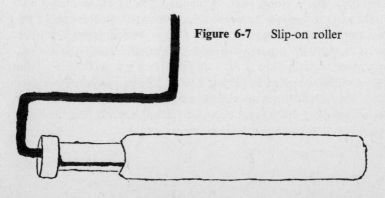

Figure 6-7   Slip-on roller

paint), if you prefer. Special roller-cleaning materials are available, if you need them. Filler-type rollers must be completely disassembled for cleaning. If you do clean your rollers, wrap them in foil or paper when not in use. The same roller should not be used for oil and water paints, and rollers should not be used at all for fast-drying paints, like shellac, lacquer, and some primers. Tell your dealer what kind of paint you are planning to use, and let him advise you about rollers.

Brushes should be of the best quality, for good-quality brushes will do a better job without excessive dripping and splattering, and will last indefinitely if properly cared-for. The price of a brush is usually a reasonable indication of its quality. A good bristle brush should feel springy and elastic, and bristles should be straight and well set into the metal ferrule. The ends of bristles should be split. Excellent nylon brushes are also on the market. (Caution: Do not use these for shellac.) Nylon brushes stand up better than bristle brushes when used continually in water-thinned paints.

You will need several brushes: a four-inch brush for large, flat surfaces; a 2-inch brush for woodwork, trim, and small corners; and a 1-inch brush (flat or oval) for sash. Enamel, varnish, or lacquer should be applied with a flat varnish brush. If you have used a brush for varnish, keep it for varnish alone; shellac brushes should be reserved for shellac; lacquer brushes for lacquer; paint brushes for paint. Some painters even keep separate brushes for oil-thinned and water-thinned paints. Label the handle of each, so you won't confuse them.

Use the same thinner you used for the paint (turpentine, water, lacquer thinner, or alcohol) to clean the brush thoroughly when you are through. Then wash it thoroughly with mild soap and warm water (but do not soak) and wrap in foil or paper, making sure bristles remain straight.

Stiff, sticky bristles (the result of poor cleaning or no cleaning) make a brush unfit for use. If it was a good-quality brush in the first place, you may be able to reclaim it. (If the brush was cheap in the first place, throw it away and get a new one.) Soak the brush in paint remover for 10 to 30 minutes or until it softens to jelly consistency. Remove paint with an old comb, rinse in turpentine, and comb again. Repeat as often as necessary. Wear rubber gloves for this job. After all paint has been removed, wash with a mixture of one quart soapy water and one cup turpentine. Rinse in clear water, straighten out the bristles, and wrap in foil to store.

An old brush that contains no dried paint, but has lost its shape from improper cleaning and storage, can be restored by soaking for half an hour in linseed oil, then wrapping in foil with the bristles straight. Remove the oil with turpentine after forty-eight hours.

If a nylon brush is used in shellac by mistake, place the bristles in boiling water for half an hour and let dry overnight.

6.12 | How to paint a room with brush and roller. Paint the ceiling first. Before you begin, mix paint thoroughly with a stick, even if you had it machine-mixed at the store. Then start painting across the width of the ceiling—not the length—in strips two to three feet wide. If you are using a roller, paint the edges of the immediate ceiling area where you are working with a brush first, then work rapidly with the roller so you can roll into the brushed edge while the paint is still completely wet.

Never begin painting a ceiling unless you have time to finish the job. Work from side to side, brushing and rolling until you have finished the full length of the ceiling. If the edges of your paint job dry, lap marks will show. Lap and brush marks are least likely to show when you are using a latex paint that dries out to a very flat finish.

If you are using a roller, do not overload it with paint, don't press on it too hard, and do not spin it at the end of a stroke. Fill the paint pan until half the sloping bottom is covered. Roll the roller back and forth in paint once or twice, then shake the excess back into the tray. With a newly loaded roller, begin stroking away from the already painted surface. As you paint, work the roller first in one direction, then at right angles to the first stroke, but always end by stroking in the same direction. Overlap strips about 50 per cent, because paint will be heavier in the middle of the roller.

If you are using a brush, use enough paint to load it fully, but not enough to make it drip. Don't press too hard when stroking. Use the largest size brush you can handle comfortably, and hold it lightly, with the handle between your thumb and first finger. Use long, steady strokes, lifting the brush gradually at the end of each stroke. To fill the brush, dip bristles halfway into paint, then gently tap against side of the can to remove excess. (Do not wipe brush on rim of can.)

If the ceiling requires two coats, wait until both coats are on and dry before doing the walls.

When you paint the walls, handle your brush and roller in exactly the way you did for the ceiling. Begin in an upper corner and paint a strip about 3 feet wide down to the baseboard. Always brush from the dry area into the wet area. When you come to an area that includes door or window, paint the edge of the trim with a small brush, then fill in with the large brush or roller. (Leave doors and windows until the end.) If you must stop before the job is finished, do so only at a corner where lap marks will not be evident. (If you stop for an hour or less, the brush can be left in the paint without any ill effects.)

If you are using enamel, work just as rapidly as possible to avoid lap marks. If the edges dry, you'll have lap marks.

Paint door casing and trim first, then the door edge, then the door. Do not close the door until it is completely dry. The easiest way to paint windows is to paint the frame, sill, and casing trim first, then paint the sash with a 1-inch brush. If you are only going to paint a few windows don't worry about getting paint on the glass—when the paint is dry take a single-edge razor blade and scrape excess paint off the glass, then clean the whole window. If you are going to paint a lot of windows that have a great many panes, you can apply masking tape, or you can make a shield the size of the pane out of sheet metal and glue a handle to it with epoxy adhesive. Then when you paint the sash, you hold the shield against the glass as you paint the muntins (the vertical and horizontal wood pieces holding the glass). (See Fig. 6-8.) Don't paint the window so it won't open—keep paint off weatherstripping and out of the track in which the window sash slides.

Figure 6-8 Metal shield for painting windows

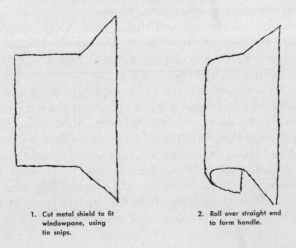

1. Cut metal shield to fit windowpane, using tin snips.

2. Roll over straight end to form handle.

Last of all, paint the baseboards with a 3-inch brush. Use masking tape along the floor at the edge of the toe molding to prevent paint from getting on the floor. If you don't cover the floor with dropcloths, keep a rag handy to remove any accidental paint spots. If you are using an oil paint, a rag with some paint thinner on it will take up spots even a few hours after painting. Water will take up latex paints within a half hour of painting.

6.13 | Spray painting. If you have a big paint job, like the complete walls and ceilings of a number of rooms all to be painted the same color, you can save a lot of time by spray painting. If you have just one room you won't save much time, so don't bother.

You can rent or purchase spray equipment at your hardware or paint dealer's. He'll show you how to operate the equipment he has. There are a number of different systems for spray painting, ranging from simple spray with a cannister of paint fastened to the gun to very specialized equipment that should not be used by anyone but a professional.

The simplest type of spray gun, which almost anyone can use, is the spray attachment used on the vacuum cleaner. This should be used with only light water-base paints—oil paints are too heavy. A somewhat more efficient spray is the electric spray, sometimes called a vibrator spray, which holds the paint in a cannister right under the gun and is simply plugged into any convenient outlet to operate. Generally speaking, both these types of equipment are good only for small jobs, like painting louvered doors—it's very difficult to get between all the louvers with a paint brush.

For any big exterior job you should rent compressor equipment, and be sure you only use it outdoors. This involves drums of paint, an air compressor, hoses, and a big commercial gun. Ask your dealer about this equipment. (See Sec. 12.8.)

There are a number of points about spray painting that you must keep in mind no matter what kind of equipment you use. Always hold the gun perpendicular to, or directly facing, whatever you are painting. Keep the spray no more than 6 to 10 inches from the object being painted. Don't swing the gun in an arc, move it straight across or up and down—doing one section after another. Don't spray too much paint into one area or the paint film will drip and sag. You can regulate the paint flow by adjustments to the gun (your dealer will show you how). Don't forget to cover and mask whatever you don't want to paint in the room, and wear a painter's mask. For more tips on spray painting, see Section 12.8.

There are special paints and formulations that you can use with spray equipment that you cannot use with brushes and rollers. Ask your dealer about them. One of them is speckled paint—a kind of paint with particles of color in it which won't dissolve into the main body of the paint. There is a wide range of color in this paint and it is very good for covering blemishes in old walls and woodwork— the color texture completely camouflages the blemishes.

WALLPAPER

6.14 | It isn't difficult to paper a wall if you work carefully and follow the rules. However, don't attempt to paper a ceiling if you have never hung wallpaper before. You will be better off painting the ceiling and papering only the walls.

For your first try at paperhanging, it is wise to select a washable paper. Paste smears can be easily removed from these and they are easier to hang. Nonwashable papers are fragile and tear easily during handling. Nonwashable papers should never be used in bathrooms, kitchens, or children's rooms.

Most wallpapers come with white borders at the edges which must be trimmed off before hanging. When you buy wallpaper, have it machine-trimmed at the store. (There is no charge for this.) Canvas-backed papers and other fabric wall coverings are pretrimmed. These are excellent for covering uneven plaster on old walls. A few papers are ready-pasted and need only be brushed with water before being applied to the wall.

Wallpapers vary in width from 18 inches to 30 inches. A single roll of 18-inch paper is 24 feet long; a double roll is 48 feet long. The average roll of American-made wallpaper contains 36 square feet.

To estimate how much paper you will need, measure the length and width of the room and height from top of baseboard to the picture molding (if there is one) around the ceiling. Don't bother deducting for windows and doors unless the proportion of these is extremely high—you'll need as much as 20 per cent extra for waste and matching, anyway. Divide by 30 and this will tell you how many single rolls you need.

Or, if you prefer, take your measurements to the wallpaper store and let the dealer tell you how many rolls to buy. If in doubt, take an extra roll. You may need some later for patching.

6.15 | Preparing the surface for wallpaper. The preliminary work is much like that done before painting. (See Sec. 6.10.) All surfaces must be dry, smooth, and even. You can hang new paper over old wallpaper if the surface is neat, untorn, has butt joints (not lapped), and is not a plastic- or fabric-surfaced paper. (New paper won't adhere to these surfaces, or to anything that has been painted with any paint except water-thinned paint.) If the seams were lapped, you can strip them with a razor and sand them smooth. Remove any other loose bits of paper. If the surface is very rough, you should use a fabric or heavily textured paper.

Loose, peeling, or heavily textured wallpaper, or wallpaper that is several layers thick or has been waxed or painted (with anything except water-thinned paint), should be completely removed before repapering. (But if your walls are very old, remove only the loose parts and use a textured canvas paper. See Sec. 6.10.) Work one section of a wall at a time, in vertical strips, soaking with a sponge or brush and warm water to soften the old paste underneath. A handful of soda (or a detergent or wallpaper remover) to a gallon of warm water makes the job easier, but do not let this mixture settle on woodwork or floors as it will damage the finish. (You can cover the floor with several layers of newspapers.) Peel the paper off in strips, and scrape away stubborn pieces with a putty knife. It may be easier to scrape off one layer at a time. If the paper is especially difficult to remove, or if there are several layers, you may want to rent a steam remover from your local hardware store.

Before the wall dries, wash it with clear water to remove paste and small bits of paper. Stainless steel or nylon kitchen scouring pads are good for cleaning walls. When dry, smooth with sandpaper or an electric sander. Fill in any cracks and holes before proceeding. (See Sec. 6.3.)

If you are removing wallpaper from drywall, be careful not to use too much water or steam, as the surface may be damaged. After paper has been removed, the drywall surface should be allowed to dry thoroughly and then primed with a thin coat of shellac or varnish.

Washable papers are waterproof, so before removing with steam or hot water you must cut the surface by rubbing with rough sandpaper to let moisture get beneath the paper.

If you are going to hang wallpaper over a painted wall, wash the wall thoroughly first. Glossy surfaces must be dulled by applying a solution of one half cup trisodium phosphate to a gallon of hot water. Rinse the solution off carefully or the paper may become discolored.

Before papering over plywood walls, special preparation is necessary. Fill joints with Swedish putty. Coat the surfaces with a half-and-half mixture of wallpaper paste and glue size, and apply a layer of smooth felt or wall-lining canvas (ask your wallpaper dealer). Joints must be neatly butted, not lapped.

When all preparation has been completed, you are ready to size the wall. Size is like a thin paste that gives a better bond for the wallpaper paste. In some cases, all-in-one wallpaper size and paste may be used when hanging the paper—ask your wallpaper dealer. If you are using regular size, you will need a 10-quart pail and a large spoon to mix it with. One package of size will make enough for a room 15 x 15 feet. Mix according to package directions and apply the size with a 4-inch brush—professionals use a larger size, but it is too difficult for the amateur to manipulate. Before you paint on the size, remove switch and outlet covers and removable light fixtures from the wall.

As you apply the size, keep the handle of the brush as nearly horizontal as you can to prevent excessive dripping. Protect furniture, rugs, and floors with newspapers or dropcloths and wipe up spots from woodwork before they dry. When you are finished, wash the brush carefully in water.

6.16 | Getting ready to hang wallpaper. Assemble everything you need before you begin. You will need a 6-foot table for cutting and pasting, a clean galvanized 10-quart pail for paste, paste brush, large scissors, a folding rule, sponge, seam roller, plumb bob and chalk line, straight edge, a smoothing brush (10 or 12 inches wide), clean rags, and a roller cutter. (See Fig. 6-9.)

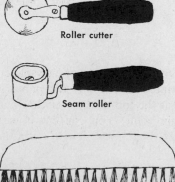

Figure 6-9 Wallpaper tools

Roller cutter

Seam roller

Smoothing brush

Anything you do not have can be purchased at the hardware or paint store. Some dealers also rent kits containing all the tools needed for wallpapering.

Purchase prepared wallpaper paste (your dealer will tell you how much you need) and mix it according to the package directions. If there are lumps, stir vigorously with a wire whisk or egg beater.

Select the most prominent window in the room as your starting point. (By working away from the light, you avoid having shadows cast by lapped edges.) Take your plumb bob and chalk line and snap a vertical line on the right of the window—17 inches away from the frame if you are using 18-inch paper, 23 inches away if you are using 24-inch paper, and so on. (See Fig. 6-10.) Measure the distance from the top of the baseboard to the picture molding or ceiling.

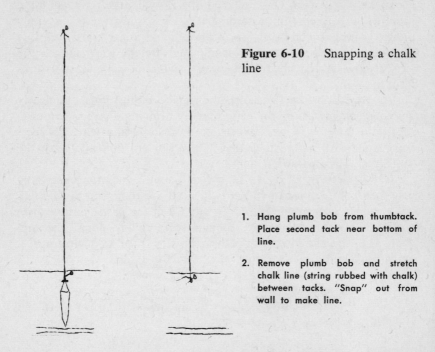

Figure 6-10   Snapping a chalk line

1. Hang plumb bob from thumbtack. Place second tack near bottom of line.

2. Remove plumb bob and stretch chalk line (string rubbed with chalk) between tacks. "Snap" out from wall to make line.

Cover your 6-foot table with several thicknesses of newspaper, and unroll about a yard of paper, printed side up. If the paper is patterned, decide what part should be at the top of the wall and tear off the paper an inch or so *above* this point. You can cut it with scissors or tear it against a straightedge.

Now unroll the paper and measure a piece a few inches longer than the height of the wall you are covering, and tear or cut it. Cut four or five strips at a time, laying one on top of the other, being careful to match the left edge of the piece you are cutting with the right edge of the top piece on the table.

To remove curl from the paper, roll the paper up opposite to the original direction of rolling; then unroll it printed side down on the table. (The first strip you cut will now be on top, with its back side showing.) Pull the top strip over so its long edge is even with the table edge nearest you. Apply paste with your paste brush smoothly, stroking diagonally from the vertical center of the strip toward the edges. Leave an inch free of paste at the top of strip, to be used as a handle later on.

When about half the length of the strip is covered with paste, fold (but do not crease) the top end over, paste to paste, to the middle of the strip. Now continue pasting until you have covered the entire strip. Fold this end up as you did the top. (See Fig. 6-11.)

See that the stepladder is placed where you can reach the top of the wall near the window, but leave as much space between ladder and wall as you can. Place the smoothing brush where you can reach it from the ladder.

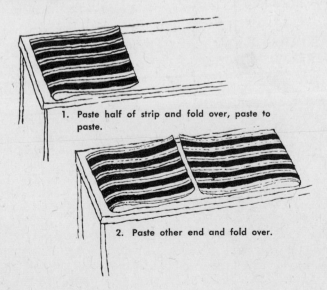

1. Paste half of strip and fold over, paste to paste.

2. Paste other end and fold over.

Figure 6-11   Pasting a strip of wallpaper

6.17 | Hanging wallpaper. Take the pasted strip and when you are on the ladder, unfold the top portion. Paste top portion in place carefully, with the right edge at the guide line, the top edge overlapping the ceiling, and about an inch overlapping the window frame on the left. If the paper doesn't line up with the guide line, pull it off the wall and try again. If it needs moving only a short distance, you can slide it with your hand.

With your smoothing brush, smooth the paper from the center toward the edges and down, being careful to eliminate all air bubbles. (If the right edge strays from the guide line, readjust it.) Unfold the bottom part of the strip, apply to the wall, and smooth out.

For washable and fabric papers, crease the top of the strip exactly at the ceiling line and at the baseboard with the back of a scissors blade, and pull the paper back off the wall just far enough to cut with a scissors. For ordinary papers, cut along the crease with the roller cutter and peel off the excess. (If the cutter isn't very sharp, it won't work right. In this case, use the scissors as for fabric papers. See Fig. 6-12.)

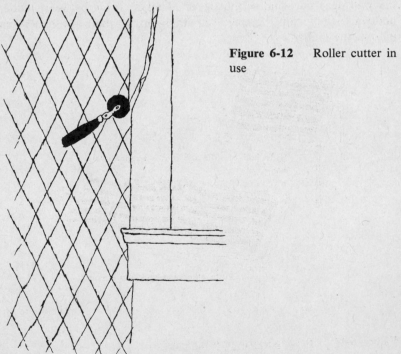

Figure 6-12   Roller cutter in use

Now you are ready to hang the second strip at the right of the first. For a lapped edge, overlap about 1/16 inch. (This is advised for the novice, as butt joints are more difficult. However, they *must* be used with fabric or heavily textured paper.) Smooth seams with your seam roller, unless paper is embossed.

After you have used up the first batch of strips you cut, put clean newspapers on your table and cut a new batch.

Continue hanging paper until you are halfway around the room, choosing as the halfway mark a doorway or other good spot where joining will not be obvious if the design isn't perfectly matched. Now go back to your starting point and begin working from the left side of the window, after making a new plumb line as you did the first time.

When you approach a corner, trim the corner piece of paper vertically before hanging—leaving half an inch to extend around the corner. Overlap the next strip so its edge fits along the corner line.

When you come to a door or window, measure from the edge of strip to the frame, leaving about an inch to spare for overlap, and cut the strip vertically before hanging. Trim off the overlap by creasing and cutting after paper is in place. When cutting strips horizontally to go over and under windows, remember to match designs on the lower half as well as the upper half.

6.18 | **Hanging paper on ceilings** is hard work. If it's possible to paint the ceiling—that is, if the surface is not too rough—paint it. But if the ceiling surface is old, cracked, and uneven, a canvas paper is your best bet to make it look right.

Paper a ceiling across the width, not the length. This will keep your lengths of paper shorter and easier to handle. Use two step-ladders to make a scaffold, resting a 2 x 12 across the bottom steps, so that the top of your head almost touches the ceiling. If you are lower down than this, your arms will tire very quickly as you try to hang the paper.

Figure 6-13 Accordion fold for ceiling paper

Snap a line at right angles to the side walls of the room, at a distance one inch less than the width of the paper from the end of the room. (See Sec. 6.16.) Cut several strips of paper the right length. When you paste the paper, fold it up accordion fashion so you can unfold it in small sections at a time, pasting it up as you work across the room on your scaffold. (See Fig. 6-13.) Continue hanging paper as in Section 6.17.

WALL PANELING

6.19 | Choosing paneling and preparing to install it. No great skill, strength, or experience is needed to install paneling. Ask your lumber dealer to show you the many types of prefinished and unfinished paneling materials available. (Some types are plastic-coated and may even be used in the bathroom.) The easiest type of board paneling to apply comes with ready-made tongue-and-groove joints, but it is possible to use any vertical board—provided it is better than No. 3 grade. (Lower grades have too many knots, splits, and may warp badly.) When using knotty pine, be sure knots are small and do not protrude on either side. Plywood and hardboard paneling comes in 4' x 8' sheets. These go up faster and provide big unbroken surfaces that make a room look bigger. They often come with special mounting systems or clips that make installation easier, or they can be glued to the furring strips so you have no nailheads to worry about. (See Sec. 6.21.)

When you are ready to buy, measure the room in running feet and multiply by the height of the ceiling or the height of the paneling (if it is to cover only the lower half of the wall). Take these figures to the lumber dealer's, together with window and door measurements, and have the boards precut to fit. They should be ¼ inch less than actual height, to allow for possible expansion. The gap will be covered by molding at top and bottom, as will the corner joints in most cases.

In addition to molding, you will need furring strips for most installations. (If the wall is perfectly flat you may be able to glue paneling directly to it—see Sec. 6.21. Or, in the unlikely event that you are installing paneling horizontally, you can nail it directly to the studs.) Some paneling is sold in kits complete with molding and furring. Otherwise, buy standard 1" x 2" rough fir furring strips, or 2" x 2" plywood furring strips, for paneling on plaster, drywall, or exposed frame walls. Your dealer can tell you how much furring to buy.

When the paneling is delivered, paint the back side with a wood preservative—ask your dealer what to use—to protect it from moisture, unless it is guaranteed moistureproof by the manufacturer. Then stack the lumber with small blocks of wood between, so air can reach all sides. Let it dry for a week before using. You may want to finish it before you install it. (See Sec. 6.22.)

While the paneling dries, you can install the furring strips. First place a strip at ends of each wall. Then install strips right around the jamb, sill, and head of any windows or doors (you'll have to remove casing and trim before doing this)—using toggle bolts if necessary. (See Fig. 6-6.) Next, fasten horizontal strips to the studs about 16 inches apart, using 8d nails. The top and bottom strips should be placed so they will be just behind the top and bottom edges of the paneling. (See Fig. 6-14.) If you are using sheet paneling, nail short strips of vertical furring behind where the joints between sheets will fall. If there isn't a solid base to nail them to, use toggle bolts.

Figure 6-14   Furring strips

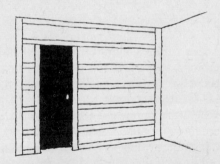

Before installing each piece of furring, check to see that the wall is straight by holding a flat board against it. Sand down any high spots, or whittle out the backs of furring pieces to fit. Fill in any low spots. Use a plumb line as you work to be sure furring surface is always flat and vertical.

If you are applying paneling to a masonry wall, use 1″ x 3″ rough fir furring strips 24 inches apart, attached with expansion plugs. (See Fig. 6-6.) On basement walls, the interior surface may have to be coated with a waterproofing compound (Sec. 10.1) before furring is applied.

6.20 │ Nailing paneling in place. If you are using a paneling kit including clips, follow the manufacturer's instructions. Clips can be used only for paneling designed to be installed this way. If you are fastening paneling with contact cement, follow instructions in next section.

If you are nailing the paneling in place, place the first board in one corner with the tongue edge out (if there is one), making sure it is perfectly vertical by checking with a plumb line. On a straight edged panel use 4d nails 6 inches apart, 1 inch in from the corner. On the tongue edge use 8d or 10d finishing nails, driving them in through the furring at an angle. (See Fig. 6-15.) Countersink nails below the surface (Sec. 6.5). Press the next board into place, fitting the groove over the tongue and tapping it into place with a block of wood. Nail through the tongue into the furring as you did before, sink the nails, and proceed.

Figure 6-15 Nailing through tongue into furring strip

When paneling with boards or 4' x 8' sheets that are not provided with tongue and grooves, leave 1/16 inch between. (Later, after baseboard and ceiling moldings are in place, you can cover the gaps with molding strips cut to fit.) Or you can bevel both sides of the boards before applying so they form a V-joint. (But this way you'll have many more nail holes to cover up later.) When using hardboard paneling, allow plenty of room (⅛ inch) at the edges for expansion and contraction with humidity changes.

When you come to a corner, butt the ends of adjoining boards together. (You may have to cut the paneling vertically to come out even.) Nail the edges 1 inch in from the corner. At doors and windows, bring paneling right up to the outside edge of the jamb and head. (You should have already removed casing trim as in the preceding section.) When you've installed all the paneling, build up jambs and heads with strips of wood so they come flush with the surface of the paneling. Then refasten the old casing, or use new casings that can be stained like the paneling. (See Fig. 6-16.)

The last step is to apply baseboard moldings and ceiling moldings, and then corner moldings. If you are paneling only the lower

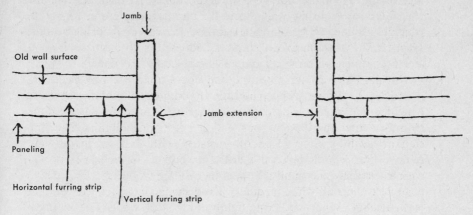

Figure 6-16   Fattening window jamb out to paneling

part of the wall, the top molding will be a cap to hide tops of panels. If you are using molding to cover joints between boards or sheets, nail it in place after baseboard and ceiling moldings are up. Finally, check to see if there are any exposed nailheads. If you find any, countersink them and fill the holes with putty.

6.21 | Applying paneling with contact cement. Contact cement is an alternative method of fastening paneling to the wall. It is possible to apply the panels directly to exposed studs, drywall, or new plaster (but not over old plaster), but it is preferable to use furring strips.

When using this adhesive, the room temperature must be at least 70° Fahrenheit. It must also be very well ventilated, unless you are using one of the new contact cements that are nonflammable and nontoxic. The amount of cement you'll need depends on whether you are using furring strips or not. Let your dealer advise you.

Cement is applied to both surfaces (front of furring and back of paneling where it will touch furring) and let dry. Then surfaces are pressed together. Once in contact they are bonded permanently exactly as you placed them—so you must work carefully. Here's how to align paneling perfectly:

Cut the first piece of paneling to fit exactly. Then cut a shim out of scrap lumber which, when placed under the bottom edge of the sheet on the floor, will bring the sheet into its exact position. Apply adhesive to both furring and sheet and let it set. Then place the bottom of the panel on the shim, with the upper part leaning against you and away from the wall. Raise the panel, aligning one edge with your plumb line. Swing the panel against the wall like closing a door. Then tap the panel in hard against the adhesive with a block of wood and a hammer, working all over the surface of the panel.

Fit around corners, windows, and doors as in preceding section.

6.22 | Finishing wood paneling. If you installed unfinished wood paneling, you have a wide choice in finishing. Finishing may be done before or after installation—it's easiest before installation. The first step in finishing is to clean all surfaces with fine sandpaper and remove grease with mineral spirits, turpentine, or benzene. If you wish to preserve the natural appearance of the wood, use one or two coats of clear, dull white lacquer, or use shellac cut back 50 per cent with alcohol. When dry, rub lightly with steel wool. For a hand-rubbed finish, the final step is to apply paste wax.

To darken the color somewhat, use one part orange shellac to two parts white shellac. Then finish as above. If you want the wood still darker, use a wood stain before applying the shellac. If you want the grain to show but prefer a more colorful treatment, you can purchase ready-made colorful stains in bright and pastel colors. (If you prefer, create your own color by mixing oil-thinned paint with turpentine, benzene, or other thinner.) To apply, brush the stain on and rub off excess with a soft cloth. When dry, apply a coat of lacquer sealer. Finally, sand with fine sandpaper and apply two or more coats of shellac or lacquer.

Paneling may, of course, be painted like any other surface. (See Secs. 6.8 through 6.12.) Remember that knotholes must be sealed with aluminum paint or they may run sap and ruin the surface later.

6.23 | Refinishing old paneling requires some preparation beforehand. If it is merely to be painted, follow instructions in Section 6.10. To restore the natural beauty of old wood, however, it is necessary to remove the old finish completely. Before you attempt this make sure the wood is worth restoring, or you'll have a lot of work for nothing.

The easiest way to remove the finish is to remove the old paneling from the wall and use lye on it as in the following section. (If the finish is only shellac, wood alcohol will remove it.) If it cannot be taken down, use a commercial paint remover. Apply as the manufacturer directs, and scrape off with a wide scraper. Be careful not to gouge holes in the wood or make scratches as this will make the job twice as hard later on. Several applications of remover may be needed. Removers are flammable, so the room must be well ventilated.

Stubborn spots can be taken off with steel wool soaked with paint remover. A file or the serrated edge of a steak knife is useful in small crevices. Neutralize the surface as directed by the manufacturer. Be sure to get off all remover, or the new finish will be spoiled.

When the surface is dry, give it a preliminary sanding with rough sandpaper on an electric sander—you can rent one at the hardware store. (The job can be done by hand, but takes much longer.) If there are any holes, fill them with wood putty, let them dry, and sand them down. If the putty isn't the same color as the wood, stain it to match. (This isn't as easy as it sounds, so avoid making holes.)

Finish your sanding with fine sandpaper. Always sand in the direction of the grain. Don't neglect the sanding—this is the most important part of the job. When you have a smooth, even surface, finish the wood as though it were new. (See preceding section.)

6.24 | Using lye in refinishing wood. The most efficient method of removing paint or varnish is to use a solution of ordinary lye. (Shellac may be removed with wood alcohol.) This will not harm the wood. Take down doors to be refinished, remove knobs and hardware, and take the doors outside to work.

Caution: Use rubber gloves, and never allow lye to touch skin or eyes. Do not let children come near while you are working, as lye is one of the deadliest poisons.

Lye saponifies, or makes soap out of paint and varnish. (Lye, grease, and wood ashes used to be the recipe for soap.) This means that a solution of lye on a paint film will make it suds and allow you to wash it off with a hose. No scrubbing or scraping is necessary. If there are many paint films on an old piece of wood, you may have to work on it quite a while with lye.

Mix your lye solution at a ratio of about one half pound lye to five gallons of water. Use an iron or porcelain bucket—lye will dissolve many other metals. It will also kill grass, so set up your work on some sawhorses in the driveway, and swab it with the lye solution with cotton rags (wool will dissolve) tied on a stick. Hose down the work from time to time as you swab it, until all paint is removed.

If you have a great deal of paint removing to do, you can make a lye pit by digging a hole in the ground and lining it with 45- or 90-pound roll roofing and then a layer of 6-mil polyethlene (a plastic film that lye does not attack) from the hardware store. You can fill the pit with lye solution and immerse the wood pieces one at a time. After the lye treatment, wash the wood with dilute muriatic acid— 1 per cent solution—to neutralize the lye.

Wood that has been treated with lye is a little darker that it would ordinarily be, but if you are adding any color at all to your finish, even a little orange shellac, this will make little difference.

WALL TILES

6.25 | How to install plastic or ceramic tile with adhesive. Measure the area of the wall to be tiled and the approximate space taken up by windows and fixture, and let your dealer tell you how much tile and adhesive to buy. (If you are using. ceramic tile, you'll need grout—the mixture that fills cracks between tiles—as well.)

Before installing plastic or ceramic (or metal) tiles, patch all cracks and holes as in Sections 6.3 and 6.4. Remove wallpaper if there is any (Sec. 6.15). Cut out a quarter-inch trench of plaster around the tub and lavatory, so adhesive can get in the crack to assure a tight seal.

When patches are completely dry, prime the wall with a sealer, either one specified on the back of the adhesive can, an oil-base paint or varnish, or a skim coat—a smooth coat 1/16-inch thick—of the adhesive itself.

When you're ready to begin, the first step is to plan exactly where each tile will go. Ceramic tiles have small nubs on their sides for spacing, but they can be placed farther apart than this if necessary to make them come out even. Check fixtures, walls, and corners for straightness with a plumb line and level. When you know where tiles will go, apply adhesive according to directions on the can. Start spreading with a notched spreader in a corner that's exactly vertical, and work along a base line—like the top of a tub or a chalked, level line—that's perfectly level. Apply only as much adhesive as you can cover with tile in 30 to 45 minutes. Place tiles in this area, then spread adhesive on a new area, and continue working in this fashion until you have finished.

Measure tiles to fit around edges and fixtures as in Figure 6-17. Plastic and metal tiles can be cut with a hacksaw. Ceramic tile must be cut by snipping out small pieces of the tile with pliers or by scoring it with a glass cutter and snapping it over a nail—see Figure 6-18. This isn't easy to do, so if you are using ceramic tiles, plan your spacing so you'll have as little cutting as possible.

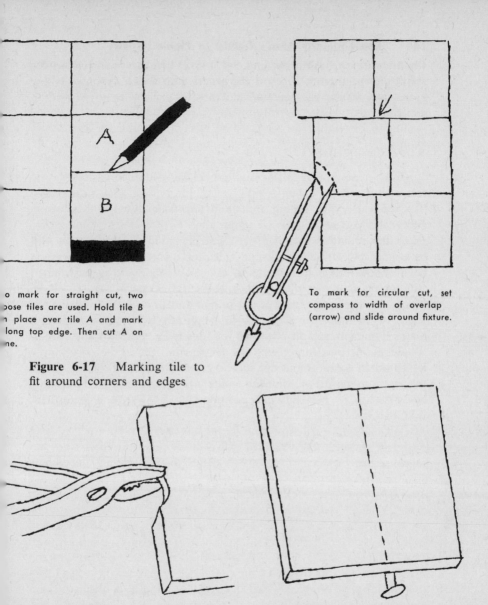

To mark for straight cut, two loose tiles are used. Hold tile B in place over tile A and mark long top edge. Then cut A on the line.

Figure 6-17 Marking tile to fit around corners and edges

To mark for circular cut, set compass to width of overlap (arrow) and slide around fixture.

Figure 6-18 Cutting ceramic tile

Score straight cut with glass cutter and snap over nail.

Grout can be applied to ceramic tile joints after the tile has set for twenty-four hours. Grout is mixed to the consistency of heavy cream and applied to joints with a sponge. Joints are dampened first so the tile doesn't draw water out of the grout. Wear rubber gloves when grouting to avoid burning the skin. When the grout has set for about fifteen minutes, wipe off the excess with a clean sponge. If any grout hardens on the face of the tiles, it can be removed with a scouring pad.

NEW CEILINGS

6.26 | How to install acoustical ceiling tile. The easiest way to restore a cracked, peeling ceiling to new life is with acoustical ceiling tiles. Measure your ceiling area, and your dealer will tell you how many tiles you need.

If the ceiling is level and in relatively good condition, tiles can be applied directly to the surface. (Scrape off loose paint before you begin, and fill in holes as in Sec. 6.3. Wallpaper and water-thinned paints must be removed. See Secs. 6.10 and 6.15.)

Locate the center lines of the ceiling and draw them in, using the "3, 4, 5" method of making a right angle. (See Fig. 6-19.) Using a tile as a guide, mark off positions for tiles from center to one corner.

Beginning in a corner with the nearest full tile to the edge, apply walnut-sized dabs of adhesive to corners and center of the tile. Press the tile into position along the guide line and the edge of ceiling, being sure to get it exactly into position. Work toward the center line,

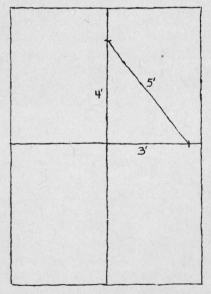

Figure 6-19 Laying out ceiling tile

Locate center points of walls and draw connecting lines on ceiling. Mark off 3 feet from center on one line and 4 feet on adjacent line. Connect points. This line should measure exactly 5 feet. If it doesn't, adjust bisecting lines until measurements are 3 feet, 4 feet, and 5 feet as indicated.

one row at a time. (If the ceiling is slightly uneven, tiles can be leveled out by a heavier application of adhesive.) Then go back and do another row, working toward the center again. When half the ceiling has been completed, begin in a corner of the other half. Install all full tiles first—then cut tiles, if necessary, to fit around the edges. They are soft and may be cut easily with a sharp knife. Measure and score tiles as you would a bathroom tile. (See Fig. 6-17.)

Furring strips of seasoned 1" x 3" wood should be installed on ceilings that are very uneven or in unsound condition, or if the paint or wallpaper is in bad condition and it's not practical to remove it. (See Sec. 6.19.) Mark off guide lines on the ceiling, as above. Now locate all joists (see Sec. 6.29) and mark them with another color from the guide lines. Attach furring strips at right angles to joists with 2½-inch nails. Place the strips so joints between tiles will fall on their centers: if you are using 16-inch tiles, place them 16 inches apart, center to center; for 12-inch tiles, place them 12 inches apart. Fatten out low spots by using small, thin strips of wood between ceiling and furring strips. Use a level to check strips as you nail them up.

Tiles can be attached to furring strips with small nails, with staples, or with clips. Some tiles are provided with tongue and groove, so they need be nailed or stapled on two sides only. Ask your dealer for advice on which type of fastener to use with the tile you select.

6.27 | Installing drywall on a ceiling can be hard work if you don't start right. First of all, unless you are going to remove the old ceiling completely and reveal the ceiling joists (to which you could nail the new ceiling), you must install furring strips at 16-inch centers. Nail them at right angles to the joists, as in the preceding section.

You will need at least one strong ablebodied man to help you hold up a sheet of drywall while you nail it, and you will also need some T-supports, as in Figure 6-20. If your drywall is 6 or 8 feet long, you can manage with only one T-support. If it is more than

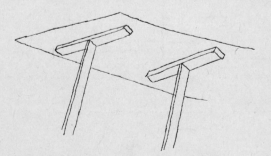

Figure 6-20
T-supports for ceiling drywall

8 feet long, you will need two T-supports (and two helpers). Use the longest size drywall possible, because the joints between the ends of drywall sheets are hard to cover up later.

If your ceiling joists are wider apart than 16 inches, you should use ½-inch drywall so you won't get any sag between joists. For 16-inch spacing, ⅜-inch drywall is thick enough, and it's a lot lighter to install.

When you are ready to put up the drywall, rest one end of it on your T-support (which is just short of ceiling height) and have your helper hold the support steady about one third the distance in from the end. To finish out ends and sides of ceiling, you can cut drywall by scoring it deeply with a knife and then breaking it along the score. When you have installed all the drywall, finish the ceiling as in Section 6.32.

6.28 | Installing luminous ceilings. Luminous ceilings usually come in a kit that includes the plastic grid or plastic sheet that forms the ceiling, the aluminum tees of channels that support the plastic,

Figure 6-21   How luminous ceiling is installed

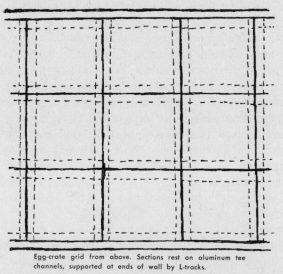

Egg-crate grid from above. Sections rest on aluminum tee channels, supported at ends of wall by L-tracks.

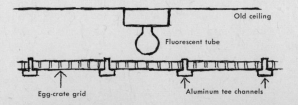

and the light fixtures or fluorescent lights that are mounted flat against your present ceiling (above the plastic). (See Fig. 6-21.) The grid or eggcrate type of diffuser is preferable to a plastic sheet because bugs and dirt can fall through.

Ask your hardware dealer about plastic luminous ceiling kits. If he dosen't carry what you need, you may be able to buy the plastic grid and mount it in aluminum tees or over a wood frame. The plastic should simply be seated on the framework so it can be removed if necessary. If you have a ceiling fixture, you can often make it work to handle two fluorescent tubes. To do this, see Chapter 2. (After pulling the fuse controlling the light fixture, you remove the fixture and mount the fluorescent strips according to manufacturer's directions to the ceiling. Then you run short extensions of armored cable from the existing box to the fluorescent strips and splice black wires together and white wires together, using wire nuts. Install the remaining parts of the fluorescents, and the job is done.)

REMOVING OLD WALLS AND ADDING NEW

6.29 | **Removing an existing interior wall.** You'll need a building permit for this work or that of the following section. (See Introduction, "The law and your house.") If your wall is nonbearing you can simply rip it out. To find out if it is bearing or nonbearing, find out how your ceiling joists lie. (See Fig. 7-1.) If they lie parallel to the wall on both sides, even though one may be right on top of the wall, it's nonbearing. (You may have to punch a hole in the ceiling big enough to put either a mirror or your head up there to see which way the joists lie on both sides of the wall.) If the joists lie perpendicular to the wall and joists lap or end at the wall, it's a bearing wall. See next section.

To remove a nonbearing wall, first remove any doors in it, trim, and baseboard. Then with a hammer punch a line of holes in plaster or wallboard down along a stud and across the top of the wall and at midpoint for the width of a stud space. Pull away this section of wall. This will show you what pattern you could best use to punch out and pull away sections of plaster or wallboard. Remove studs by hammering the foot of the stud loose from the plate. Then remove the top and bottom plate. You may have to patch the floor, or the finish floor may run right under the wall. At the ceiling, you can use expanded wire mesh and plaster of Paris to make a good tight patch where the wall was. (See Sec. 6.4.)

6.30 | How to remove an inside bearing wall. The first thing you have to do is install a beam and its supporting columns right beside the wall you want to remove. Unless you are really experienced and handy, it's best to let a professional do this job because it's hard, tricky work. The size of the beam varies with the span and the load it will have to carry—it may be two 2 x 6's, 2 x 8's, or 2 x 12's. The beam is supported on structural columns, usually 4 x 4's, at the sides of the room.

Before you can install the beam, you must remove ceiling plaster and lath in a strip slightly wider than your beam will be, right beside the existing wall. Lay bare the ceiling joists in this strip so that your beam can come right up against them for bearing. With temporary supports work your beam up into position against the joists, then position your supporting columns under the ends of the beam. The columns should fit so tightly that you have to drive the column foot into position with a sledge hammer. Place the head in position first and fasten it in place with finishing nails under the beam.

When the columns are in position under the beam, remove the temporary supports and wreck out the bearing wall as in the preceding section.

6.31 | How to build a new inside wall. This is relatively easy. Measure the distance between floor and ceiling exactly at the point where you want the wall. Plan to have the wall either directly under a ceiling joist or running at right angles to the joists. (To locate the joists, see Sec. 6.29.)

Prefabricate your wall on the floor, either in sections or all in one. (See Fig. 6-22.) Nail into the foot and head of studs through the top and bottom plate, countersinking nails in bottom plate so the floor isn't scratched when you raise the frame into position. The wall frame should be ⅛-inch higher than the ceiling. If there is to be a

Figure 6-22   Prefabricated wall section. Studs are toenailed to sole and plate at 16-inch intervals (center to center).

door in the wall, prefabricate the frame in two sections—one for either side of the door—and build in the part over the door after the wall sections are in place.

Raise the wall frame so the top is in its exact position on the ceiling and drive the foot into position with a sledge hammer. Nail the top plate to the joists, bottom plate to the floor. If there is a door opening, frame in the wall section above it and hang the door as in Section 8.9.

Finally, put up drywall and finish as in next section; then install baseboard and toe molding.

6.32 | Installing and finishing drywall. Sheets of drywall should be installed vertically, using short, ringed nails (they look like thin screws) that will not penetrate the stud more than an inch. If you are installing drywall over old plaster or drywall, instead of on new wall framing, nails can be a little longer to allow for depth of the old wall surface. Space the nails 8 to 12 inches apart and drive them just below the surface of the drywall so you can cover the nailheads neatly with joint cement later.

To make a straight cut on drywall, score it with a knife point on one side, then snap the drywall back from the score, and slide through the paper backing with your knife point. If you have to cut corners or irregular shapes, use an old keyhole saw.

For finishing, you will need joint cement and paper tape from your hardware store or lumber dealer. Mix the joint cement according to instructions on the bag and let it set for half an hour before using. Apply cement directly over nailheads with a broad, flexible knife. Then "butter" joints between the sheets of drywall with a fat bead of cement, then place a strip of paper tape in the cement down the length of the joint. Cover the tape with another layer of cement, then remove excess with your knife. Let the first application of cement dry for twenty-four hours. Then apply a second coat with the flexible knife, feathering it out evenly into the flat surface of the drywall. When this dries, a special topping coat—ask your dealer— can be applied, or you can use a third coat of the same cement. Make joints neat and flat as possible to minimize sanding. When final coat is dry, sand until perfectly smooth if it isn't already.

On outside corners, instead of paper tape use a metal corner bead with paper edges that are feathered into the surface of drywall. The corner bead is placed on a thick bead of joint cement, just like the paper joint tape. On inside corners you can use regular paper tape folded on the center line.

7 FLOORS AND STAIRS

STRUCTURAL PROBLEMS

7.1 | Floor structure. The backbone of a floor is the framework of joists that support the surface you walk on. Joists are 2 x 6's, 2 x 8's, or 2 x 12's, depending on the span, and they are usually spaced 16 inches apart. (See Fig. 7-1.) In most construction, bridging between joists is used to stiffen the floor.

Figure 7-1   Typical floor framing

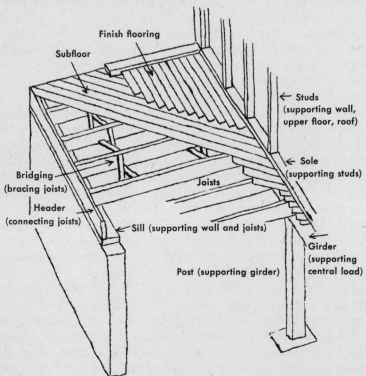

154

Resting on the joists is the subfloor, made of plywood or 1 x 6 boards, nailed diagonally across the joists for greater stiffness. The finish floor rests on the subfloor, at right angles to the joists underneath. (Sometimes there is a layer of building paper between finish floor and subfloor to keep out dust and dirt.) Finish flooring (wood, tiles, etc.) is nailed or cemented to the subfloor. In some construction, especially in old houses, the finish flooring is nailed directly to the joists.

Floors that are on concrete slabs—you can tell by the "feel" of the floor—rarely have any squeaks or vibrations. If they do, you have a major problem—the failure of the whole slab—and you'd better call in an expert.

7.2 | If you have a squeak in the floor, it is due to movement that shouldn't be there. Go into the basement or crawl space and have someone walk over the squeaky spot so you can locate it in relation to the floor joists. If it seems to be over a joist, drill two tiny holes through the floor from below and next to the joist so you can locate the joist's exact position from above. If the underside is not exposed, as in a second floor or a first floor over a finished basement ceiling, you will have to check position of the joists by measuring in at 16-inch intervals from the face of an outside-wall baseboard. (Remember that finish flooring boards usually run at right angles to the joists.)

If the squeaky spot is over a joist or within a few inches of one, you may be able to eliminate the noise by merely nailing the flooring back in place. (Slight shrinkage or warping of joists or subfloor can prevent the subfloor from resting directly on the joist.) Have someone stand on the spot and drive two 2-inch hardened steel nails (sold especially for oak flooring) through the face of the board at opposite angles in the form of an X. (See Fig. 7-2a.) Take care to avoid hammer marks, and use a nailset to countersink the nails. Fill nail holes afterward with plastic wood. If nails won't do the trick, try flathead wood screws about 1½ inches long. (See Sec. 7.5.)

An alternative method, if the underside is exposed, is to insert a wedge between joist and subfloor. A wood shingle makes a good wedge. (See Fig. 7-2b.) Put some epoxy glue on the end of the shingle before driving it into place. Or, if several boards squeak, you can raise them slightly with a strip of hardwood nailed to the joist (forcing it with a wedge set on the floor while you nail the strip in place. See Fig. 7-2c.)

If the squeaky spot is located between joists, and is confined to

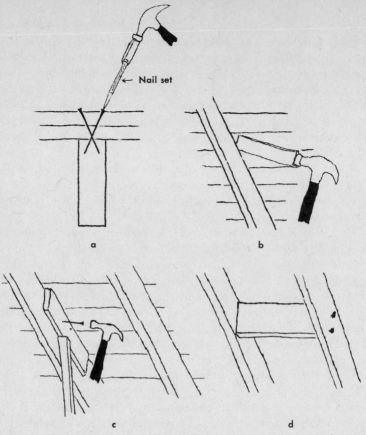

Figure 7-2 Ways to eliminate squeaks

one board, you can install a length of 2 x 4 or 2 x 6 between the joists, flush against the subfloor. Fasten with nails, two at each end. Then drive a glue-coated wooden shingle between wedge and subfloor. (See Fig. 7-2*d*.)

Squeaks caused by two boards rubbing together can sometimes be silenced by lubricating the floor cracks near the squeak with powdered graphite (from the hardware store). Or if the wood has shrunk and open cracks move a bit, you can sometimes use a two-part epoxy glue in the crack to make it solid again and prevent squeaking.

Ends of boards that have curled up from the floor and cause squeaking can simply be nailed back again to the subfloor. (See Sec. 7.5.)

156

7.3 | **If there's widespread vibration or sagging in your floor,** you probably have a serious structural defect. Unless you are an accomplished handyman, call a contractor to look into this for you. Here are the possibilities he will point out to you:

If you have an old house or one that is cheaply constructed, there may be no bridging. Or the bridging may be poorly fitted or loose. New bridging will add strength to weak floors; 1 x 3 or 2 x 3 stock should be toenailed diagnally to the studs. (See Fig. 7-3.)

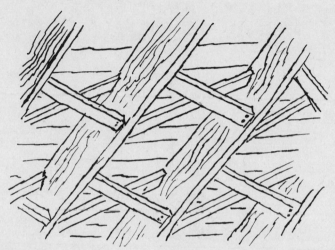

Figure 7-3 Bridging

If the floor sags in the center of the house, the center girders have probably sagged and must be propped up with a column. If the house is old and has a dirt floor in the basement, or a weak and crumbly concrete floor, new footings will have to be put in first. A hole 18 to 24 inches square is dug (to about the same depth as width) and filled with concrete which is troweled off smoothly at the top.

If your basement has a good concrete floor, the column can be installed without any extra footing, but holes in the concrete are chipped out with a star drill so the lug-plate bolts can be set in concrete. (See Fig. 7-4.) The metal lug plate keeps the lally column in place, so be sure you get a column that has one. It should also have a screw-jack top that is tightened in place by turning.

If the girder (see Fig. 7-1) is damaged and must be replaced, see Section 10.8. If the girder is not damaged, and is already sup-

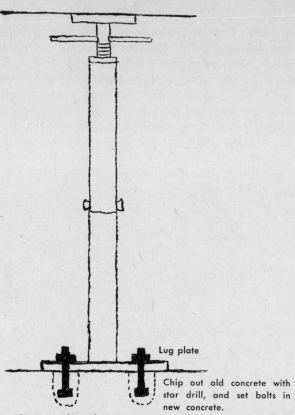

Lug plate

Chip out old concrete with star drill, and set bolts in new concrete.

Figure 7-4   Lally column on lug plate

ported by a column, the footings under the column may have crumbled. Temporary supports must be used to hold up the girder while new footings are put in.

If the sagging is at the outside end of joists or girders, the foundation may have crumbled. If girder or joists rest on a wood sill supported by the foundation, the sill may be damaged or rotted. In either case, complicated (and expensive) maneuvers are called for. This is not work for the amateur.

7.4 | **When the second floor sags,** corrective measures are even more difficult and complicated. It is necessary to remove either the flooring above or the ceiling below so that bridging or additional joists may be inserted. Do not attempt this work yourself, unless you have first been assured by an expert that the sag is due to simple timber shrinkage—not structural weaknesses. In this case, you can remove the finish floor and level it off by inserting furring strips between it and the subfloor at right angles to finish flooring. Strips must be tapered to correct for the sag—check with a level as you work.

7.5 | Repairing and replacing damaged floor boards. If a floor board is merely warped, you may be able to repair it by soaking it, then screwing it tightly to the subfloor. Use flathead steel wood screws about 1½ inches long. Drill holes in the floor board slightly smaller than the screws, so you won't split the boards, then screw them in with a screw bit on a brace. (See Fig. 7-5.) Countersink them (screw them in beneath the surface) so you can cap screw heads with plastic wood.

Figure 7-5   Rachet brace with screwdriver bit

If cracks develop along the grain of the wood, force two-part epoxy glue into the cracks. Cracks between the boards that develop when the wood shrinks during dry weather should be filled with plastic wood or other prepared crack filler (ask your hardware dealer). Permanent cracks between the boards of old floors can be filled by strips of hardwood cut to fit and glued or nailed in place.

Rotted or badly damaged boards should be removed and replaced. If there is a subfloor, any portion of any board may be removed. If there is no subfloor, ends of the new piece of floor board must, of course, meet over the floor joists.

Cut a new piece of the same type of floor board—the same size as the piece to be replaced, *plus* the extra length of a bevel of 45 degrees at one end. Using the new piece as a guide, mark the piece to be removed. Cut a hole just inside each corner with a large bit, being careful not to cut into the subfloor. Cut the board between drilled holes with a sharp chisel and hammer. Be sure not to damage the tongue and groove of adjoining boards. Undercut one end at a 45-degree angle so the replacement board will fit in snugly. (See Fig. 7-6.) Plane off the underside of groove on the replacement board so it can be fitted over tongue of adjacent board.

Figure 7-6   Making beveled edge with wood chisel

Place the beveled edge under the beveled undercut and tap the other end gently in place using a block of wood between hammer and board to avoid making hammer marks. Drill at least four holes slightly smaller than the screws or finishing nails you are using. Hammer nails in, countersink them, and fill holes with plastic wood. If necessary, sand the board down to level of existing floor, and finish to match other floor boards.

7.6 | Replacing worn or damaged thresholds. If a threshold is badly worn, it must be replaced. This is particularly true if the threshold is on an exterior door, for there it will allow rain and dirt to penetrate under the door.

Take down the door. (See Sec. 8.1.) Remove the door stop by prying it away from the jamb with a chisel or pry bar, not a screwdriver (which might dent or damage the stop). Start at the bottom and pry out only ¼ inch at a time to prevent cracking. With the stop off you may be able to pry out the threshold in one piece. (See Fig. 7-7a.)

If the edges of the threshold rest under the jamb and you cannot pull it out, cut it out with a handsaw and chisel. (Fig. 7-7*b*.) Be careful not to damage the floor. If possible, remove pieces of threshold under the jamb so you can cut a new threshold (of oak) that will exactly replace the old one. If you can't get these pieces out from under the jamb, cut a new threshold to fit in flush with the jamb. Drill holes near the outside edges of the new threshold, staggering holes on the opposite sides, so you can screw it down to the structural plate (usually a 2 x 4 right under the threshold). Fasten the new threshold with wood screws and finish to match existing floor. (See Secs. 7.13 and 7.14.)

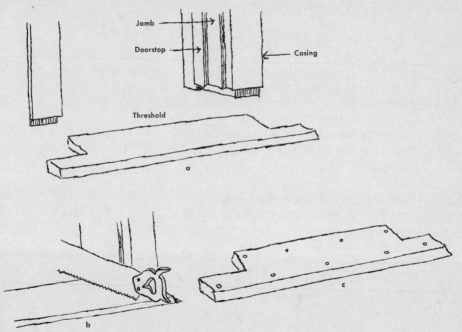

Figure 7-7   Replacing a threshold

7.7 | **If your stairs creak,** they can be repaired in much the same manner as squeaky floor boards. (See Sec. 7.2.) Screw squeaky treads to risers with wood screws, first drilling holes—slightly smaller than screws—in at angles to avoid splitting the wood. Countersink screws and fill holes with plastic wood or dowel plugs.

If the underside of a stairway is exposed, you can eliminate

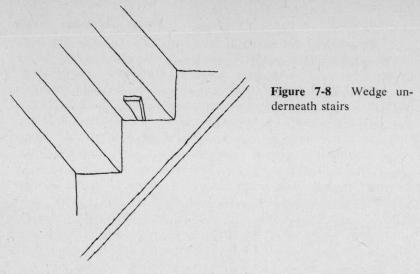

Figure 7-8 Wedge underneath stairs

squeak-making movement with wedges to wedge tread tighter to stringer. (Fig. 7-8.) (Treads and risers fit into routed-out channels in stringer.)

7.8 | **Replacing a worn-out tread.** Care must be taken in removing the old tread so you don't split or break risers or balusters. First, remove the balusters by removing the end piece of trim on the tread, if there is one. (See Fig. 7-9.) If they are toenailed to the tread, cut

Figure 7-9 Replacing a tread

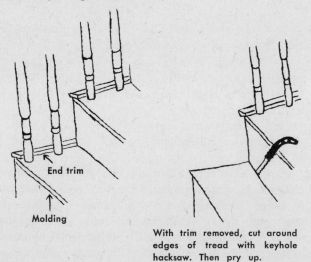

End trim

Molding

With trim removed, cut around edges of tread with keyhole hacksaw. Then pry up.

under them, flush with the tread, with a keyhole hacksaw. The tops of the balusters can simply be twisted out of the hand railing.

Next, remove any moldings under the front edge of the tread, and then see that the back edge is clear of the riser behind it by cutting all along its length with a keyhole hacksaw. Now pry up the tread and work it loose from the wall side.

Cut your new tread to exact size, and drill holes for wood screws before installing. Fasten to stringers and risers, and countersink screws. Replace balusters by toenailing them to new tread, and finish tread as in Section 7.13.

7.9 | Remodeling a stairway. You may want to do this either because your old stairs are worn out or you just don't like the looks of them. It can be a very big job depending on your plans. If you do have big plans for remodeling your stairs, and you are not particularly handy, you should call in a professional to do the job. You may want to get bids from several contractors—see Chapter 17.

At any rate, your present stairs will probably have to be ripped out down to the basic structure—the stringers. (See Fig. 7-10.) On this framework the stairs can be rebuilt with any risers, treads, rails, and balusters you wish. Consult your lumber dealer about new materials before you begin wrecking, if you are doing the job yourself.

If you want to widen your stairs, straighten them, stretch them out, or make them turn a corner, basic structural changes in the house itself will be involved. It's essential to get a contractor in this case.

7.10 | Building a new stairway. If your stringers on first floor, basement, or porch stairs are rotted out, they should be replaced before somebody breaks a leg. First wreck out or remove all the treads, risers, and so forth, down to the stringers—see preceding section. If you want to reuse treads and risers, be sure not to damage them when you remove them.

Then carefully remove all rotted structural parts so you can use them as templates for cutting new pieces out of structural lumber. If this process is impossible because the stringers are too badly out of shape, or if it would put the stairs out of commission too long, you have to make an accurate plan so you can precut stringers to exact size before you wreck out the treads.

To make such a plan, remove all side trim on stairs so you can see the whole stringer, then measure the vertical height of stringer from its foot, and the exact horizontal length of the stringer. (See

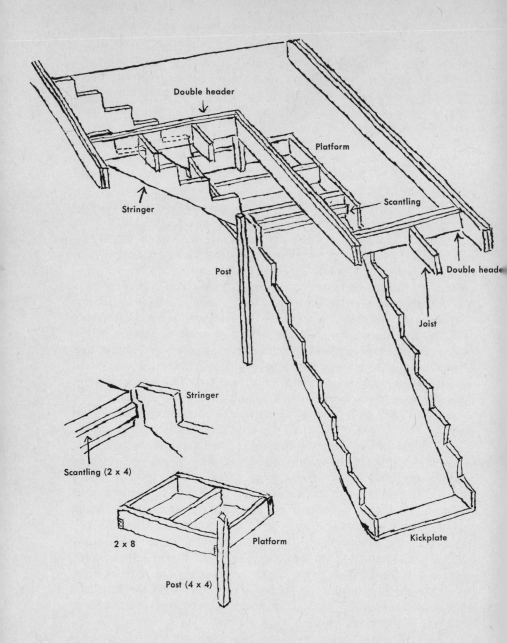

Figure 7-10   Stair structure

164

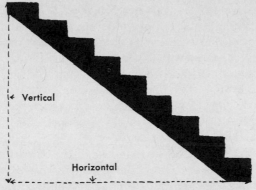

Use plumb line and carpenter's level to establish
perfect vertical and horizontal. Then lay out design
for stringer to exact scale on graph paper.

Figure 7-11   Measuring for new stringer

Fig. 7-11.) You will have to use a plumb bob and a level to be sure
you have the right measurements. Now lay these out to scale on a
piece of paper and scale off the runs and rises in the stringer. When
you are through, you should have an accurate scale drawing of the
stringer. You can cut new risers from this and have them all ready
to install when you wreck out the old stairs. Install new treads by
first drilling holes in them as in Section 7.8.

If you want to create a new stairway where there was none
before, call a contractor, as this involves a great deal of structural
work.

FINISHING AND REFINISHING WOOD FLOORS

7.11 | Scratches and spots on wood floors. Most wooden floors
are made of oak, usually in strips or boards, but sometimes in blocks
or parquet, either prefinished or finished in place. Other hardwoods,
like pecan, hickory, maple, and beech (all light), are sometimes used,
in parquet floors especially. Dark woods used in parquet are usually
walnut, teak, or cherry. Generally speaking, any kind of finish can
be used on hardwood floors—new plastic finishes, varnishes, paints,
or just wax.

Some floors and stairs in older homes are made of various kinds
of pine or fir. These softwoods are usually laid in wide planks and
should be finished with stains and wax. Tight film finishes like paints

and varnishes give too much beneath a footfall or a table leg and this will soon break the finish film and let it chip off.

If surface scratches occur in a wood floor, they can be removed with steel wool dampened with liquid cleaning fluid, such as Carbona, rubbing with the grain. Smooth with a dry pad of fine steel wool. Deeper scratches must be filled with plastic wood, then sanded smooth with sandpaper. The damaged area can then be finished with the same finish used on the original floor, or just stained and waxed to match. If you use a regular floor finish, brush the edges of the patch out to blend with the surrounding area. When dry, rub with fine steel wool if it looks too new compared with the rest of the floor.

A badly scratched floor or one that has become darkened and stained must be completely refinished.

7.12 | **Removing old floor finish.** Sanding and scraping is the best, and usually the cheapest, way to remove old finish. Rent a power sander and an edger sander from your local hardware store. (It is absolutely pointless to attempt this job without the proper equipment.) You will need coarse sandpaper for the first "cut," medium for the next, and fine for the last going-over. Tell your hardware dealer the age and type of your floors and he'll know the exact papers you should use. (See Fig. 7-12.)

Before you begin to sand, check for protruding nails and loose boards, and make any necessary repairs. (See Secs. 7.2 and 7.5.) Countersink all visible nailheads (they'll ruin sander and paper) and

Hand scraper for small corners

Power sander   Disc sander for edging

Figure 7-12   Sanding equipment

fill holes with plastic wood. Fill cracks, if any. (See Sec. 7.5.) Your job will be easier if you remove the toe molding so you can sand up near the baseboard. When you have refinished the floor, you can replace the old molding or install a new one finished to match the floor.

Always sand with the grain—lengthwise along the boards, working from one end of the room to the other and then back again. Never stop in one spot with the sander running. Sand edges, baseboards, stair treads, and other inaccessible corners with the edger. You may have to hand-sand or use a scraper in the corners or under radiators. As you work, clean up loose sand and sawdust with the brush attachment of your vacuum cleaner. Vacuum thoroughly when sanding is finished.

7.13 | **Easiest and toughest floor finishes** to apply and care for are the new plastic finishes. These are clear, varnish-type finishes that will last for years, need no waxing, and can be simply wet-mopped when necessary.

You can identify these finishes by looking on the back of the can, or by asking your hardware dealer. There are two basic types: One has a polyester and acetate base, the other a urethane base. Both are good, and other new types of synthetic finishes just as good are finding their way to the market every year. Even the old type of floor-finishing varnishes now have tough new synthetic plastics as part of their base.

If you want to darken the wood before using one of these clear finishes, you can use a pigmented sealer for the first coat. Oak floors with their open grain should be sealed with a liquid or paste sealer before the finish is applied in any case. Most other types of wood floors do not require a sealer for a good-looking finish. If you want to use a stain, ask your dealer what kind should be used with the finish you plan to apply.

When applying sealer, put it on liberally with a brush or cloth, and wipe off the excess after about fifteen minutes (it will be slightly sticky). Let dry overnight and sand lightly with fine sandpaper. Then, if the floor seems to need it, apply a second coat, let dry, and sand again lightly. Finally, apply finish according to directions on the can.

7.14 | **Other floor finishes you can use.** Floors with the richest, deepest luster are almost always floors with a good application of paste wax. (The plastic finishes, mentioned in the preceding section, have a hard, high gloss.) To prepare a floor for paste wax, be sure it is absolutely clean. If the old finish has been taken off, or if it is a new floor, use a sealer, with or without stain (see preceding section), or a light coat of varnish thinned with turpentine. Or, if the grain is tight, you can use just a stain. When this dries, sand it lightly. Then apply paste wax with a rag. When it dries, in about 15 or 20 minutes, buff it down with an electric buffer. If you can't get an electric buffer, or if your floors are very old and uneven, you can get sheepskin slippers at the hardware stores which go on over your shoes. Put them on and "skate" around the floor to polish it.

There are on the market a number of combination sealer-wax-stain materials that are wiped on the floor and polished with a cloth when dry. They are good but not as durable or as rich as a paste wax finish. However, they are much easier to apply.

Don't use shellac as a floor finish. It is easily damaged by water or alcohol, and scratches very easily.

INSTALLING WOOD FLOORS

7.15 | How to install strip flooring. Strip flooring comes with tongue and grooves and is available in many styles. Ask your lumber dealer to show them to you. You can buy it either prefinished or unfinished. The unfinished kind is less expensive but must be sanded and finished after it is installed. If you are laying the floor over an uneven old floor or on concrete, use strips at least 5⁄8-inch thick. Thinner material may be used over a smooth subfloor or old finish floor.

If you are installing strip flooring over an old floor, there is no need to take up the old surface or smooth out irregularities—5⁄8-inch strips will easily span it. First nail down any exposed nailheads and remove the toe molding around the edge of the baseboard. Clean the old floor thoroughly and cover it with asphalt building paper (it comes in rolls 36 inches wide) lapping the edges about 4 inches.

Have your flooring strips delivered in dry weather, and stack them loosely in a well-ventilated place at about 70 degrees for several days before installation (Caution: If walls or ceiling of the room have been recently plastered, do not install flooring until the plaster has completely dried—a period of several months.)

Nail your first row of strip flooring across the room at right angles to the old floor and parallel to one wall. Start with a row about ½ inch from the baseboard with grooves facing the walls, lining the strips up with a string stretched taut along the floor. The toe molding will cover the crack between flooring and baseboard. Each row of strip flooring should be nailed complete from one end of the room to the other before beginning a new strip. Nail at 6-inch intervals and within 4 inches of ends of strips. Space joints in adjoining strips at least 8 inches apart. (See Fig. 7-13.) You can get a nailing template from your dealer that will make it easier to get nails into

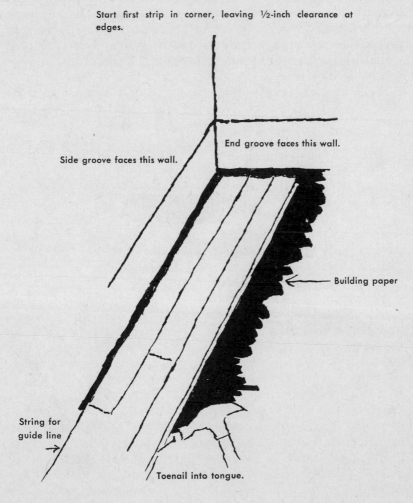

Figure 7-13   Strip oak installation

the tongue of the strips without damaging the floor surface. Or you can rent a special nailing tool that is loaded with nails, placed on the strip, and hit with a rubber mallet to drive the nail in at exactly the right angle.

To install strip flooring over a concrete floor, first spread asphalt mastic (ask your hardware or lumber dealer) over the floor to form a vapor barrier and a glue surface for the screeds. Screeds (short lengths of 2 x 4's) are laid in the mastic in rows 12 inches apart, staggered and lapped as in Figure 7-14. Place continuous lengths of 2 x 4's against the walls at the two ends parallel to direction of screeds. Flooring is then nailed to end supports and screeds as shown.

After flooring has been installed and sanded, but before finishing, nail toe molding in place.

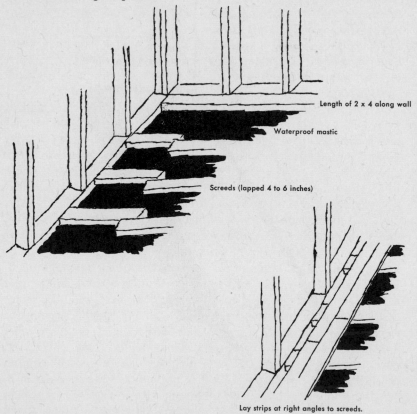

Length of 2 x 4 along wall

Waterproof mastic

Screeds (lapped 4 to 6 inches)

Lay strips at right angles to screeds.

Figure 7-14   Laying strip flooring on concrete

7.16 | Installing wood block and parquet flooring. These materials can be installed directly without nailing (they are glued) over concrete, plywood, asphalt tile, or any wood floor, provided the floor is sound and smooth. However, they should not be installed over radiantly heated slabs and cannot be glued over old vinyl or linoleum.

The reason wood block and parquet can be glued directly to the floor surface underneath, whereas strip flooring cannot be, is that they expand and contract very little with changes of humidity—they are dimensionally stable. Block flooring is usually three-ply, like plywood, and comes in squares 9″ x 9″. Parquet patterns of small pieces of hardwood usually come in small sheets up to 16 inches square. Thicknesses of both materials run from ⅜ to 25/32 inch.

Your first step is to prepare the surface. Clean it thoroughly by rough sanding or scrubbing with a solution of one pound of lye in three gallons of hot water. (Wear rubber gloves, and take care to avoid splashes.) If the floor is asphalt tile, sand it smooth (mostly to get the old wax and shine off), then scrub with water and scouring powder. Rinse and let dry thoroughly and you are ready to install your flooring.

If the floor is covered with resilient flooring other than asphalt (vinyl, linoleum, or rubber) you can remove the old covering and then scrub with lye solution as above. Or you can cover it with ⅜-inch-thick Grade C-D sanded plywood sheets. Nail these down through the floor after removing the toe molding. This will result in a higher level of floor in this room than in adjacent rooms, but you can install a sloping threshold to bring the two levels together.

On a concrete floor, you must first fill in low spots with patching mix (ask your hardware dealer for an epoxy or latex type) and level high spots with a carborundum grinder or a floor sander or hammer and chisel. Vacuum the surface thoroughly before proceeding. If the concrete is in contact with earth, you must damp-proof it as follows. First apply a coat of asphalt primer (you'll need approximately a gallon for every 150 square feet) and let dry four to eight hours. Then apply a layer of hot mastic (ask your dealer what kind) with a spreader with quarter-inch teeth. (One gallon will cover 25 to 35 square feet.) The mastic can be heated over an outside fire. Be careful not to boil it, and not to get any water in it. When the floor is covered with mastic, overlay it with No. 15 asphalt saturated felt, butting seams (no overlap). Now apply a second coat of hot mastic and again overlay with felt, this time starting with a half-width strip of felt at the same wall where you began before. This insures that seams of the second layer will not be over seams of the first layer. Then proceed as below.

Wood block flooring should be stored in the room in which it is being installed for several days beforehand. When you are ready to install the blocks, figure out how you want to lay them—squarely or diagonally. (If the length of the room is more than one and a half times its width, the diagonal pattern will best minimize risk of overexpansion and possible buckling. See also Sec. 7.20.) To establish your guide line for a square pattern, start at the center of the threshold of the main door and place two rows of loose blocks about four feet long. Snap a chalk line at this point parallel to the entrance wall. Store all materials and tools in this two-row strip across one end of the room. Now apply mastic (use the kind your flooring dealer recommends) to the rest of the room with a notched spreader, and leave it to dry according to directions on the can. Place the first block in position approximately in line with the center of the doorway, with the side along your guide line. Place two or three blocks on either side of it, aligning edges with your guide line. To place a block in position, fit it into groove of last tile and drop it into place. (If you try to slide it into place, you'll end up with mastic in the grooves and on the surface as well.) Tap gently on the opposite edge to get it tightly into place.

After placing about five blocks along your guide line, place one above the first block. Continue working in pyramid style. (See Fig. 7-15.) When you have a large enough area laid to transfer tools and materials, do so, then spread mastic in the two-row storage strip.

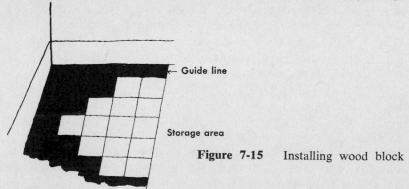

Guide line

Storage area

Figure 7-15   Installing wood block

Return to work on the main area, laying all full blocks first—then trimming blocks to fit edges and corners. Leave a half-inch space at the edges to be covered by toe molding later. If there are any pipes, hearths, columns, and so forth to fit around, leave $\frac{1}{16}$-inch clearance between block and object for each foot of distance between it and nearest wall.

By the time you finish laying all blocks in the main area, the storage area mastic should be dry and you can proceed to lay blocks there.

If you are laying your blocks or parquet diagonally, establish right angles at the center of the floor according to the "3-4-5" method —see Section 6.26 and Figure 6-19. Then divide the right angles in half with 45 per cent diagonals. (See Fig. 7-16.) These angle-dividing lines are your guide lines. Pick out their end points on the baseboard

Figure 7-16   Installing block diagonally

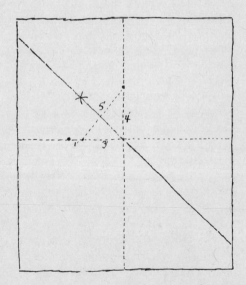

To establish guide lines for laying block diagonally, first connect midpoints of walls and form perfect right angle by "3–4–5" method. Then bisect right angle with overlapping area drawn from points equidistant from center point, using chalk on a string as your compass. Connect points to form 45° angle and use this line for guide line.

with small nails, then apply your mastic (leaving one corner for a storage area) and let dry. Begin laying block or parquet at the nearest diagonal to the door, pyramiding out as above. Transfer tools from the storage area and apply mastic there, and proceed.

Nail toe molding in place after all flooring has been installed.

RESILIENT FLOORS

7.17 | Basic facts about resilient floors. Vinyl asbestos tiles are the most popular in use today. They are inexpensive, look good, wear well, are resistant to grease, and easy to take care of.

Asphalt tiles are the cheapest resilient flooring you can lay. In many ways they are as good as vinyl, but unless they are specified as "greaseproof" they won't be and spots from food will wear through the shiny finish. They don't come in as many bright colors as the vinyls and are harder to install.

Linoleum tile and sheet is very good-looking, long-wearing, very tough, and costs accordingly.

Vinyl (pure vinyl) tile and sheet are also expensive, but come in a wealth of colors, patterns, and even rich semitransparent marble and wood effects. They are highly decorative, wear well, and come in thinner grades than linoleum.

Rubber tile is very much like pure vinyl. It's expensive and colorful, but is limited largely to opaque colors.

Most tiles are 9″ x 9″, but they may be priced by the square foot rather than by the tile. Tiles are easier for the amateur to install than sheet flooring (linoleum or sheet vinyl). However, sheet flooring is now available in 2-foot wide rolls, which simplifies the process considerably. Surface-printed sheet flooring, whether vinyl or linoleum, is much cheaper than "inlaid"—which means that the design goes all through the thickness of the material. However, in the long run, surface-printed sheets are not economical, because once the surface is marred little can be done to repair its appearance.

7.18 | Care and repair of resilient flooring. Newly laid resilient flooring should not be washed until the adhesive has set thoroughly— for four or five days at least. After this period, wash, let dry, and wax. (Use the kind of wax your flooring dealer recommends.)

Spots can be removed with scouring powder when necessary. (If flooring is surface-printed, remember you may wear off the surface and the decoration.) Difficult spots on inlaid flooring may be scraped off with a razor blade or stainless steel scouring pad and water. Do not use strong soaps regularly on any resilient flooring. Chlorine bleaches take the color out of some surfaces. If the surface becomes coated with old wax, apply a commercial wax remover according to directions on the can.

If a few tiles become damaged, you can pry them up with a chisel and scrape out the old adhesive underneath. Carefully sand the edges of the new tiles until they fit exactly in spaces left by the ones you removed. Then apply the manufacturer's recommended adhesive and fit tile in place.

To replace a worn-out section of linoleum, cut the damaged piece out with a sharp knife. Use a straightedge (preferably metal) as a cutting guide, so edges will be absolutely straight. Replace the worn-out piece with another cut to the same size. If necessary, place one or more layers of lining felt underneath (see next section) to raise the new linoleum level with the old.

Use the proper adhesive (ask your flooring dealer) to cement lining, if any, and linoleum patch in place. Weight down the patch until the cement is dry. If any oozes out, remove it with a rag and scouring powder before it dries.

If sheet flooring bulges between the seams, force adhesive underneath with a spatula or kitchen knife, press into contact, and weight down. If the bulge is not at a seam, make a slit straight across the bulge and force cement under it. If possible, follow lines of a pattern when making your slit, so patch will be less obvious.

7.19 | Preparing the surface for new resilient flooring. This is an important part of the job, because if there are any irregularities in the surface beneath, they will show up in the flooring after it has been installed.

Before you begin work, remove all removable fixtures and furniture, and remove the toe molding around the baseboard if there is any.

If you are installing the new flooring over an old wooden finish floor in good condition, with boards less than three inches wide, rent a heavy-duty sander at the hardware store and rough-sand the floor. Before you sand, repair any loose boards or protruding nails. When the floor is smooth and clean (use a vacuum cleaner), the next step is to apply felt underlayment. (Your flooring dealer will tell you what kind to use.) Place the first strip at one edge of the room, cut to the proper length. Roll up halfway, apply adhesive (use the one your dealer recommends) to the floor with a trowel-type spreader, and smooth the felt in place. Then roll up the other end and repeat the process. Smooth down each strip with a roller (rent it from your dealer)—see Figure 7-17. Cover the whole floor with

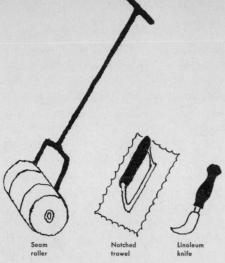

Figure 7-17 Tools for laying resilient flooring

Seam roller   Notched trowel   Linoleum knife

felt, butting the strips together—no overlap at seams. Then you are ready to install tile.

If you are going to install tile or sheet where there is old resilient flooring, remove the old surface down to good wood and proceed as explained.

If tile is being installed over a subfloor, over old flooring in poor condition, or flooring with wide boards, more preparation is required. First, a layer of felt is laid loose, not glued in place. Over this, nail a layer of ⅛- to ¼-inch hardboard or Grade C-D sanded plywood. If you are laying it over a subfloor, make sure joints do not lie directly over subfloor joints. Very uneven floors take even thicker plywood. Be sure nailheads are driven just slightly below the surface of the underlayment. The resilient flooring can be cemented directly to the plywood underlayment, but for the best job you should lay a felt underlayment between plywood and tile. Glue this layer of felt in place—see page 175.

If the flooring is to be laid over concrete, asphalt and some types of rubber tiles are the only suitable kinds. The surface must first be smoothed and cracks filled with a concrete patching compound. (Ask your dealer what kind—the epoxies or latex-base types are best.) See Section 7.16 for details on how to smooth uneven concrete floors. Make sure floor is completely waterproof before installing tiles; see Section 10.1. No underlayment is required on concrete, but a special adhesive must be used.

7.20 | How to install resilient tiles. When tiles are installed, room temperature should be 70 degrees or above.

When your underlayment is in place, establish guide lines by stretching strings from the mid-points of opposite walls. They will intersect at the exact center of the room. Use a carpenter's square to make sure angles are 90 degrees, or use the system shown in Figure 6-10. Chalk the lines and snap them so they are marked on the underlayment.

"Rough in" a row of tiles with edges along the guide lines. If the space left between the wall and last tile in the row is over 8 inches or under 2 inches, adjust the center guide lines so you come out with either a whole tile or about half a tile at each end. This will look better and avoid the necessity of cutting narrow strips of tile—which can be a very difficult task.

If you want to install tiles diagonally, lay out guide lines as explained in Section 7.16.

When guide lines have been adjusted to provide the desired borders around the edges, stretch one line taught across the room again. Apply adhesive (use the kind your dealer recommends) with a notched spreader to one half the room, stopping just past the center guide line. (Run adhesive under the line.) Let adhesive set if the manufacturer says to do so. (When using asphalt tile, adhesive must set for several hours.) Then resnap your taut chalk line on the adhesive and remove the line. Lay one complete row of tiles first, placing them carefully along the guide line. Place the two center tiles first. Butt tiles together snugly and lay them in place—do not slide. If any adhesive gets on the surface, wipe it up immediately with a rag and scouring powder.

When one row has been laid, go back to the center and work in pyramid fashion until all full tiles have been laid. (See Fig. 7-16.) To measure tile to fit around the edges, place the tile to be cut exactly over the last tile laid. Now take another tile and place it on top of the first, but with its edge flush against the wall. Score or draw a line on the first tile along edge of the upper one. (See Fig. 6-17.) Mark tiles for curved edges around fixtures and pipes as also shown in Figure 6-17. To fit around pipes out from the wall requiring a cut-out in the tile, first make a paper pattern as in Figure 7-18a.

Linoleum, cork, vinyl, or rubber tile can be cut with a linoleum knife or scissors, or any very sharp knife. (If the tile seems hard to cut, warm it.) To make a straight cut on asphalt or vinyl asbestos tile, score on the line with a sharp knife or awl and place the tile between two wooden blocks with scored line at the edge. (See Fig. 7-18b.)

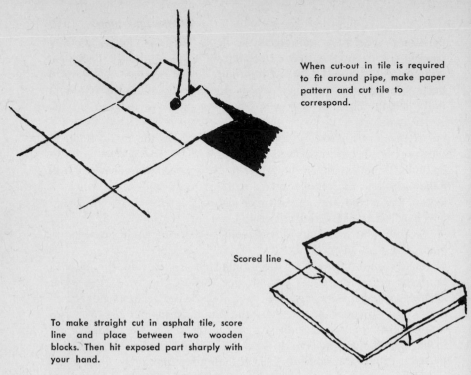

When cut-out in tile is required to fit around pipe, make paper pattern and cut tile to correspond.

Scored line

To make straight cut in asphalt tile, score line and place between two wooden blocks. Then hit exposed part sharply with your hand.

Figure 7-18   Fitting and cutting asphalt tile

Hit the exposed portion sharply with your hand, and it will break cleanly with a straight edge. To cut a curve in asphalt or vinyl asbestos tile, you must heat it until it is soft—either with a torch (be very careful) or over a range top. Wear work gloves for this job and turn the tile as you warm it. Then cut with a scissors or sharp knife.

When all tiles have been laid on the first half of the room, apply mastic to the other half and lay tiles as above. If the mastic must set more than a few minutes, you will probably want to transfer equipment to the tiled area as soon as it is large enough, then apply mastic to the second half of the room so it can set while you fit tiles around the edges of the first half.

7.21 | **Installing sheet flooring.** To fit sheet flooring properly, you must make a paper pattern out of building paper. When your floor is prepared as in Section 7-19, take a role of building paper and begin laying it out in strips, flush against one wall and butted evenly against adjoining walls. To get the exact line of the wall against the end of the paper, crease the paper exactly with the point of a pair of scissors where the wall meets the floor. Then cut the paper. You can cut the paper slightly short of the wall, because the toe molding will cover the gap. But be sure you cut it exactly where you want it because once the sheet of flooring is down in the adhesive, you can't move it.

Continue laying strips of paper across the room, lapping the edges and taping them together with masking tape. Thumbtack your pattern to the floor or weight it down with books so it can't move as you fit it. To fit around uneven walls or fixtures, cut as in Figure 7-19.

Figure 7-19   Making a paper pattern

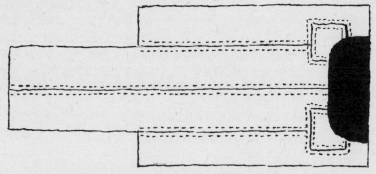

1. Cover floor with strips of building paper, fitting around curves with small pieces of paper cut to fit exactly. Tape all joints with masking tape *(dotted lines)*.

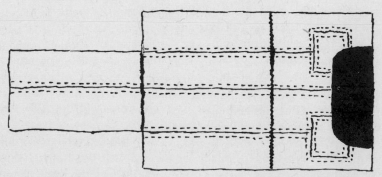

2. Cut pattern into widths corresponding to flooring width *(heavy black wiggly lines)*.

When you have finished making your pattern, check to be sure the floor is covered completely, with all joints taped throughout their length, and the paper completely flat in all spots. Then you are ready to cut the pattern into widths matching the width of your sheet flooring. Before you start cutting, carefully figure out the most economical use of the flooring. For fixtures not against the wall (toilets and pipes), make one straight slit behind the fixture to the wall. (See Fig. 7-18a.) When you have cut the pattern into the proper widths, cut your sheet flooring into corresponding pieces with a sharp knife.

When all flooring has been cut to fit your pattern, apply the adhesive according to manufacturer's directions to a strip along the wall the width of one pattern piece. Let it set if required. Then take your strip of flooring, cut to size, and hold it up so the far edge drops in position against the wall. Don't place sheet all the way down until you are certain edge is exactly in the right position. Then lower it into place. Continue working across the room in this fashion. When your flooring is all down, roll it with a heavy roller you can rent from your dealer. (See Fig. 7-17.)

CERAMIC AND STONE FLOORING

7.22 | Preparing a base for ceramic tile. Ceramic tile floors are ideal for bathrooms because standing water can't affect them. They are less ideal for kitchens because dropped glasses and plates will break easily on them, and food stains are likely to take hold in their slightly porous surfaces.

The easiest way to install ceramic tile is with a waterproof adhesive especially made for it. Ask your dealer to show it to you. If you decide to use it, you must first prepare the floor as though you were laying resilient tile—see Section 7.19. Remember that ceramic tiles are usually 3/16- to ¼-inch thick. So unless you remove the old finish floor and install underlayment of the right thickness, you will have to install a sloping threshold to adjust the different floor levels. If the bathroom door opens in instead of out, you may have to cut the door bottom down.

The best and most permanent way to install ceramic floor tile is in mortar. This will give you a floor that time, rough use, and all kinds of adverse conditions cannot affect. To install tile this way you must remove the door, threshold, toe molding, and baseboard so tile can extend to the wall. Take up the old floor covering or finish floor and expose the subfloor. Check the subfloor for rot, warped or damaged boards, and make repairs or replacements if needed. Then jack up radiators and remove all movable fixtures, including the toilet. (You will have to raise your bowl flange to reseat the toilet—see Chapter I. If you can't raise the flange and reseat the toilet, have a plumber do it before you put down your mortar.) Next, spread a layer of heavy asphalt-impregnated felt over the floor, lapping the joints two inches and turning edges up slightly at the walls and around fixed objects like the tub. Over the felt nail down expanded

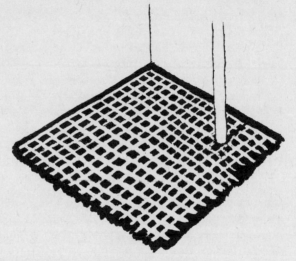

Figure 7-20 Preparing floor for ceramic tile laid in mortar

metal lath—it looks like diamond screening for gigantic bugs. Use galvanized nails at 6-inch intervals. Cut the lath with tin snips to fit around fixtures and into corners. (See Fig. 7-20.)

7.23 | Installing ceramic tiles. Placing the tiles is comparatively easy, except for fitting around edges and fixtures. Tiles come in sheets, with a number of individual tiles glued together to a backing sheet or a web of paper cords. If the backing is of paper, the tile is put down with the backing side up. (The backing is removed later.) If the backing is of cord, the cord side goes down into the adhesive and you don't have to remove it later. (But you can't use tile backed with cord in cement mortar.)

Before you lay any adhesive or mortar, cover the floor with sheets of tile, lining them up to fit exactly, then numbering them and marking their position on the floor. The smaller the tiles, the easier it is to cut sheets to fit the whole floor exactly so you don't have to snip a lot of individual tiles at the end. (This is quite difficult.) Now stack the sheets in order, with the first ones to be used at the top of the pile.

Spread the adhesive according to the manufacturer's directions, covering only about a square yard at a time so it doesn't dry out before you get the tile down. If tile coves (like a tile baseboard) are to be used against the walls, install these first and align them with a straightedge. Then start applying your tile sheets, starting in a square corner. Leave about ⅛ inch from the wall or cove edge for a grout joint. Be sure to keep the same distance between sheets as the distance between tiles on a sheet.

If it is necessary to cut tiles to fit around fixtures and edges, follow method shown in Figure 6-18.

When you have laid all the tiles, let them set about an hour. Then dampen the backing paper and remove it, using a scraper if necessary. Then let the tiles set for twenty-four hours before grouting the joints. Mix the grout according to manufacturer's instructions and use a kitchen sponge to force it into place between the tiles. When grout has set about twenty minutes, remove the excess with a damp cloth or sponge. Then polish the surface with a dry cloth, and cover with wet papers for three days. Wear rubber gloves when working with grout or you may burn your hands.

If you are installing tiles in mortar, first mark tiles and stack as above. Mix one part cement to three parts sand, add a quarter-part of lime, and enough water to make a sandy—not a soupy—mixture. If you get it too soupy, add more cement and sand. Or you can use a ready-mixed mortar from your masonry supply dealer. You can make the mixture in several buckets or in a steel wheelbarrow— but be sure your container doesn't leak. Spread mortar over the metal lath surface to a depth of ¾ inch, and level it off with a straight piece of board that is short enough to manipulate around the bathroom floor. If the floor is large, you may want to use wood grounds at intervals to be sure you are getting the right level. (See Fig. 7-21.) When your mortar sets—don't give it more than fifteen minutes—remove the grounds and fill their spaces with more of the mortar.

Now lay your tiles according to the method described above, and level the sheets by tapping them with a hammer on a flat 2 x 4,

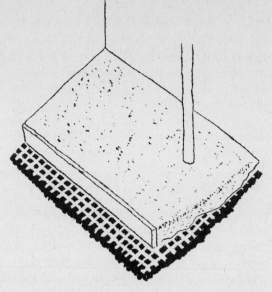

Figure 7-21 Wood grounds in mortar

sliding it around to be sure there are no humps. Check level with a carpenter's level.

Fit around fixtures and edges, described in Figure 6-18, and remove backing paper when all sheets have been laid. You can grout between tiles after about an hour—see above. Then let the floor cure for three days with wet newspapers as above. If you have to walk on newly installed tiles, lay a board down to spread you weight where you walk.

7.24 | Installing flagstone, brick, slate, and quarry tile floors. These materials are all installed roughly in the same manner as ceramic tile in mortar—see preceding sections. Remove flooring down to the subfloor and prepare the base as above, using metal lath. Lay stones or bricks in cement as before, but use a thin mortar (the consistency of thick pea soup) for joints, instead of grout. Try to pour the mortar between stones or bricks without spilling it on them, for it is hard to get off. When the joints set, smooth them with a mason's joint tool or (if the joints are large) the back of a large serving spoon. On large joints be careful not to create too deep a depression —it will catch dirt.

When the job is finished, you'll have to install a sloping threshold or step to take up the difference in floor levels between the masonry floor and wood floors in adjoining rooms. If there are any hardened mortar stains on the surface, you can remove them with sulfamic acid or diluted muriatic acid (from the hardware store).

183

8 DOORS AND WINDOWS

DOORS

8.1 | **If there are wide cracks around a door**—and it's an outside door that lets in drafts—they can usually be fixed by weatherstripping. The best type to use for doors is a spring metal kind that comes in strips, is nailed to the doorjamb, and holds itself against the door (when the door is closed) by spring action. (See Fig. 8-1.) When installing this type of weatherstripping, be sure the strip clears the doorstop—if the edge of the strip touches the stop, it won't work right.

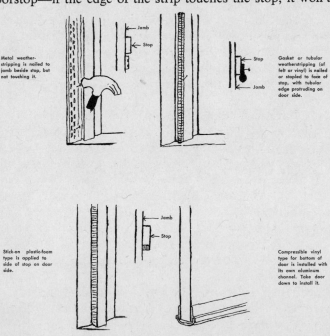

Metal weather-stripping is nailed to jamb beside stop, but not touching it.

← Jamb

← Stop

← Stop

← Jamb

Gasket or tubular weatherstripping (of felt or vinyl) is nailed or stapled to face of stop, with tubular edge protruding on door side.

Stick-on plastic-foam type is applied to side of stop on door side.

← Jamb

← Stop

Compressible vinyl type for bottom of door is installed with its own aluminum channel. Take door down to install it.

Figure 8-1   Types of weatherstripping

184

Most other types of weatherstripping are usually applied to the stop itself. Follow the manufacturer's directions for installation if you decide to use one of these kinds. (See Fig. 8-1.)

If there is a crack under an outside door less than ⅜ inch deep, you can close it up with a piece of compressible vinyl weatherstripping. (It looks like a long, thin half-section of a balloon.) To install it, take down the door, as in Figure 8-2, and nail the weatherstripping to the bottom of the door.

Figure 8-2   Removing a door

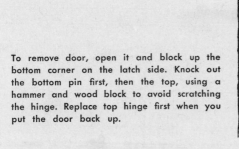

To remove door, open it and block up the bottom corner on the latch side. Knock out the bottom pin first, then the top, using a hammer and wood block to avoid scratching the hinge. Replace top hinge first when you put the door back up.

On interior doors, cracks on the latch side can often be closed up by shimming out the hinges. (See Fig. 8-3.) If the crack is only at the top, shim out only the top hinge; if it's only at the bottom,

Figure 8-3   Shimming out a hinge

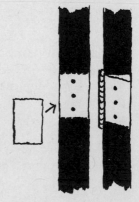

To close crack by shimming out hinges, open door and block up bottom corner on the latch side. Unscrew bottom hinge on wall side, insert cardboard shim cut to fit, then replace hinge. Then do the top hinge. If this isn't enough, use thicker shims or use shims on the door side too.

just shim out the bottom one. You can also conceal cracks by using a wider stop (the wooden strip nailed to the jamb, against which door closes).

Wide cracks around a door that cannot be corrected by any of these methods usually indicate that the door no longer fits the frame. The easiest solution to the problem is to purchase a new door a little larger than the opening, and plane it to fit exactly. (See Sec. 8.10.) The alternative is to readjust the frame to fit the door. If the frame is badly out of alignment, this is what you should do: Take the door down by removing the hinge pins—see Figure 8-2. Then remove the casing on both sides of the door head by prying it off with a chisel. (Finish nails left in the head can be pulled out afterward.) Then cut the jamb down so the head can be lowered and wedged tight in its new position. Refasten the casing and the job is done. (See Fig. 8-4.)

Figure 8-4   Lowering head casing

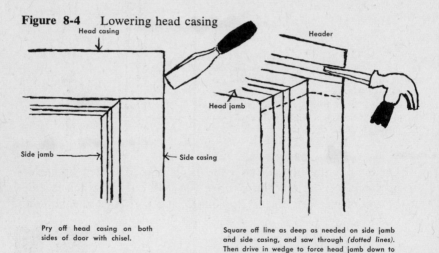

Pry off head casing on both sides of door with chisel.

Square off line as deep as needed on side jamb and side casing, and saw through *(dotted lines)*. Then drive in wedge to force head jamb down to new level. Replace casings.

8.2 │ If water comes in at the door, it is most often because the threshold doesn't slope enough. You can correct this by putting down compressible vinyl weatherstripping as in the preceding section, by installing a metal drip cap on the outside of the door at the bottom, as in Figure 8-5, or by putting in a new threshold, as in Section 7.6.

If water comes in through the wall or casing at the head of the door, you probably need new flashing (a strip of sheet metal, aluminum, or copper 18 to 24 inches wide, used under the siding to

Metal drip cap is nailed to bottom of door on outside.

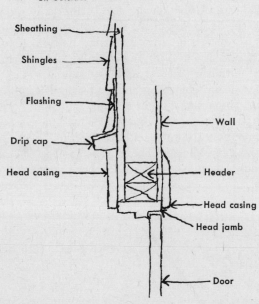

Figure 8-5   Drip caps and flashing

keep water out) or a drip cap over the door. (See Fig. 8-5.) If you have clapboard siding, drive the nails holding the piece over the door in place all the way into the wall with a nail set. Then you can work a piece of flashing (wider than the door by 6 inches on either side) up behind the siding. If the siding is shingle, you'll have to remove some shingles. If your outside wall is brick, you'd better call a mason, unless you're good at removing and replacing brick.

If water comes in through the wall at the jamb and jamb casing, recaulk the outside joint between siding and casing.

8.3 | If a door warps so it doesn't close against a stop on the hinge side, you can add a third hinge midway between the top and bottom hinges. (See Sec. 8.10.) First mark the hinge position, with the door closed, exactly at the top and bottom of hinge leaves on both door and jamb. Then remove the door, as in Figure 8-2. Install new hinge leaves on the door and jamb, lining them up with the other hinges. Rehang the door on old hinges, and force it into position so you can drop in the new hinge pin.

If a door warps on the latch side, you can make it close more easily by resetting the stop. First pry the stop loose and then, with the door closed, draw a line on the side of the jamb along the inside or stop side of the door. Renail the stop on this line.

If a door is warped all over you may be able to restore it by taking it down, and drying it in the sun, bulge side up. If this doesn't work, place it between sawhorses, bulge side up, and put enough bricks or other heavy objects in the center to flatten it out. Leave it this way for about twenty-four hours.

Doors warped unevenly can be pulled into shape by inserting big screw eyes in opposite corners and connecting them with a small cable or wire and turnbuckle. (See Fig. 8-6.) Don't use this method on a front door: it's ugly. If a front door is warped out of shape, replace it.

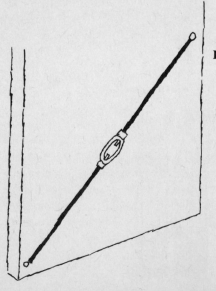

Figure 8-6   Turnbuckle on door

Warping is caused by penetration of moisture into unpainted tops, sides, and bottoms of the door. Prevent future warping on doors you've repaired or replaced by carefully painting or varnishing all these neglected surfaces.

8.4 | If a door sticks, the first thing to check is the hinge screws. Tighten them as much as possible. If screws won't hold, remove screws and hinges. Fill the holes by driving plugs of glue-coated wood (wooden matchsticks are often just right) into them with a hammer. (See Fig. 8-7.) Then remount the hinges, tightening the screws into the plugged holes.

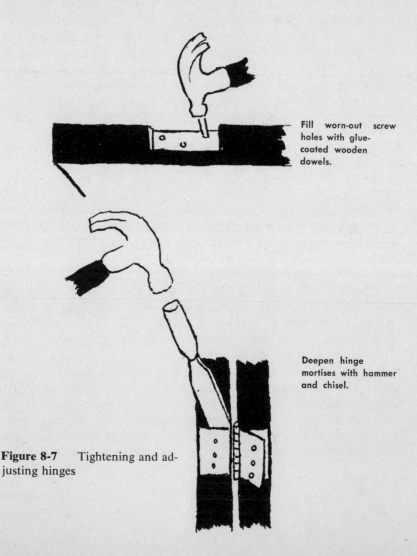

Fill worn-out screw holes with glue-coated wooden dowels.

Deepen hinge mortises with hammer and chisel.

Figure 8-7 Tightening and adjusting hinges

If the hinges are tight but the door sticks on the latch side, unscrew both hinges—one at a time—and deepen the mortises. Then replace the hinges. (See Fig. 8-7.) If the door sticks on the hinge side, the hinges are probably set too deeply. Shim them out with pieces of cardboard. (See Fig. 8-3.) If the door rubs against the frame, but doesn't really stick, rub the offending edges with paraffin or soap.

If the door sticks at top or bottom, you can first try shimming out the hinges one at a time. If it sticks at the top, shim out the top hinge; if at bottom, shim out bottom hinge. If this doesn't do the trick, unscrew the other hinge and cut a deeper mortise in the wall side. A heavy door that sags can frequently be cured by shimming out the lower hinge and deepening the mortise on the upper hinge.

If a door is hung too high or too low, so that it scrapes at top or bottom and gaps at the other extremity, remove door and enlarge mortises up or down, as necessary. (See Fig. 8-7.) Rehang the door, fill up unused mortise space with plastic wood, and touch up with paint. If the old screw holes are worn out, fill them with wooden plugs as in Figure 8-7.

As a result of hinge adjustment, you may find that the latch no longer strikes the right spot. If so, see Section 8.7.

If shimming or hinge adjustment will not cure sticking, try sanding the offending edge. With the door closed, find the spot of contact by sliding a piece of cardboard along the crack.

If you can't remove enough wood by sanding, you can plane off the edge, being careful to shave off no more than needed. On top and bottom, sanding is usually better since planing across the grain of the wood may split off slivers of wood.

Caution: Do no more planing or sanding than absolutely necessary, especially on outside doors. Remember that doors shrink in dry or cold weather and swell in wet or hot weather.

8.5 | If a sliding door squeaks or sticks, rub frame and track with paraffin or soap. If the door really binds on the bottom, the hangers that support it from the track at top must be taken up. If it's a closet door, the hangers are often accessible from the closet side—a small nut on the hanger is tightened to raise the door. If there are moldings on both sides of the door, one of these must be removed (pry it off gently with a big chisel), then pull out nails left behind in the wood frame to get at the hanger. (See Fig. 8-8.)

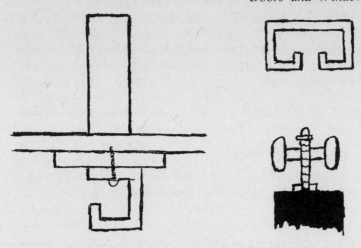

Double-track type cannot be adjusted from either side. Trim board at ends must be removable for adjustment.

Commonest type of sliding-door track is open on one side (usually closet side). Tighten bolt in hanger to raise door.

Figure 8-8 Sliding door mechanism

If a sliding door is warped, there's not much you can do but replace it. Pry off the molding at the top, detach the hanger from the door, insert the new door, and fasten the hanger to it. Adjust the hanger for proper height and action. Before putting up the new sliding door, paint all the edges to prevent any excess moisture accumulation that might cause more warping.

If a swinging door squeaks or sticks, remove one of the side plates of the swinging hinge and clean out dirt. Lubricate with powdered graphite. (Don't use oil, as this will attract more dirt and gum up the works again later.)

8.6 | **If a hinge sticks, squeaks, or is loose,** apply a few drops of oil around hinge pins and move the door to let oil work down into the hinge. If this doesn't do the job, remove the hinge pins, as in Figure 8-2, and apply oil to both pin and hinge before rehanging the door. Clean the pins thoroughly with steel wool if they are rusty or dirty. Powdered graphite or petroleum jelly can be used in place of oil.

If a hinge is loose, check to see if the screw holes are worn out in the door or the door jamb. If they are, drive wood plugs in holes and remount hinges. (See Fig. 8-7.) If the screws seem tight but the hinge is loose anyway, it is probably deformed and must be replaced with a new one. With a good new hinge in place, you may find that the door binds. (This is what deformed the old hinge.) If so, the door is warped (see Sec. 8.3) or the door or doorstop are out of line and must be moved slightly. (See Secs. 8.1 and 8.4.)

8.7 | If a latch doesn't work properly, perhaps the latch tongue (in the door) and the opening in the strike plate (metal piece on the doorjamb) do not line up. Enlarge the opening with a file and chisel if necessary. If the alignment is more than ¼ inch off, better remove the strike plate, extend the mortise up or down as needed by using a hammer and chisel, replace the plate, and fill in the exposed part of mortise with plastic wood. (See Fig. 8-7.)

If the latch tongue doesn't reach the strike plate, and the latch won't catch, unscrew the strike plate and shim it out with a piece of cardboard the same size. Place the cardboard in the mortise and then replace the strike plate. If the latch still won't reach, shim out the hinges of the door, as in Figure 8-3.

If the latch trouble isn't due to poor alignment, it may be that the latch needs to be lubricated. Apply powdered graphite (it comes in a "puffer" stick at the hardware store) into the lock works and around the knob. If knobs are loose or rattle, loosen the setscrew on the knob's collar, and screw the knob up tighter on the shank. If this doesn't work, put some putty or small pebbles in the shank hole in the knob, so the knob can tighten up against something.

If all these measures fail, you need a new latch. You can put a new lockset over the old one, leaving the old one in the door, or you can remove the old one. If there's a setscrew on the knob collar, remove it, unscrew the knob, pull out the shank, remove screws from face of the unit, and remove the lockset. If there are screws in the metal plate under the knob, remove them, pull out both knobs, then remove screws from face of lockset in side of the door and remove the unit. Take the unit down to your hardware store so you can get the type best fitted to replace it. If your door and lock are very old, you may have to cut out the lock section of the door and glue in a new piece of wood shaped to fit. (Use a two-part epoxy glue.) Then you can drill in the new piece for the new lockset.

8.8 | Installing a new lockset is relatively easy. Most new locks only call for a 2-inch round hole through the door and a ⅝-inch-round hole from the face edge of the door back to the 2-inch hole. You'll need a brace and a 2-inch and a ⅝-inch bit, a screwdriver, and a hammer and chisel. (You'll only need the hammer and chisel if you have a rectangular latch face.) With the new lockset you'll get instructions that are very easy to follow; you'll also get a template for positioning the holes in the door.

8.9 | Installing a spring-latch lock. If you have an outside door that is opened with an old-fashioned skeleton-type key, but the lock is in good condition and you don't want to replace it, you can give yourself additional protection by installing a cylinder spring-latch lock. (See Fig. 8-9.) You can get a complete unit and installing it will only take an hour or so.

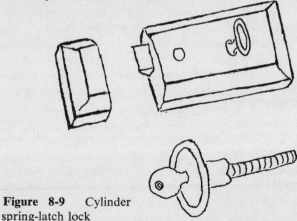

Figure 8-9 Cylinder spring-latch lock

Decide on a convenient location for the new lock, and read the manufacturer's directions carefully. Installation will be easiest if you make a paper template of the latch case (the large part that goes on the inside of the door) and thumbtack it to the door in the proper position. Now bore the hole for the lock unit. (The directions will tell you what diameter hole you need.) You probably won't have a bit large enough, so drill a small hole near the outside rim of the needed circle, then cut it to the right size with a keyhole saw. Now slip the lock unit into place from the outside, with the trim unit in place. On the inside of the door, put metal plate in place with mounting bolts and lock shaft extending through. Tighten bolts and break off unneeded shaft length with your pliers. (It comes notched so it can easily be broken to fit the depth of door.) Put the latch case in place, making sure shaft enters it on an absolutely straight line. Mark positions for the wood screws with a pencil. Remove latch case and drill holes for screws.

Fasten latch case in place and carefully line up the strike plate. Cut mortise with chisel if required. (Manufacturer's directions will tell you if you should do so.)

8.10 | How to install a new door. Measure your door opening exactly where the door will sit, and buy a door just a bit larger or the exact size from your lumber dealer. Trim the door with plane, saw, and sandpaper so it fits easily in the opening without any binding. (Don't trim it too much or you'll have big cracks around the door.) Take the door out and cut mortises for the hinges on only the door itself, using a hammer and chisel. (See Fig. 8-7.) Then shim up the door on a few pieces of cardboard under the threshold, and mark exactly against the jamb where the hinges fall. Remove the door, mortise the jamb, and fasten hinge leaves in place, leaving the screws slightly loose. Then put door in place, and drop in hinge pins. Tighten screws in the jamb leaves. If the door binds, see Section 8.4. If your marking for hinge position wasn't quite right, you can move the hinge leaf by enlarging the mortise and plugging screw holes with wooden dowels. (See Fig. 8-7.)

Louver doors are installed the same way as regular doors. Swinging doors are mounted on special hinges installed at the bottom of the door and in the floor, and in the top of the door and the head jamb.

8-11 | Installing a sliding or folding door is not difficult. If you are cutting a new opening, see Section 8.31. If the opening is already there, take its exact measurements to the hardware or lumber store. Your dealer can help you choose the hardware, track, and door that will do the job best for your opening. Follow manufacturer's directions for installation. Tracks for sliding doors are installed on a nailer —see Figure 8-8—which is fastened to the ceiling with toggle bolts or nailed through the ceiling to a joist above. Rollers are installed on the door before hanging it, if there is room to slide rollers into the track with the door attached. Otherwise, the roller is put into its track, the door held in position, and roller attached to the door.

If there are floor guides to guide the bottom of the door, they should be placed first. Use a plumb bob to make sure they are directly below the track. Then fit the door into the bottom guide and fasten it to its rollers. Add moldings to conceal hardware and the job is done.

Folding doors are installed in almost the same way. They usually come with complete hardware, track, and door all in one package.

8.12 | Painting doors inside and out. Doors should always be painted with a gloss or semigloss paint to prevent too many finger marks. Trim or kitchen enamel can be used on any interior door. Outside doors must have exterior enamel on the outside face and all edges of the door—otherwise, they may warp. If there is sap running out of a knot or a sap crack in a door, wipe it off with benzene or paint thinner and paint the knot with aluminum paint before painting the rest of the door. Otherwise the sap will burn through the paint film and the knot will show up clearly.

WINDOWS

8.13 | How to replace broken glass. Remove all broken glass, glazier's points (the little triangular pieces of metal that help to hold glass in place), and old putty. Wear work gloves to protect your hands from broken glass. You may have to dig putty out with a chisel—a little at a time to avoid chipping wood. Or you can use a file or rasp on its edge in the groove. If the frame is metal, remove spring clips holding glass in place, if there are any.

If you are buying a new piece of glass, have it cut to size at the hardware store or glazier's. (It should be about 1/16 inch smaller than the inside of the frame it fits in.)

It isn't easy to cut glass, especially on the first try. However, if you have some spare glass and want to attempt it, you will need a good glass cutter. Cover your work surface with a layer of newspapers. Be sure cutter and glass are absolutely free of dust and grit. This is the key to accurate cutting. Mark your lines for cutting on the reverse side of the glass with a crayon. Hold a straight-edged cutting guide of metal or wood in place, and score with a single stroke and an even pressure, holding the cutter almost perpendicular to the glass and drawing it toward you.

Now place the glass *over* your cutting guide, with the scored line directly over the edge of the guide (or over the edge of a table). Press down gently and glass should break in two. (See Fig. 8-10.) Never score a second line before you have broken the first. If the piece of waste glass is too small to be grasped, you can break it off after scoring with pliers—a little bit at a time.

Figure 8-10   Cutting glass

Use metal straightedge for guide when cutting glass.

Before placing the glass in the frame, paint wood with linseed oil or wood preservative to give putty a good bond. When dry, apply a layer of putty or glazier's compound (you can buy both at the hardware store) or, if window is metal, a special metal-window putty, about ⅛ inch thick, to the area where window will sit. Then set glass in place. If the frame is of wood, secure glass with glazier's points about 4 inches apart. Push them in first with your finger, then press them in about halfway with side of a chisel or screwdriver. On metal frames, press spring clips into position after inserting glass. (See Fig. 8-11.)

To finish the job, lay a ½-inch rope of putty or glazing compound along all sides of the window, press against wood and glass, and smooth with putty knife. Paint when firm.

On wooden sash, lay in bead of putty, insert glass, and fasten with glazier's points. Then apply putty on top of glass and smooth with putty knife.

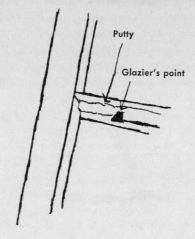

Do metal sash the same way, but use metal clips to hold glass in place.

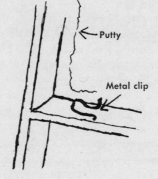

Figure 8-11   Setting glass in putty

8.14 | **If windows are drafty,** they probably need to be weather-stripped. This is much like weatherstripping a door. (See Fig. 8-1.)

To weatherstrip a double-hung window with spring-type metal stripping, raise the bottom sash all the way and nail the stripping in place in the track where sash runs. Finish the bottom tracks first, then lower the window and apply stripping to top sash. Nail stripping to sill or bottom of window—it's less conspicuous that way. Where top and bottom sash meet, fasten stripping to the top rail of lower sash.

Weatherstripping metal casement or awning windows is tricky

because weatherstripping may warp the window. Very often, multiple coats of paint, especially on steel casement windows, will gradually reach matching configurations on sash and frame so they are practically airtight when the window is closed. If there are cracks, however, spring-type stainless steel weatherstripping should be used. Ask your hardware dealer for the best kind for your particular windows.

Drafty windows that need not be opened in winter may be caulked with outside tube-type caulking. Gaps between frame and siding should be caulked too. If old caulking shrinks or pulls away, it should be removed and replaced.

Leaks around panes of glass, or rattling panes, are caused by loose putty. Remove it and apply new. Be sure to paint the exposed wood with linseed oil, or new putty will not stick well.

8.15 | **If water comes in around a window** at the top, check the flashing and drip cap. (See Sec. 8.2.) If it comes in at sides or sill, recaulk between siding and outside casing and sill. If the sill does not slope out, put in a new section or build it up with a sloping piece of wood. Caulk between the jamb and new sill sections.

8.16 | **If a window works stiffly,** rub the tracks with paraffin or soap, or lubricate with powdered graphite. Pull down the upper half of the window to rub the upper tracks. Put a drop of oil on each side of the pulley shafts if they are exposed.

On metal windows, clean off dirt and grime with steel wool, then wipe with a light machine oil.

If the window still doesn't move freely after being lubricated, you can expand the frame slightly by cutting a small block of wood to the width of the window track. Slide the block along the track, tapping it gently with a hammer.

Loose weatherstripping can keep the window from working properly. Renail or replace it if necessary.

As a last resort, remove the sash from the frame by carefully removing the stop on the side jamb. (See Sec. 8.21.) With stop off, try moving the sash up and down. If it moves freely, the stop was binding it. Replace the stop, nailing it slightly away from its original position.

If sash doesn't move freely when you take off the stop, lift sash out of place, sand the inside of the track, and scrape away any hardened paint or dirt. Replace sash and try it again. If it is still hard to work, plane the sides of the sash a little at a time, testing as you work and stopping as soon as it will move freely. Don't plane it too much, especially if it has swollen as the result of a damp season.

While the window is out, treat bare edges of sash and track with linseed oil or wood preservative. Then lubricate with paraffin, soap, or powdered graphite. Replace sash in frame and renail the stop.

In a window fitted with metal weatherstripping, you may have to remove the weatherstripping as well as the stop to get the sash out. When the stop is off, pry off the strip, working down from the top with the sash closed. To free the lower end, slide the sash to the top. Handle strip carefully to avoid kinking. When you have repaired the window, replace the strip or install a new one if necessary.

8.17 | **If a double-hung window is stuck,** look for hardened paint around the window and cut it with a sharp knife, using only as much force as needed. If this doesn't free the window, go to the outside and loosen it by inserting a chisel under the bottom of the sash. This will avoid scarring the inside paint job.

If you can't loosen the sash from the outside, drive your chisel in with a hammer about ½ inch from the inside, right at the stuck spot or spots. Rock it back and forth gently. (Never use a screwdriver, as this will mar the surface.) If you can't loosen it by working on the bottom sash alone, try using the chisel at the sides as well. You can also try moving a block of wood along the side of the sash next to the molding, tapping with a hammer as you move it.

8.18 | **When awning, casement, or sliding windows are stuck,** it's usually a matter of lubrication. Clean out tracks, scrape away old paint, and lubricate thoroughly with oil or graphite at moving joints. If you use oil, wipe up the excess or it will gather dust and cause more trouble later.

Stiff adjusting arms on casements and awning windows must not be neglected because they can pull screws loose, even damage the sash.

8.19 | **If lock on a double-hung window doesn't work.** The most common causes of lock trouble are paint and rust. If your lock won't close and it is heavily coated with either paint or rust, remove it with a screwdriver (and a chisel if necessary). Soak it in paint remover or rust solvent, if for some reason you want to put the same lock back on. Otherwise, install a new lock from the hardware store.

Occasionally a window swells enough to prevent a lock from closing. If this occurs during a damp or rainy period, wait to see if it shrinks back in place before making any repairs. If it doesn't, remove the part of the lock on top part of lower sash, and plane the surface of the wood lightly. Replace the lock and try it. If it still doesn't work, take it off again and plane it a little more.

8.20 If a double-hung window won't stay open, either the sash-weight cord or the spring balance is broken. (You have one or the other, unless your window is very old.) To repair it see Section 8.2 1 or 8.23, depending on the type of balance. You can replace a broken sash cord with a spring balance of the flat or ribbon type if you want to.

You don't have to repair cords or balances if you don't want to, however. Instead, you can install a simple clamp fastened to the side of the window stop. (See Fig. 8-12.) When pushed down, the clamp

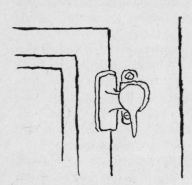

Figure 8-12   Window clamp on jamb

forces the sash against the parting strip between sashes and holds the window open. Your hardware dealer carries them. If your windows are very old, you may have clamps instead of weights or balances anyway.

If you do decide to install a clamp instead of replacing a broken sash-weight cord, the loose ends of the cord may possibly cause trouble. It may be necessary to remove the sash (see next section) to cut off the broken cord. This is still easier than replacing the sash cord.

If awning or casement windows won't stay open, first try tightening up the arms and turn the handle mechanisms with screwdriver and pliers. If this doesn't work, then the mechanism is broken and will have to be replaced. Your hardware or lumber dealer can help you get the right parts. Tell him the type of window, size, and manufacturer. You may have to replace the whole sash in some cases. (See Sec. 8.31.)

8.21 | Replacing a broken sash cord can be a lot of trouble if you try to do it in a hurry. So take your time. First remove the sash from the frame by taking off the stop on the side opposite the broken sash cord. Work a putty knife or other thin blade under the stop at the bottom, and pry it out about half an inch. Then pry at the next nail about half an inch. Continue prying, a little at a time, until the stop is free. Nails should come away with it.

With the stop off, remove the sash part way by pulling the sash toward the side where you removed the stop. Unfasten the unbroken sash cord from the sash by pulling the knot down until it can be removed from the pocket inside the sash. Hold knot and gradually lower the weight all the way. Then remove the sash entirely. Take off the pocket cover around the weight on the broken cord side. (See Fig. 8-13.) If there is metal weatherstripping on the window, you will have to remove it to get at the pocket cover.

Figure 8-13   Replacing broken sash cord

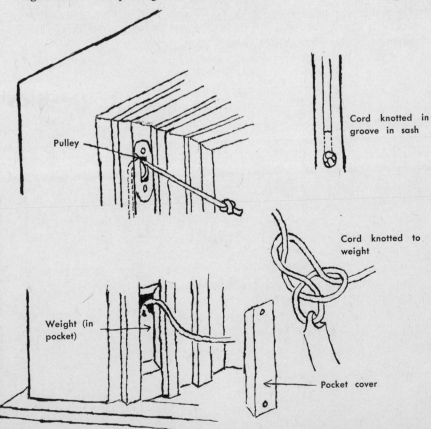

Pulley

Cord knotted in groove in sash

Cord knotted to weight

Weight (in pocket)

Pocket cover

Cut off the old cord. The easiest way to insert the new cord (or sash chain, which won't break) is to tie a small string to the end of it and a small nail to the end of the string. Drop the nail through the pulley hole and pull the cord out through the pocket. Now remove the string, fasten the new cord to the sash weight, and put the weight back in the pocket.

Now place sash on the sill. Pull the new cord until the weight is at the top of window against the pulley. Cut cord off 3 inches below the socket in the sash. Tie a knot in that end and insert the knot in the socket, being sure it fits snugly.

Place the sash back in the groove and move it up and down to be sure the cord is the right length. The weight should not touch the pulley when the sash is closed, or rest on the bottom of the pocket when the sash is raised. When it is properly adjusted, take the sash out again and replace the pocket cover. Put the sash in place and nail the molding back with new nails.

8.22 | **Installing a new spring balance.** Most balances are cylindrical and fit in a round groove at the side of the sash. If one won't work it should be replaced with another of the same type. Your hardware or lumber dealer carries them.

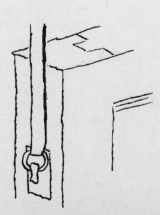

Figure 8-14   Jamb-type balance

To install a new balance, remove the sash as in Section 8.21, then remove the broken balance. Drive wood plugs in the old screw holes holding the balance in place (see Fig. 8-7) so new screws can get a good hold. Install the new balance according to the manufacturer's directions.

If your window had sash cords and weights, or no balance at all, you can install a jamb-type balance. (See Fig. 8-14.) In windows formerly equipped with sash weights and cords, the spring casing fits in the slot that held the pulley. In windows with no balance, you will have to cut a slot for the spring case in the top of the window jamb.

8.23 | **If the top sash can't be closed,** its sash cord or spring balance is broken. Repairs are made in the same way as to a lower sash. To get at the broken cord or balance, you must first remove the lower sash as in Section 8.21. Then take off the parting bead between sashes on the unbroken side so you can remove the upper sash. Then repair the cord or balance as in Section 8.21 or 8.22.

If you don't have time for a permanent repair, you can shut the window temporarily by nailing in a thin finishing nail (one with no head) part way through the sash, at an angle. Or you can install a clamp as in Section 8.21.

8.24 | **If sash is badly out of shape,** broken, or rotted, it should be replaced. Take its exact measurements to the lumberyard and get a new sash. Then remove the old sash, as in Section 8.21, and insert the new one. If the old sash had weights, get the new one with spring balances.

If the sash happens to be a rare size that can't be replaced, you can repair it much as you would a screen or storm sash. (See Sec. 8.30.) If you're going to do this, remove the glass first. Your lumber dealer can get or make for you the new wooden parts (rails, muntins, and stiles) needed to replace rotted ones.

8.25 | **If frame is badly out of shape,** the entire window should be replaced with a complete new unit. A frame that has rotted away at the sill or warped out of shape at the jamb is not worth bothering with. Unless you are fairly handy at building, don't try to replace the unit yourself—get some professional help.

Prehung window units, with the sash already in place, are the best and easiest to work with. Measure your old window and then consult your lumber dealer as to what size of unit you need. To measure correctly you'll have to chop holes around the old window in the inside wall—then measure the window opening from face to face of studs and structural plates surrounding the opening. (See Fig. 8-19 in Sec. 8.31, following.)

When choosing your new window be sure you select one that matches or goes well with other windows in the house, and be sure it has outside trim that matches the rest of the trim on the house.

When you have your new window unit, remove the old window. First take off the casing or trim inside and out with a screwdriver, hammer, and wrecking bar. Chop out any plaster sticking into the opening where the window sits, back to the edges of the structural frame around the window. Pry off stops and remove sash, then tear out the old jambs, head, and sill. When the rough opening is clear you can insert the new window unit, cutting away any siding on the outside that gets in the way of the sill or casing. (See Sec. 8.31.) Put in new flashing above the window—see Section 8.2 and Figure 8-5. Caulk between siding and jamb and sill. Put up inside trim. (This should cover the space between the jamb and plaster.) Countersink nail holes and fill with plastic wood before painting.

8.26 | If double-glazed windows cloud up, air and moisture are getting in between the panes. In manufactured double glass—two plates of glass joined, with a sealed partial vacuum between—this can practically never happen. If it does, the glass must be replaced because there is a leak in the vacuum.

If you have a picture window that is not double-glazed but merely has storm sash permanently attached, however, it's a different story. After a few years air and moisture will certainly get between the panes, making them look dirty and cloudy. The only solution is to make the sash removable so it can be taken down periodically for cleaning. (Or, of course, you could replace it with manufactured double glass.) If the window is very large, and very tightly fastened together, you will probably need the help of a carpenter or glazier to take it down, clean it, and put it back together. Don't have it put back as it was. Have it reinstalled in such a way that next time you can take it down and clean it yourself, even if this means having the glass cut into sections and reframed.

8.27 | Window shade and blind problems. When a roller shade doesn't wind up properly, pull it all the way down. Take it out of brackets and roll the shade up by hand. Replace it and try again. If it still isn't tight enough, repeat the procedure. If the tension is too great, raise shade all the way, remove from bracket, and unroll part way by hand. Replace and test. If a shade rolls crookedly, take it down, unroll it, and remove tacks or clips holding shade to roller. Straighten out the end and retack or staple.

If venetian-blind tapes break, you can replace them with new tapes from the hardware or dime store. They come with directions for assembling. First of all, take the blinds down, untie cords and remove them, and remove slats from the old tape. Wash slats thoroughly before inserting in new tapes, and touch them up with paint if needed.

When nailing up brackets for shades, blinds, or drapery, predrill holes for nails or wood screws to avoid splitting the wood.

SCREENS AND STORM SASH

8.28 | If there are holes in screens. Small holes can be repaired by painting over the hole with colorless epoxy glue. Larger holes will have to be patched. Cut a patch of screening material an inch or two bigger around than the hole, and ravel the ends. You can bend the wire ends into the screening around the hole to hold the patch in place, or you can attach it with colorless epoxy glue.

If the screen is in poor condition all over, purchase new screening material. (It is available in bronze, copper, galvanized steel, aluminum, and plastic.) To replace screening, lay the screen on a flat surface and remove inside and center moldings. Use a chisel or putty knife to loosen them, starting at the center of each and working gradually to the end. Pry out only a small fraction of an inch at a time, or the moldings will break. Move along from nail to nail until the whole molding has been loosened. If necessary, break the paint seal between molding and frame with a sharp knife.

If only half the screen is bad, cut away the damaged part under the central brace with heavy shears or tin snips. Remove old tacks or staples.

If the new screening it too wide to fit the frame, cut it to fit, allowing enough at the sides and ends for tacking to the frame. Stretch screening over the frame as in Figure 8-15. Then staple it to the frame with a stapling gun. (If you don't own one, you can rent one from the hardware store.) Trim off excess screening and replace the moldings, using small finishing nails. If the old moldings are in bad condition, cut new ones to fit.

Place screen frame on two supports (or a table) with 1-inch board under each end.

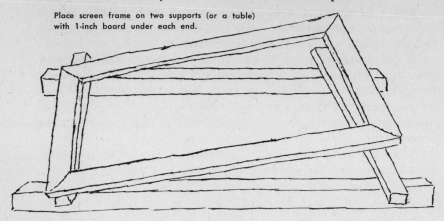

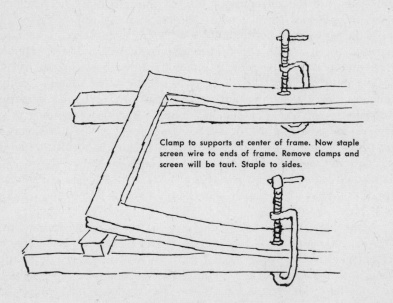

Clamp to supports at center of frame. Now staple screen wire to ends of frame. Remove clamps and screen will be taut. Staple to sides.

Figure 8-15   Replacing screen wire

8.29 | Installing screens and storm sash. Storm windows and doors that are well fitted can save you as much as 30 per cent of your fuel bills every winter. On this basis, ordinary storms and screens easily pay for themselves in only two heating seasons. Combination metal storms and screens (all-in-one permanent units) are somewhat more expensive, but worth considering if you have neither storms nor screens.

Wood storms and screens are simply installed with hangers against the blind stop on the outside of the window. (See Fig. 8-16.) If you have double-hung windows or sliding windows with no blind stop or molding to mount a storm or screen in, you can fasten moldings to your casing, or outside trim, underneath the drip cap. Or you can get storm windows just enough bigger to hang over the trim itself, so the storm sash actually covers the trim or casing on both sides of the window. Then if you have a conspicuous gap between sash and

Figure 8-16   Hanging storms and screens

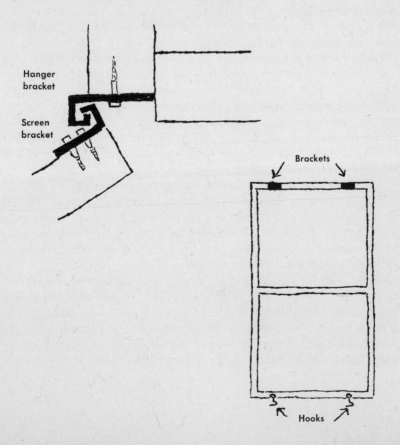

trim, you can caulk it with rope-type putty. This can be taken down at the end of the season and used again the following year. However, you shouldn't caulk up every window; for ventilation, install a "hold open" bracket on at least one window in each room. These let you swing out the storm window about 8 inches from the window sill. (The bracket will hold the window steady in this position.) Your hardware store carries the brackets and they are easily installed. Don't depend on them to hold in a heavy wind, though—better close the window.

If you have casement or awning windows, the sash itself may have provision (like brackets or clips on the sides) for mounting special screens and storm sash on each section of the window. These allow you to open the window as freely as if there were no storm sash or screen. If there are such clips on your window, be sure you get the screens and storms designed for your particular size and brand. (Ask your hardware or lumber dealer.) If your casement windows have no such provision, you can mount storm sash on the outside, as for a double-hung window, but then you cannot open the windows for ventilation. If you want to keep the windows so they can be opened, you can mount storms or screens on the inside. Use handles and simple catches for mounting so they can be taken down easily.

Combination storm doors (they're called combination because they come with a screen panel and storm panel that fit interchangeably in the frame) should be mounted on all exterior doors. You can get the right size by taking the measurements of your door and a sketch of your doorjamb to your lumber dealer. For hanging, see Section 8.10. Door-closers, rather than springs, should be mounted at the top of the door according to the manufacturer's directions.

When not in use, store storms and screens in the nearest place to where they belong: put upstairs windows in the attic, downstairs ones in the basement. The easiest way to get each one back in the right place next season is to install numbered tacks (they come in pairs at the hardware store). Put a number in every sill and its mate in the screen or storm for that window.

8.30 | How to repair and square up sagging screens and storms. If you have a loose corner joint, the easiest and best way to repair it is with a metal corner brace. (See Fig. 8-17.) If you have to replace a badly rotted or damaged section of a window or a screen, you can fasten the corners together with a corner brace or by any of the methods shown in Figure 8-18. The strongest joint is the mortise

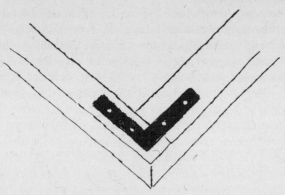

Figure 8-17   Metal corner brace

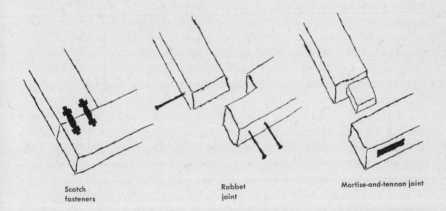

Scotch
fasteners

Rabbet
joint

Mortise-and-tennon joint

Figure 8-18   Joints for screen and storm sash

and tenon, but this is difficult without power tools. Next best: the rabbet joint.

To be sure your joint is square, lay out two strips of wood on a work surface to make a right-angle corner. (Use a carpenter's square.) Fasten the strips to the work surface and hold the corner of the window that's being repaired tight against the strips while you fasten its joint.

To prevent rotting, wood screens and storms should be painted every few years with exterior paint. Paint them only when completely dry, and don't forget the edges.

If your screens are plastic, the screening itself should not be painted. Bronze or copper screening should be shellacked or varnished to prevent staining. Galvanized steel screening should be painted with screen enamel about every other season.

To paint a screen, first brush away all dust from the screen wire and sand old paint off the edges of the frame. After painting the screen wire on one side, turn it over and go over the other side with your brush, not filling the brush with paint. This will get clogged paint out of the openings and spread out the paint as needed. Extend paint into the joints at the edges.

ALTERATIONS

8.31 | How to make a doorway or a window. If you want to create a new door, window, or sliding glass wall, you must first check to see if the wall is a bearing wall (one that helps hold up the roof or the floor above). Determine which way the joists in the ceiling run. If they run perpendicular to the wall, it's a bearing wall, and the ends of the joists rest on the wall. If they run parallel to the wall, with their ends resting on another wall, the wall is nonbearing. (See Sec. 6.29 and Fig. 7-1.)

If the wall is a bearing wall and the opening you plan is a wide one (3 feet or over), you'd better get some professional help and advice from a carpenter or contractor. In such a case, you'll need a heavy header beam to carry the ceiling load over your new opening. Installing and supporting big beams like this (usually two 2 x 12's) is hard and tricky work and shouldn't be tackled by anyone without experience in building. A building permit is required, too—see Introduction, "The law and your house."

If there are any electrical or plumbing lines in the wall, they will have to be relocated below the floor. It may be easier to revise your plans than to make such extensive (and expensive) alterations.

Openings in nonbearing walls (whether exterior walls or interior partitions) and openings less than 3 feet wide in bearing walls are fairly easily handled. Determine where the studs are and what width of rough opening (see Fig. 8-19) will call for the least amount of new framing around the door or window. Then start on the inside (assuming it is an exterior wall) and cut away plaster or drywall with a hammer and old saw. (Don't use a good one—you may ruin it.) Cut the plaster back flush on each side to the face of existing studs,

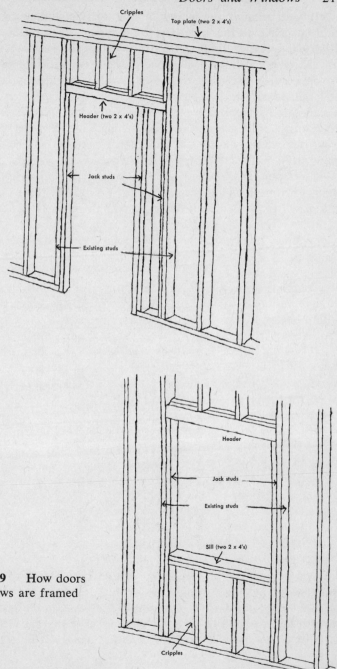

Cripples

Top plate (two 2 x 4's)

Header (two 2 x 4's)

Jack studs

Existing studs

Header

Jack studs

Existing studs

Sill (two 2 x 4's)

Cripples

Figure 8-19   How doors and windows are framed

and to the ceiling. Don't open up the outside siding and sheathing until you have all the materials you'll need.

Next, decide on the height of the opening, and the location of the sill if you are making a window. Take these measurements and a sketch of your existing framing to your lumber dealer and he can help you select the unit best fitted to your framing. If you can, get prehung doors or windows that come with the jambs all set. All you have to do is put the unit in the opening and nail it in place (after your jack studs, header, sill, and cripples are in place). The job is then virtually done except for patching and trim. If you can't get a prehung door to fit, you'll have to use a door package with jambs, head, and threshold supplied separately. Assemble these on the floor and install them as a unit, leveling and shimming as in Figure 8-20.

Figure 8-20   Shimming and leveling jamb

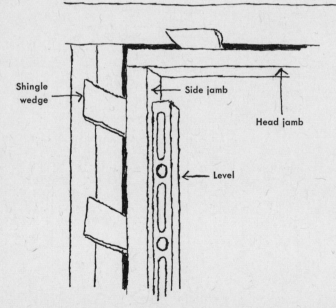

When you have your window or door unit ready to install, cut away the siding and sheathing to exactly fit the casing or outside trim of your unit. Start early in the morning so you can close up the unit by nightfall. (See Fig. 8-21.) To see how windows and doors should fit at drip cap and sill, see Figures 8-5 and 8-22. Use a plumb bob

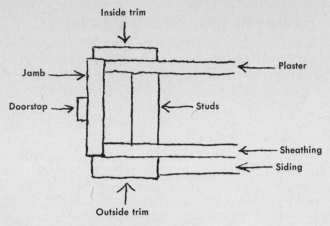

Inside trim

Jamb

Doorstop

Outside trim

Plaster

Studs

Sheathing

Siding

Figure 8-21   Top view of casing and jamb

Figure 8-22   How window sills and doorsills fit

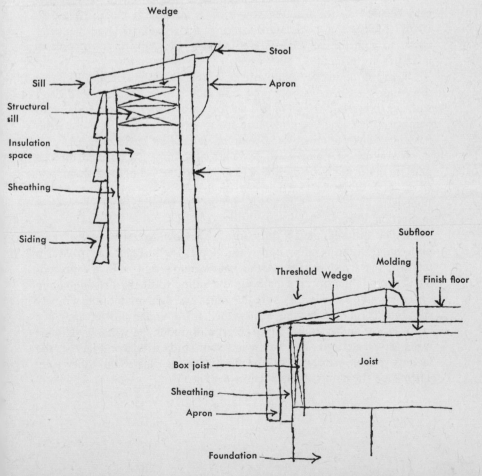

Wedge

Stool

Sill

Apron

Structural sill

Insulation space

Sheathing

Siding

Subfloor

Molding

Threshold   Wedge

Finish floor

Box joist

Joist

Sheathing

Apron

Foundation

and carpenter's level to make sure your cuts are straight and level. The easiest way to cut siding is with a power handsaw. You can set the level or depth of cut so you can cut away the siding to the outside width of the casing, then cut the sheathing to the width of the jambs. (You'll later nail the casing to the sheathing.) If your siding is brick veneer, cut it with a power saw and a carborundum blade. (This is hard, hot work.)

Next, saw away any intervening framing and install the header, sill, and jack studs as in Figure 8-19. Toenail these members (drive the nails at an angle) to the existing framing. Then set your unit in place. Don't forget to flash the top of all outside openings—see Section 8.2. Then install trim inside and out. If the inside trim doesn't cover all the chopped plaster, patch it as in Chapter 6. Caulk between casing and siding on the outside.

8.32 | **Making a window into a door, or vice versa,** is relatively easy because all the framing you need is already in place. (See Fig. 8-19.) Measure the existing door or window and take the measurements to your lumber dealer. He'll supply you with the right unit to install in its place.

Remove the inside casing and trim first, then the outside. Remove the window sash as in Section 8.21. Take out jambs, sill, and head with wrecking bar. If there is flashing over the drip cap, try not to damage it, because you can reuse it for your new unit. If there is no flashing, or you damage what's there, reflash as in Section 8.2.

If you are changing a window into a door, you'll have to remove plaster, the framing below the window, and the siding and sheathing, all as in Section 8.31. Then put in the necessary new framing (if door is to be narrower than the old window), and install the unit as in Section 8.31.

If you are changing a door into a window, you'll have to frame up to support the window unit with cripples, as in Figure 8-19. When this framing is in position, install your window unit as in the preceding section. Then install sheathing and siding to fit the existing siding on either side exactly. Be sure it comes up tight under the window sill. Finally, nail batt-type insulation with a vapor barrier in place from inside, and install a piece of drywall under the window. If your walls are plaster, you can fatten out your studs with wood lath so the face of your new drywall will be flush with the plaster on either side. Then tape the joints as in Section 6.32.

8.33 | **Closing up an existing door or window** is not difficult at all. First remove the door or window, its casings, trim, and so forth as in Section 8.32. Then install new studs on 16-inch centers by nailing them into structural sill and headers. (See Fig. 8-23.)

Figure 8-23 Placing framing for closing up window or door opening

Toenail new studs
to existing framing.

In an outside wall, you may want to install extra studs to give yourself a nailing base for new siding and sheathing. You'll need insulation too. (See last paragraph of Sec. 8.32.) Put up drywall on inside walls, fattening out the studs if necessary as above.

8.34 | How to make a window larger. You have to approach this job as if you were making a window where there was none before. You'll need a new header across the top of the new window unit. You'll probably want to remove the old header first, unless you want the head of the new window lower than the head of the old window. When you've framed in the opening, install the window and finish the job as in Section 8.31.

8.35 | How to install a skylight. If you have a room directly under the roof where extra daylight is needed, you can install a skylight. Plastic skylights are usually best because they give better insulation and won't break.

Figure 8-24   Skylight framing

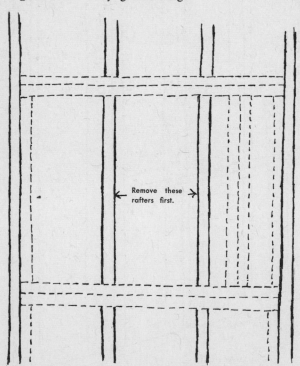

← Remove these rafters first. →

Saw out rafters in skylight area, then install new framing members (*indicated by dotted lines*).

If you want to install a skylight wider than four feet you should get a contractor to do the job, because framing and handling the unit is a heavy and tricky job. If you want to install a small skylight you can do it fairly easily yourself. (But you may need a building permit —see Introduction, "The law and your house.") You can get the unit from your lumber dealer or from a mail-order house, and it will come with full instructions. The first thing to do is open up your roof. The shingles and siding must be removed in an area slightly bigger than the rough opening for your skylight. It's a good idea to have a sheet of heavy polyethylene plastic handy so you can cover up the opening at night or if it rains, unless you are absolutely sure you can finish up in one day.

Then you'll have to frame in a rough opening like that in Figure 8-24. Follow manufacturer's instructions for installation. Skylights should be flashed with aluminum or copper flashing into the roof shingles, and all joints should be well caulked. Inside, you can finish off the well of the skylight with plaster, wood paneling, or any trim you choose.

⑨ FIREPLACES AND CHIMNEYS

9.1 | Keeping a fireplace and its chimney clean is essential for efficient operation. If your fireplace has an ash trap (metal opening in the fireplace floor) empty it several times a season. Otherwise, scoop out the ashes into a pail (wet them down first with a few cups of water to cut down the dust). Always leave an inch-thick blanket of ashes on the fireplace floor to help the fire burn more steadily. (See next section.)

About once every two years, your chimney should be cleaned. (An old fireplace that has been neglected should be cleaned annually for a while.) Otherwise it will be partially clogged with soot and will not draw well. The best way is to have a professional chimney cleaner do the job. (If none is listed in your yellow pages, ask your heating fuel dealer to recommend one.) It isn't expensive. If you prefer to do the job yourself, though, you can climb up on the roof and drop a length of tire skid chain attached to a rope down the chimney opening. Pull it up and down rapidly and it should knock the soot and scaly deposit loose from the sides. Be sure the damper is tightly closed during this process, or you'll have soot all over the house. If you have no damper, stretch an old, wet blanket or sheet tightly over the fireplace opening. (Instead of a chain, you can use a burlap sack weighted with stone and stuffed with straw. Tie a rope to its top and work it up and down in the chimney from above.)

You can partially check soot formation in the chimney by occasionally burning old flashlight cells or rock salt in the fireplace.

If you let too much soot accumulate in the chimney, it may cause a chimney fire. You can't always tell if you have one—the only evidence may be a lot of sparks coming out the top of the chimney. A box of table salt sprinkled over the fire in the fireplace will put out a chimney fire, or you can first quench the fireplace fire and then hold a wet blanket over the fireplace opening to shut off the air. Don't light a fire again until you've cleaned your chimney.

9.2 | If some fires smoke and some don't, your trouble is in mak-

218

ing a fire the right way. To draw well, a fire must be properly laid. It should be well to the rear of the fireplace. Begin with a few pieces of crumpled newspaper. Then make a "log cabin" of small kindling pieces, with ends of the first ones resting on andirons or bricks. (See Fig. 9-1.) Place a large log on top of the kindling but toward the rear

Figure 9-1 How to lay a fire

wall. After the fire gets going you can add more logs. Always make sure there is plenty of "air space" between logs so the fire can draw. Opening a door or window will usually help get the fire started. Or, if necessary, you can hold a piece of newspaper up in front of the fire, but not extending quite all the way down to the floor. It's best to keep a bed of ashes about an inch thick in the fireplace to let fires start faster and make the fire smoke less by insulating it against the cold hearth.

Before lighting the fire, make sure the damper is opened all the way. When no fire is burning, the damper should be closed. Otherwise, a great deal of house heat will escape up the chimney in winter.

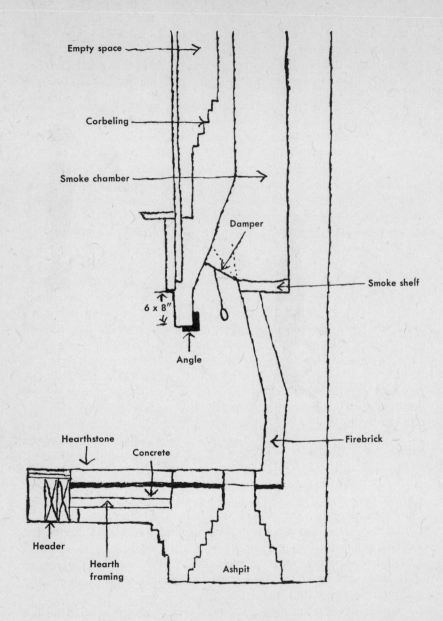

Empty space

Corbeling

Smoke chamber

Damper

Smoke shelf

6 x 8"

Angle

Hearthstone

Concrete

Firebrick

Header

Hearth
framing

Ashpit

Figure 9-2 Cross section of traditional fireplace

220

Firewood should be seasoned (dried) at least a year before burning. Do not burn wet wood. Avoid burning pine and fir in large quantities, as they will cause a disproportionate amount of soot and scale in your chimney. Slow-burning hardwoods are much more satisfactory.

9.3 | **If a fireplace smokes all the time,** first check to see if the chimney needs cleaning (Sec. 9.1) or if the damper is open all the way. Sometimes the damper gets loose and does not work properly. If there is any soot at the base of the damper, scrape it away. If the damper is removable, take it out and clean it.

Another possibility is that the damper was not placed correctly when the fireplace was built. It should be near the front of the fireplace, but not too low in the opening. (See Fig. 9-2.) If it is too low, some smoke will go out the front of the fireplace as it rises toward the smoke opening.

If smoke rolls out of the top of your fireplace, the first remedial measure is to take a strip of sheet metal and hold it across the top. (See Fig. 9-3.) Gradually lower the metal, while the fire is burning, until you have a good draft and no smoke coming out. Now mark the place where the bottom edge of the sheet metal touches the sides of the fireplace. Your fireplace should be covered to this extent. The easiest way to cover it is to have a piece of block iron made that will fit into the fireplace opening (Fig. 9-3) and can be bolted to the masonry on either side with expansion bolts. (Drill a hole in the masonry with a star or carborundum drill, insert the sleeve of the fastener, then put in the screw and tighten it.)

A fireplace that is too large for its flue will smoke too. Generally, the area of a flue opening should never be less than 1/12, preferably 1/10, of the opening of the fireplace. In other words, it is better to have your fireplace opening less than twelve times as large as the flue opening. If your fireplace opening is too big, you can experiment with making it smaller by placing a layer of loose brick on the floor and up the sides of the fireplace. If this improves the draft and eliminates smoke, you should install a layer of *firebrick* on the sides and bottom of the fireplace. (Don't try to use ordinary brick—it can't stand the high temperatures for long, and will gradually disintegrate.) Use fireclay, not cement mortar, to lay the brick—mortar will fall apart under intense heat. If you are not handy at masonry, you should get a mason to do the job for you.

Sometimes downdrafts that blow smoke back into the room are caused by nearby trees that tend to deflect winds downward. If a tree

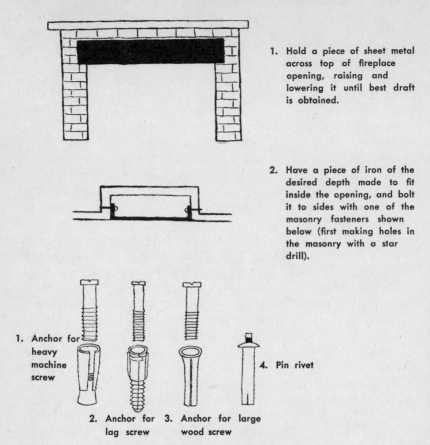

1. Hold a piece of sheet metal across top of fireplace opening, raising and lowering it until best draft is obtained.

2. Have a piece of iron of the desired depth made to fit inside the opening, and bolt it to sides with one of the masonry fasteners shown below (first making holes in the masonry with a star drill).

1. Anchor for heavy machine screw

2. Anchor for lag screw

3. Anchor for large wood screw

4. Pin rivet

Figure 9-3   Fastening metal hood across top of fireplace

is close to the top of your chimney and higher than the chimney, the cheapest solution is to cut the tree back. If you can't do this, try putting a hood over your chimney. (See Fig. 9-4.)

Finally, the fireplace will smoke if the chimney isn't high enough. This is rarely the case in two-story or split-level houses, but may occur in a ranch house. If you feel your chimney is too low, you can have a mason extend it upward.

9.4 | Some danger signals. If there are any leaks in your chimney (if smoke comes out anywhere except at the top), it is a definite fire hazard, and should be repaired at once.

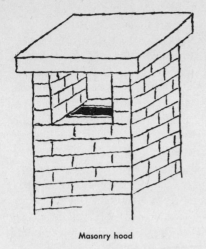

Masonry hood

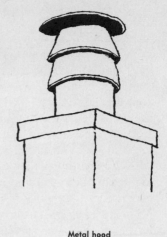

Metal hood

Figure 9-4 Chimney hoods

If you get smoke in an upstairs room when you have a fire down-stairs, put out the fire immediately; you have a leaky flue and it can set the whole house afire. You need a professional mason to take apart sections of your chimney and rebuild them.

If there are crumbling bricks in the walls of your fireplace they should be repaired at once. Better have a mason inspect the chimney too in this case—it may be crumbling also.

If a chimney fire develops (you'll see sparks coming out of the chimney), put it out as in Section 9.1, and don't build a fire again until you have had the chimney cleaned.

9.5 | **Painting a fireplace and chimney.** Woodwork and paneling around a fireplace can be painted, stained, or refinished like any other interior wood in the house. (See Secs. 6.8 through 6.12 and 6.22 through 6.24.) If you're painting, it's best to use a very washable paint, since the best of fireplaces may create a little smoke now and then. The most washable paints are the eggshell enamels. Remember that if you paint over a blistered paint surface, the new paint will blister too. If the surface previously blistered, remove old paint (Secs. 6.23 and 6.24) and use a breather paint, like an acrylic latex, instead of enamel.

All face masonry around the fireplace—not masonry that is actu-ally in the fireplace facing the fire—can be painted with interior latex paints (water-base paints). Exterior bricks or stonework on chimneys can be painted with exterior-grade acrylic latex. This is usually speci-fied for masonry right on the can. Ask your dealer about it.

Actually, it's much better practice both functionally and aestheti-cally not to paint any masonry, either inside or out. The surface of brick and stone is much tougher, easier to clean, and longer lasting than any paint film you can put on it. To remove old paint from bricks or stones, use muriatic acid. Ask your hardware dealer about using this. It's dangerous and should be used in fairly dilute solutions. You will need rubber gloves and plenty of fresh water to sluice off the acid. Keep the windows open so the fumes don't make you sick.

9.6 | Putting a new face on a fireplace. If your fireplace doesn't look like much, you can make a great deal more of it by extending the mantle, adding bigger side pilasters, or by making a bigger hearth. Millwork pilasters (from your lumber dealer) can be applied simply to the sides of the fireplace (nailed or toggle-bolted in place) and painted—see preceding section.

New mantles are a little harder to handle. Tearing off the old mantle carefully with a wrecking bar and screwdriver (a back mold-ing usually comes off first) will show you how it was attached to the wall above the fireplace. The same supports or holes in paneling or framing can be used to install a new mantle. First take out your old one, draw a sketch of what you have left in the way of structure for installing a new mantle, and take your sketch to the lumberyard. They can order the right mantle to fit or be adapted to your conditions.

If the woodwork around your fireplace is very old or in poor condition, or if it is old-fashioned in an unattractive way, you can restore it to traditional, colonial, or modern paneling—see Figure 9-5. The first step is to remove the old mantle. If it is wooden, the job is easily done—see above. Then remove the old paneling. Underneath you'll see the sloping outer wall of the smoke chamber. If the mantle is of stone or brick, you'll have to take it down piece by piece with a cold chisel and hammer.

The next step is to install furring strips behind all edges of abut-ting panels in your design. (See Fig. 9-5.) Furring strips are installed as in Section 6.19 and Figure 6-14. If the wall you are working on is flush and even with the front of the fireplace opening, use 1 x 3's fastened to the wall with nails or expansion anchors. Then install your paneling. If the furring must come out from the wall and stand free to be flush with the face of the fireplace, use 2 x 4's. This is usually the case when you remove very old paneling.

Figure 9-5   Traditional paneled fireplace

Making and installing colonial paneling like that in Figure 9-5 is a job for a professional woodworker or the expert woodworking hobbyist, so choose a simpler style if you are inexperienced and want to do the job yourself.

It's usually best to finish the edge of your paneling job (around the fireplace opening) with glazed tiles, brick, or stone mounted in a bed of mortar. (See Sec. 13.10.) First install a small steel angle (use expansion bolts) to support the masonry across the top of the fireplace, and to line up the sides. (See Fig. 9-6.) Then fasten some expanded metal lath to the face of the old fireplace with expansion bolts (Fig. 9-3). Then use mortar and dampen the tile to lay up your facing around the fireplace.

If instead of paneling and a facing of tile or brick, you want a whole new masonry veneer on your fireplace, call a professional mason, because the first thing you will probably need is a stouter

Figure 9-6   Steel angles and metal lath around fireplace opening to hold masonry in place

foundation to support the extra weight. This is also true if you want to enlarge your hearth.

9.7 | Planning for a new fireplace. If your house does not have a fireplace, or if you don't have one in the room you want one in, you can always get one built. (Don't try to do the job yourself—get a professional mason.) But there are a number of check points to keep in mind before you plan very far. First check your local codes and permit requirements. Then:

A) Don't put a fireplace in a small room. Face it the length of the room, not the width, unless it's more than 15 feet wide—the room will get too hot otherwise.

B) Be sure the fireplace is not too big for the room. Ideally, a fireplace 32″ wide by 24″ high calls for a room with at least 2,000 cubic feet—height x width x length. A 40″ x 27″ fireplace should have a room with 3,000 cubic feet; one 54″ x 31″ needs 4,000 cubic feet.

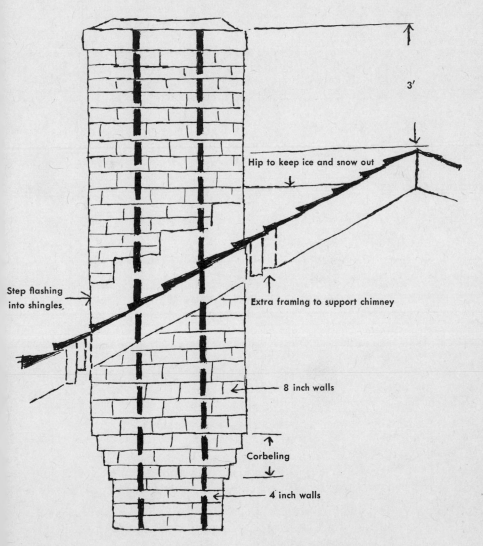

Figure 9-7   How to frame and flash chimney through roof

C) Be sure you have good chimney space overhead, and that the top of the chimney is 3 feet above the roof. (See Sec. 9.3 and Fig. 9-7.)

D) Be sure you have good foundation space for the chimney outside. To support a big hearth inside, you will have to reinforce and drop the floor framing. A good hearth is twice the width of the fireplace and should be the same depth.

E) Plan to use a pressed-steel fireplace unit that is simply set on your fireplace foundation and the fireplace, throat, and smoke shelf built around it. (See Fig. 9-8.) These units are foolproof—you *can't* build the fireplace wrong.

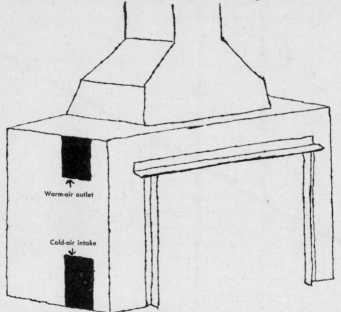

Warm-air outlet

Cold-air intake

Figure 9-8   Fireplace unit of pressed steel, which serves as a form for masonry

F) Have your mason line the chimney with flue tile. Mortar and bricks exposed to flue gases will disintegrate over the years.

G) Be sure that exterior walls of chimneys are 8 inches thick, interior walls at least 4 inches thick. If stone is used in the chimney, walls should be 12 inches thick.

H) Use a chimney cap to cut chimney maintenance. The cap slopes out and down from the chimney opening, sticks out over the outside of the chimney to form a drip cap. The slope drains off water and deflects air currents upward.

9.8 | Using prefab fireplaces. Today the handiest way to get a fireplace is to buy a prefabricated unit of steel or ceramic. (This is not the same thing as " E" above.) These high-style units can be very striking, especially in a modern decor. Your lumber dealer probably carries brochures about them. They come with prepackaged insulated chimneys approved by fire underwriters. They can sit out in the open like a piece of furniture, or they can be set against masonry panels at one side of the room. You don't need to worry about foundation problems with them. You can place them any place in the house where you can put a length of chimney up through the roof and flash it properly. Be sure you have a building permit.

Their only drawback is that you cannot build very big fires in them.

10 FOUNDATIONS

10.1 | **If your basement is continually damp or musty,** but there is no visible water penetration (check to make sure after a heavy rainstorm), you can sometimes damp-proof it by furring out the walls —using expansion bolts as in Figure 9-3 to hold framing to the masonry—and installing drywall or paneling. (See Fig. 6-15.) The most satisfactory floor treatment is to lay strip oak flooring on screeds in mastic. (See Sec. 7.15 and Fig. 7-14.) Most basement dampness is due to condensation and can be stopped by these measures.

If the dampness is really severe, however, you should first damp-proof walls and floor with one of the new synthetic damp-proofing compounds. Ask your paint or hardware dealer about them. If you damp-proof the floor this way, you can install asphalt tile instead of wood flooring if you prefer. Tile mastic can be laid right on top of the damp-proofing—see Section 7.19. (If there is water actually present in your basement, read Sec. 10.3 before you do anything.)

Sweating pipes in a damp basement should be covered with wrap-around insulation—see Section 1.36 and Figure 1-19. Finally, increase ventilation by keeping a window open (any basement will feel clammy unless it is well ventilated) and adding a ventilating fan. If necessary you can install an electric dehumidifier, but use it only when someone is in the basement—otherwise it will burn up a lot of electricity for nothing.

10.2 | **How to repair basement and foundation cracks.** If there is a crack in the basement floor, first undercut it with a cold chisel (Fig. 10-1) to widen it and let the concrete patch get a good wedged-in grip. Use a small chisel and don't widen the crack too much. When you have cleaned out and widened the crack along its full length, remove loose particles with a whisk broom and vacuum cleaner. Then mix your concrete—one part cement, three parts sand, and enough water to make it easily workable. Or you can use a ready-mixed concrete, such as Sakcrete, which contains cement and sand.

230

Figure 10-1 Undercutting crack with hammer and cold chisel

When you are ready to patch, wet down the crack and sprinkle sides and bottom of it with just cement from the bag. Then put in your concrete mix and smooth off with a trowel. After the patch has set overnight, sprinkle to wet it down again and cover it with wet newspapers so it can cure for three days.

If the crack is very small, or you just want to bring a worn-down spot up to level, it's often handier to use an epoxy patching compound. Ask your hardware dealer about these materials. They are very tough and can be applied in thin coats that will cling to the concrete. They are usually too expensive to use in very big cracks.

For patching very large cracks in the walls, buy a bag of ready-mixed mortar. This contains lime, which gives the mortar plasticity and makes it stick better to vertical surfaces until the mortar sets. Wet down your patch first, before applying mortar, and chip away any loose material at the edge of your patch. (If you have part of a sack of Sakcrete, you can simply add some hydrated lime to it— about 1/10 as much lime as Sakcrete—instead of buying a bag of ready-mixed mortar.)

10.3 | If water penetrates into the basement, you should attack the problem from two angles. First find out how the water is getting in. If there are cracks in cement or around stone foundation walls, openings around pipes and electrical conduits, cracks around windows, and so forth, they should be repaired as in the preceding section. Very small holes can be sealed with epoxy patching compounds.

If you can't locate any actual cracks or openings, water is probably coming in through the pores of the concrete because the walls were poorly constructed in the first place. You may be able to eliminate the water by applying a special waterproofing compound—ask your hardware dealer.

If you only get water in your basement in the spring when the groundwater is high and if you are on top or on the side of a hill where drainage is good, then it may pay to install some drainage channels in your basement rather than digging up around the outside basement walls (see below). If you lack confidence in yourself, hire someone to do this job. If you want to do it yourself, dig out a length of basement floor slab, against a wall or in a low spot, with a pick and crowbar. Remove the earth below it to a depth of two feet and fill the hole to floor level with clean graded 1-inch gravel. This simply makes a dry well in your basement to take care of that spring flood—it disperses the water into the well-drained soil beneath the slab. Remember, this treatment will work only if you are on high ground.

If you seem to have water in the basement off and on at any time of year, check to see whether gutters are leaking and causing water to run down the side of the building and into the basement. If so, repair them. If the ground next to basement walls slopes toward the house, it will form a pocket where water collects. Grade it the other way and place a splash block or other device to divert water from gutters and downspouts away from the house.

If you are on very level ground and heavy rains just sit on the ground or soak in, but there is no place for them to run off too easily, you will have to waterproof the full height of the foundation walls to stop leaks into the basement. In areas with clay subsoils, high water tables, or poor drainage conditions, even a reasonably well-built foundation cannot resist the force of water from the ground outside. (When building, you should find out if such conditions exist in your area, and have walls waterproofed substantially enough to withstand any groundwater condition likely to arise.) To deal with groundwater coming into an already built basement, you must dig a trench around the outside of the foundation, and wide enough to work in, to the bottom of the foundation. Place clay or fiber drain tiles on gravel in the bottom of the trench with their tops just below the top of the footing. (See Fig. 10-2.) Cover lightly with graded gravel. Now apply a coat of waterproofing mastic (ask your hardware dealer what kind)

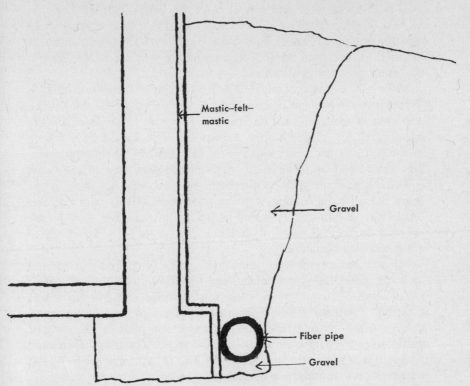

Figure 10-2   Drains at footing outside foundation

to the foundation wall. On the mastic apply a layer of asphalt roofing felt (the mastic serves as an adhesive) overlapped 6 inches at the seams. (Or you can use a polyethylene film.) Then give the felt another coat of mastic. Finally, fill the trench with dirt again, being careful not to tear the paper. Fill the upper 4 inches of the trench with gravel and slope it away from the house.

If you have tried all waterproofing methods, inside and out, and water still gets into the basement, you will have to have someone install a sump pump. Be sure you get one with a capacity large enough to handle the largest possible flow of water. Install the pump in the lowest part of the cellar (you'll find it usually slopes toward one end) in a pit 4 to 6 feet deep. Have the sides and bottom of the pit lined with concrete poured into a wooden form. The sump pump must be installed according to the manufacturer's directions.

This is all tricky work and not a job for the amateur. It will pay you to have a good plumber do this for you. The pump must be tied into the basement waste lines with backflow valves and must be adjusted to turn itself on and off automatically as the water level in the sump goes up or down.

10.4 | If crawl space is damp. If your house (or a part of it) is over a partial basement or crawl space, you may find the floor damp and cold in winter. If it's damp, the first thing to do is check the crawl space for adequate cross ventilation. You should have a vent in each side of the crawl space, near the corners. Their total openings should add up to an area 1/150 of the floor area of the crawl space. If you don't have crawl-space vents, you can get them in the same size as a foundation wall concrete block—then chip out one block with a hammer and cold chisel and install the vent in the opening. It's best if the vents are movable so they can be closed in extremely cold weather.

If you have vents and your floor is still damp due to ground moisture, cover the ground of the crawl space with 45-pound asphalt roll roofing. Seal it to foundations on all sides and overlap seams 4 inches. Then put a 2-inch layer of dry sand over it. Even better, place a 6-mil polyethylene sheet (transparent plastic) as a vapor barrier over the bare ground in the crawl space. This may be covered with a 2-inch-thick slab of concrete on top. The concrete can be left rough since it is only a ground cover.

If the floor over the crawl space is cold, you need to insulate. Use either a 4-inch batt-type insulation with vapor barrier facing up, or accordion-type aluminum insulation, applied between floor joists. Staple it on flush with lower edges. Fastening it like this will give extra insulating dead-air space between insulation and subfloor.

10.5 | How to tell if you have termites or dry rot. Termites today can be found in every state except Alaska, and more houses are susceptible to termites today than they were in the past because they have more attached porches, garages, and breezeways—which give termites easy access to the house. In addition, more houses are now built of sapwood and have central heating, both of which termites love. So it's a good idea to inspect your house from time to time for termites. If you don't have them this year, you may have them next. Much the same can be said for dry rot.

There are certain set conditions that attract termites and dry rot: If your basement or crawl space is excessively damp, if the yard is full of old stumps or scrap lumber, or if wooden parts of the house (siding, steps, basement windows) come into direct contact with the earth, it is easy for dry rot or termite damage to occur. Such damage is also invited by open downspouts that splash water back up under siding boards, cracked or damaged concrete, or badly peeling or blistered clapboards. If any of these conditions are present in your home, or if you have recently eleminated any of them by repairs, you had better check for termites or dry rot. First look in the dark places where wood touches the ground. Probe this wood with a sharp tool, such as an awl or ice pick. If you can push it more than one inch into the wood with hand pressure, the wood is so badly deteriorated either by termites or dry rot that it must be replaced.

Saw out a piece of the bad wood and inspect it. If the center is full of tunnels, you have termites. If it is spongy with many small open cells, you have dry rot.

Termites will climb the full height of a basement wall to reach wood they want to eat. You may spot their mud tubes running from

Figure 10-3   Termites

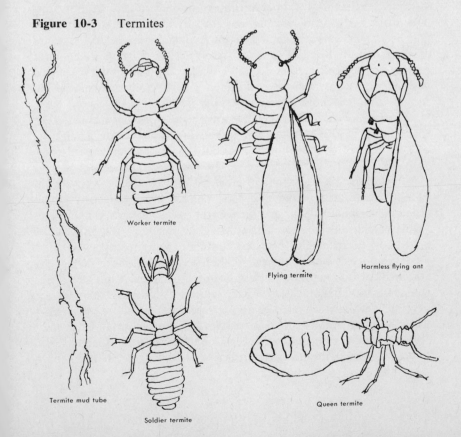

Worker termite

Flying termite

Harmless flying ant

Termite mud tube

Soldier termite

Queen termite

earth to wood along foundation walls. They build the tubes to get moisture from the ground. These tubes are quite obvious under a flashlight beam. (See Fig. 10-3.) Break them up and inspect the wood where they start—it is probably deteriorated. At certain times of the year you may also find a little pile of termite wings somewhere outside your house. If so, you probably have termites at work inside. White worker termites (see Fig. 10-3) are most likely to be seen, but you may also come across others that look like harmless flying ants. (They can be distinguished by the different-shaped body.)

In poorly built houses, termites can find enough moisture near leaking plumbing and in walls without vapor barriers, where the insulation is soaked with condensed water vapor, that they don't have to return to the ground to get the water they need to survive. In other words, you may not find any mud tubes from ground to wood in a poorly built house—yet it could be infected with termites.

If you are not sure about termite or dry rot damage, better call in an expert to assess the situation for you.

10.6 | What to do about termites and dry rot. If you have termites, hire an exterminator to get rid of them for you. (You can find exterminators listed in the yellow pages. Most of the best ones are members of the National Pest Control Association.) Damaged wood resulting from either termites or dry rot may need to be replaced by a carpenter or contractor unless you are experienced enough to do the work yourself.

The best way to get rid of termites and to protect against them in the future is to poison the soil—this does not kill the vegetation—and treat the framing lumber near the ground. Both are jobs for professionals.

Incidentally, if your house has metal termite shields you should inspect for termites anyway. Metal shields are rarely any good, because the smallest hole or crack in them will let termites through. (Most shields develop some tiny hole or crack in the process of fabrication or installation which a termite can get through.)

If you are building a new addition to your house, be sure the new structural wood sills and joists are treated with preservatives, or that the foundation wall is capped with solid concrete blocks. Don't let your contractor sell you termite shields unless they are soldered—and even then they're not foolproof. Be sure siding ends at least 6 inches above soil, and be sure at least 18 inches of space is provided between earth and floor joists in crawl spaces. (Be sure space is vented properly—at least one vent for each 25 feet of foundation.) Leave no wood in direct contact with the ground.

10.7 | Repairing crumbling piers and foundations. If the surface of foundation walls is crumbling and peeling on the inside, be sure to waterproof the outside (Sec. 10.3) before you repair them. The crumbling was caused by water coming through the wall, unless it is a very old house and mortar is simply falling off the foundation stones. If it is an old house the outside of the foundation wall needs to be waterproofed anyhow.

Before repairing the crumbling place, scrape off loose mortar and concrete with a wire brush. If there isn't much "tooth" for your patch to grip while it sets, you should fasten some expanded wire lath (see Sec. 6.4) to the patched area in the wall with expansion bolts (Fig. 9-3). Then mix up one part premixed mortar—it has cement and hydrated lime in it, and can be purchased at any building supply house—and three parts sand, and apply it with a trowel.

Figure 10-4   House jack in use

Wet the patch down first as in Section 10.2. Patching outside faces of foundation walls can be done the same way, except that you don't have to waterproof first.

If you have a pier under a porch, bay window, steps, or the middle of the floor in the basement, and it is crumbling or has mortar falling out of it, check the level of the porch or floor that the pier supports. If it does not sag, you can simply patch the mortar as above. If it does sag, the job is more complicated and will require the services of a contractor unless you are pretty handy. Planks and blocks and a house jack (Fig. 10-4) must be used to jack up the porch or floor to the proper level. (You can probably rent or borrow a house jack from your lumber dealer or hardware store if you want to do this job yourself.) When you have jacked up the superstructure to its proper level, the old pier will stand clear. Remove it down to the footing and repair and rebuild the footing as in Section 10.9. Then lay up a new pier with mortar and concrete block, working with these materials as in Section 13.10. Build the pier right up to the underside of the structural beam under the porch or floor. Remove the jack after a few days' time and the job is done.

10.8 | Replacing damaged wood posts or girders is done with the same technique shown in Figure 10-4. If a post has rotted away at any point, it's best to replace it with a masonry pier (if the post already sits on a footing or a concrete slab) or with another post treated with a preservative, such as creosote or Cuprinol. If there is no apparent sag in the superstructure resting on the post, then you should jack it up only far enough to slip a piece of paper between the top of the post and the beam resting on it. At this point the weight is off the post and you can remove it. If the footing needs repair, do the job as in Section 10.9 before putting in a new post.

If the post sits in a posthole, remove the entire post and use the hole to form a new footing, capping it off well above the ground so the post is clear of the soil. Or you can build up a masonry pier on the new footing.

Replacing a rotted girder under a porch or floor is a little more difficult and if you have any qualms about tackling it, call in a professional. First new seats (to support each end of the new girder) must be prepared alongside the spots where the present damaged girder rests. On foundation walls you have to make new pockets in the wall, or if the girder sits on piers you have to pour new footings and build up new piers as above, right alongside the old ones. Be sure the new girder is the same size as the old one, or at least of comparable strength. If there is an appreciable sag in the floor, jack it up temporarily with lally columns (Sec. 7.3) so you can get your new girder in.

Be sure that both ends of floor joists meeting over the old girder will lie over the new girder, too. Then jack up ends of the old girder (Fig. 10-4) just enough to slip the new girder in place.

10.9 | Building foundations for porches and steps. If you are adding new steps or a new porch, or repairing old ones, you have to be sure that a frost pocket (water collecting by capillary action and then freezing) cannot form under the bottom of the post or footing and throw your steps out of line. First dig a hole, or the whole area of the step to be poured, two or three feet deep. (See Fig. 10-5.) Then fill it with stones or coarse gravel (water can't travel upward through it) to within a foot of the top. Then pour your concrete footing or steps in a step form, as in Figure 10-5. Use premixed concrete, or mix portland cement (one part) and sand (three parts) and put in enough water to make the mix workable, not soupy.

If you want to, you can reinforce your steps by placing coat hangers, pieces of chicken wire, or wire mesh in the wet concrete. It may help prevent hairline temperature cracks in the concrete later on, but is not really necessary.

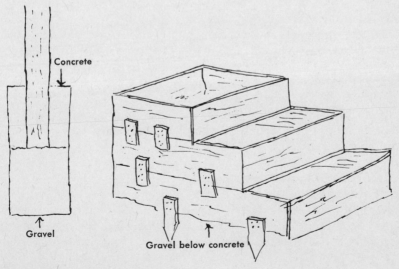

Figure 10-5   Posthole and step form

If you are going to strengthen an existing footing, dig down to the bottom of the old footing, then scoop out part way underneath it with a trowel and pour your new footing all the way around it and on top of it, reinforcing it with bits of steel wire if you want a very strong job.

11 ROOFS

11.1 | How to locate a leak. Ceiling stains and stains at the top of walls, right under the roof, come from roof leaks. Leaks may be due to shingles that are split, loose, or damaged, to rusty nails, or (very often) to defective flashing (the sheet-metal seal where the roof joins a chimney, vent pipe, or dormer, or in "valleys" where different angles of the roof meet). Gutters that are clogged and too close to the eaves can cause leaks in winter, if ice forms in the gutters and pushes water back up under the roof. (See Sec. 11.8.)

If the underside of your roof is exposed in the attic, you can locate the leak by tracing water to the spot where it comes in from outside. (This isn't necessarily the point where drops fall.) You may see pinholes where the light in coming through. When you get the leak spotted, poke a broomstraw or thin wire up through the opening so you can find it again from above.

If the underside of the roof is not exposed, you'll have to go up to the roof to look for the leaky spot. Begin over the spot where water or stains have appeared on the ceiling, and work up the roof (water may have run down a rafter before dripping off). If you see a shingle torn off or broken, you've probably found your leak.

Caution: Go up on the roof only when it is perfectly dry. Wear rubber-soled shoes to avoid slipping. When raising a ladder to the roof, place the feet against the wall and "walk" the ladder up until it is vertical. (See Fig. 11-1.) Then move the bottom out from the wall about one-fourth its length for maximum safety. Never paint a ladder, and never use one that has been painted—you can't see a faulty rung through the paint. Never reach out more than arm's length from a ladder.

11.2 | Repairing leaks in and around flashing. If you have a leak near flashing, nine times out of ten it will be at the edge of the flashing—that is, water is coming in under the flashing rather than coming through it. Figure 11-2 shows typical flashing.

Figure 11-1   How to put a ladder up

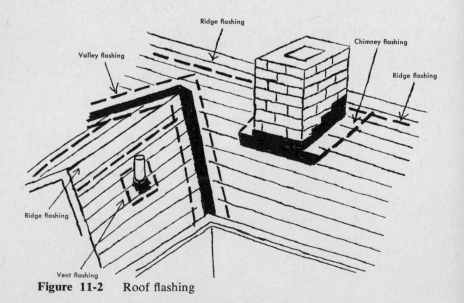

Figure 11-2   Roof flashing

When repairing faulty flashing, first examine it closely and figure out exactly where water could get under it. Usually the top edge of flashing lies well under shingles, so water couldn't get under here. If the sides are exposed, however, a driving rain may push water in under them. The best sealer for the edges of flashing is a synthetic puttylike material, applied from a tube, called Thiokol. It makes a permanently elastic rubberlike seal between flashing and shingles of any type. (Other sealing materials that can be used are caulking and asphalt roofing compound.) Before sealing, nail down loose edges of flashing with galvanized roofing nails.

Flashing at chimneys may have pulled loose from mortar joints. You can drive it back in again with a small hardwood wedge, then seal the mortar joint (with flashing in it) and the joints between flashing and roofing with a sealing compound, as above.

If flashing comes loose around a vent pipe, use the same sealing compound to fasten it back again.

If your flashing has developed holes (this doesn't happen often) you can seal them up with the same sealer used around the edges. First clean the area around the hole with steel wool, so you can have a clean metal surface for your sealing material to cling to.

It's highly unlikely, but if your flashing looks as though it has corroded away beyond repair, or if you have no flashing where you should have it, you'll have to install new flashing. Shingles at the top side of the flashing will have to be removed and replaced as in Section 11.3 or 11.4 (depending on the type of roof) to cover the top edge of flashing. Flashing should extend under the shingles to the edge of the next highest row of shingles. Nail down flashing with roofing nails. In valleys, shingles along both sides must be removed to install flashing, then replaced. If you should have to replace flashing around a vent pipe, the easiest material to use is a plastic sheet called Saraloy. This is simply pulled on over the vent pipe and glued down to the roof with the adhesive supplied with it.

Installing flashing can be a hard job, and unless you are sure of yourself you should call in a professional to do the job.

11.3 | Repairing and replacing asphalt roofing. Small holes in asphalt shingles or roll roofing can be patched with asphalt roofing compound from your lumber dealer. If there are loose or curling shingles, apply a coat of asphalt roofing compound under the edges of each one, and press it back in place. This should be done on a hot day when both shingles and compound will be pliable and easy to work with.

If the shingle is torn or seriously damaged, replace it. The best time to do this is on a hot day, when shingles are soft. Wear gloves so you don't burn your hands. You can remove shingles by lifting up the edge of shingle above and pulling out all nails in the damaged shingle. However, as asphalt shingles are 3 feet long, you may want to cut out only the damaged section. Insert the new shingle or section and nail down with roofing nails, using the old holes in the roof. Coat nailheads with roofing compound.

When making repairs on a hip roof joint (see Fig. 11-3), apply a liberal layer of roofing compound before you lay new shingles. New shingle pieces should overlap at least 2 inches. Nail down all four corners.

Figure 11-3   Hip roof ridge repairs

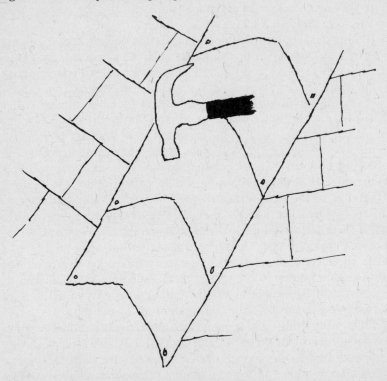

To repair hip covering, apply a layer of asphalt over hip, then nail new shingles in place—overlapping at least two inches. Nail down all four corners.

If your roof is asphalt roll roofing—big sheets that lap each other and stretch from one end of the roof to the other—it's easiest to patch any holes or damaged spots with a patch, rather than trying to replace a whole strip of roofing. Take a piece of heavy roofing felt (asphalt-impregnated paper) and cut it out slightly bigger than your patch. Then scrape away all the mineral aggregate from the damaged place in your roofing. Apply roofing compound to your patch, lay the paper in the compound, and apply more compound on top of the paper. Then sprinkle sand into the compound.

If your asphalt shingles or roll roofing are worn out (they will last ten to twenty years) you should reroof. Asphalt shingles that are buckled up, dry, and that tear or crumble when you take hold of the edges, are worn out. When choosing new shingles, consult your lumber dealer about type, style, and color. White asphalt shingles are best in a hot climate because they cut down summer heat. The heavier your shingling material, the better.

If there is just one layer of shingles or roofing, you can reroof right over the old material. Wait for a day when the roof is completely dry. Start at the eave and lay a double layer of shingles for the first row, making sure the slots in the shingles do not lie over each other. (See Fig. 11-4.)

Figure 11-4   Laying asphalt shingles

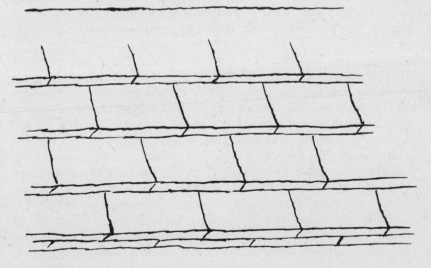

First row double

If there are already several layers of shingles on the roof, they should be removed before new roofing is installed. This is a big job and in most cases should be done by a professional.

11.4 | Repairing and replacing wood shingles. If a wood shingle is split or otherwise slightly damaged, you can slip a piece (cut to size) of aluminum flashing or roofing felt under the shingle. (It should fit under the shingle above the broken one, too.) If a shingle is badly curled, split it and treat in the same way. Nail down all loose ends with galvanized roofing nails. If a shingle is badly damaged, replace it with a new one. To remove the old shingle, slide a hacksaw blade under it to cut off the nails. Slide the new shingle in place and nail it down, using old holes in the roof if you can. When finished, coat all nailheads with asphalt roofing compound.

If a wood shingle roof is in bad condition all over, you'll have to reroof. You can use wood shingles again, or asphalt if you prefer. The new material can be laid right over the old, unless the old shingles are extremely waterlogged. (This rarely happens unless the roof is in constant shade.) If you remove the old shingles you will usually find that they were nailed to boards that had spaces between. If this is the case don't try to fill up the spaces between boards—just nail the new wood shingles to the boards that are there, as the old shingles were nailed. (This system lets the roof "breathe.") Shingling material is sold in bundles that cover 35 to 50 square feet. Shingles come in different styles and types, most of which are designed to provide a double- or triple-thick surface. Ask your lumber dealer for his recommendation.

When you are ready to reroof, be sure the roof is completely dry. (If it looks like rain, don't start the project.) When installing wood shingles, nail the upper half of each shingle to boards, using galvanized nails. Trim shingles to fit with a hatchet. Be sure solid shingles cover a joint line for the next two rows up. (See Fig. 11-5.)

In a hot, damp climate, a wood shingle roof should be treated with a wood preservative. If desired, shingles can be stained. (It's easiest to do this before installing them. Ask your lumber dealer what stain to use.) Don't paint wooden shingles, because it makes drying out after a rain slower and moisture damage more likely.

11.5 | Repairing built-up roofing. A built-up roof is made of several layers of roofing felt, liberally coated with asphalt between layers and on top with a finished surface of crushed stone or some similar aggregate. A built-up roof can have its asphalt dry out and begin a

Line up every third row so joints are staggered.

Figure 11-5   Laying wood shingles

leak here and there. The easiest way to repair this condition is to use the penetrating oils made especially for this purpose. Ask your hardware or lumber dealer.

When you are ready to patch—wait for a good dry day—sweep the loose aggregate into piles off the areas you are going to patch. Then apply the oil, right over the aggregate that still sticks to the roof. Sweep the aggregate back into position when you are through.

If you have a blister in a built-up roof, slit the blister with a knife, apply asphalt roofing compound liberally in the blister, then weight the spot down so the compound can "reglue" the layers that came apart.

Built-up roofs sometimes have a tendency to develop leaks right at the eaves, at the gravel stop. This is because there is a pocket where water can collect at this point. (See Fig. 11-6.) To repair leaks along here, wait for warm, dry weather when the roof has dried out, sweep back the aggregate, and apply roofing asphalt compound liberally all along the eave edge, at the gravel stop, back as far as water can stand. Then replace the aggregate.

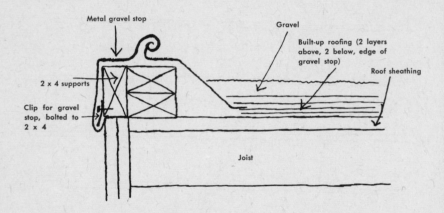

Figure 11-6   Cross section of gravel stop on built-up roof

11.6 | Repairing metal roofs is seldom necessary. A good metal roof can last a lifetime and usually the only holes it gets are those that somebody punches in them.

If you do get a hole in a metal roof, the best way to repair it is with a synthetic sealer (like Thiokol) that stays permanently elastic. You can also use putty or asphalt roofing compound. A good roofer can solder a patch on a copper or a terne-roof, but this is tricky work and should not be attempted by the amateur.

Galvanized roofing should be painted after a few years with red lead to prevent the possibility of rusting through. If it was painted before and the red lead is peeling off (this is most often true in tropical climates), scrape and brush loose paint off with a wire brush and repaint. Consult with your paint dealer about primers to use with galvanized roofing, and about new paints that can be applied over rusty surfaces without cleaning off the rust.

Copper, terne, and aluminum roofs shoud not be painted. Colored aluminum roofs have baked enamel surfaces and these should not be painted over except with special exterior paints that can form a tight bond with such smooth surfaces. Ask your paint dealer about this if you want to change your roof color.

(You can often tell what kind of metal a roof is by its color. Copper roofs have a patina of green. Terne—steel coated with lead and tin—roofs are usually slate-gray. Aluminum roofs look shiny when new, light-gray when old. Galvanized roofs are light-gray or red from red lead paint.)

11.7 | Repairing slate and tile-type roofs. Slate, glazed and unglazed clay tile, concrete tile, bermuda shingles, and asbestos cement tile roofs are all very long-lasting, like metal roofs. About the only way they can be damaged is by people walking on them, or limbs, tools, or rocks dropping on them.

If you have to repair this type of roof, wear sneakers and use a one-board ladder—Figure 11-7—so your weight is spread around and you have decent footing.

Figure 11-7   One-board ladder on roof

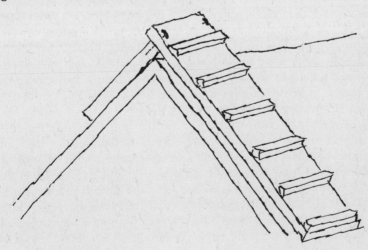

To make a one-board ladder, nail cleats to a board, then nail 2 x 4's to ends for hangers.

If a crack develops in a slate or tile roof, you can repair it with a synthetic sealer like Thiokol (Sec. 11.2) or with putty or asphalt roofing compound. A slate shingle that comes loose can be resealed with the same material.

The easiest way to replace a broken slate or roof tile of any type is to use a piece of sheet-metal flashing to hold the broken piece or the new tile in the old position. First remove the broken tile by inserting a hacksaw blade underneath the broken slate and cutting off the nails that held it in place. If the solid upper end is held fast in the roof, leave it there. Then nail in a piece of flashing so it will lie under the new tile or the broken piece, and so its lower edge can be bent up to grip the new tile in position so it can't slide out and down the roof. Study the lay of the roof and place your flashing so rain cannot leak through. Flashing may lie under or over adjoining tiles, depending on the position, so water can't get in. Treat the nail-heads holding the flashing in place with roofing compound.

Now take a new slate or tile and mark on it the exact size you need to replace the broken piece. Score deeply along the line with a screwdriver or chisel. Hold scored line over a solid straight edge and tap along the scored line with a hammer, and it will break along the line. You can tap off ragged edges with a hammer, holding the edge of the slate on a masonry surface. Lay out nail holes on tile to match existing holes in roof, and make holes in the tile by tapping a nail as you turn it, with tile laid flat on a board. Apply roofing compound to the flashing where tile will lie, insert the tile, nail it, and touch up nailheads and cracks with roofing compound or Thiokol.

11.8 | If your gutters and downspouts need repairs, the best thing to do is to replace them with aluminum gutters. Your lumber dealer sells these and will tell you how to install them. Wood and galvanized gutters eventually corrode away, but aluminum ones never do (except in seashore climates)—and the only maintenance they require is cleaning out leaves once a year.

When gutters become clogged or overflowing, water running down the side of the house may cause interior wall damage. Mud and rotting leaves will also cause all gutters except aluminum ones to rust and deteriorate. No matter what kind of gutters you have, you should inspect and clean them regularly. The time to do so is after all leaves have fallen in the autumn. You can flush the leaves away with a hose. It's also a good idea to install gutter screens that slip under shingles and over the edge of the gutter—see Figure 11-8. If

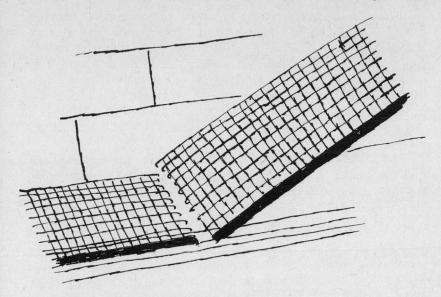

Metal gutter screens slip under edge of shingles, over edge of gutter.

Figure 11-8   Gutter screens

you don't want to install screens, you should at least fit downspouts with wire strainers (you can buy them ready-made at the hardware store). If a downspout does become clogged, you can clear it out from above with a plumber's auger. (See Fig. 1-1.)

The slope of the gutter is important for efficient draining, too. There should be a ¼-inch drop per foot toward downspouts. Gutters that are too close to the house sometimes cause leaks in winter when ice dams form in the gutter and force water back up under the eaves. If this occurs, move the gutters farther away from the edge of the roof by moving the straps out a little. Seal old nail holes with roofing compound.

If pools or puddles form in the gutter (in winter these can freeze, and the weight may break the gutter entirely) there is a sag. Raise the straps or replace rusty straps with new ones. (You can get replacements at the hardware store.) Straps are simply nailed through the roofing and the nailheads touched with roofing compound. Straps holding downspout are nailed to the wall and their heads covered with putty.

When the galvanized coating of gutters and downspouts becomes damaged, apply roofing compound to protect spots against rust. If a hole develops, you can patch it temporarily with heavy roofing paper cut to fit. Clean the spot with a wire brush and sand it to remove rust. Then coat the inside of the gutter at the damaged spot with roofing compound, and press the patch into place. Seal the edges and cover the entire patch with compound. This will prolong the gutter's life a season or so, but eventually you'll have to replace it.

11.9 | Repairing cornices and rake boards. The moldings and trim right under the edge of the roof—they're called cornices along the eave of the roof and rake boards at the end of the roof—may become damaged from too much water. If they do, what you need is a drip edge for the roof. (See Fig. 11-9.) This is usually an

Figure 11-9   Drip cap under roof

Metal drip cap extends under lowest row of shingles.

aluminum strip that can be shoved under the edge of the shingles and nailed in place. You can get one at your lumberyard. If the drip edge doesn't go under the shingle easily, clear a path for it with the end of a hacksaw blade. (This will remove any nails that are in the way.) The edge should go under the shingles far enough so that the tee on the bottom side comes up against the cornice molding. Nail it from above, into the cornice or the roof sheathing. Then touch up nailheads with roofing compound.

When waterlogged cornice and rake boards have dried out, after you've installed the drip edge, you can repaint them. If they are completely rotted, of course you should replace them before installing the drip edge.

11.10 | **Widening an overhang for more shade.** This is one of the best ways to keep your house cooler in the summer without investing in an air conditioner. Figure 11-10 shows how to add wide

Figure 11-10   Widening an overhang

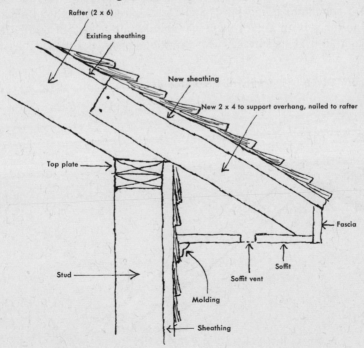

Nail molding in place before installing soffit, so molding can support house side of soffit while you nail other side to 2 x 4.

overhangs. One of the best times to do this is when you are going to reroof the house. In any case, roof shingles and roof sheathing must be cut away two or three feet in from the edge of the roof. (This is best done with an electric hand saw, with the blade set to a depth that just cuts through the sheathing and no farther.) Then the 2 x 4's for the overhang are nailed to the rafters to make the line of the rafters continue out past the house. Sheathing is nailed to the 2 x 4's. (Use thin nails so you don't have a lot of heavy hammering to do.) Then you can reroof, or patch as in Section 11.3 or 11.4. Add new trim pieces to finish the job. You don't have to install gutters if you don't want to.

Note: A building permit is required for this work. See Introduction, "The law and your house." Don't attempt the job yourself unless you are an accomplished carpenter.

11.11 | Making a flat roof into a sundeck. If you have a flat roof or one with a very slight pitch, and window or door access to the roof, you can make it into a sundeck. First be sure that the roof is in good condition. If the roofing material is roll roofing (it isn't likely to be shingles on a flat roof), you should put a layer of roofing compound all over its surface before putting down duckboards like those

Figure 11-11   Duckboard construction

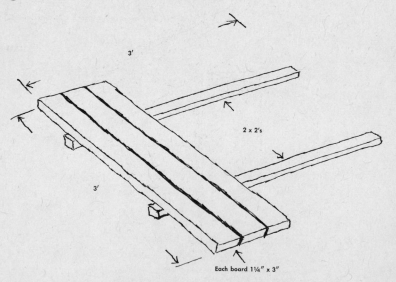

3'

2 x 2's

3'

Each board 1¼" x 3"

shown in Figure 11-11. These units are 3 feet square and are movable for roof repairs. Boards should be separated by about half an inch to let rain water drip through. The 2 x 2's forming the base for the duckboards can be slanted to match the pitch of the roof if there is one.

Don't try to use a plain roof without duckboards for a sundeck— you may damage the roof beyond repair.

12 SIDING AND TRIM

12.1 | Repairing wood siding. Most cracks, splits, and small holes are best repaired with putty or caulking compound touched up with paint. A good caulking job with a putty knife and a new coat of paint can make old siding look like new.

If a clapboard splits along its grain, wait for a dry, warm day and then gently pry the upper split piece outward. Insert waterproof epoxy glue in the crack and press the board back in place. Drive finishing nails just below the patched clapboard and bend them upward to hold it tightly in place until the glue dries. Then remove the nails and fill holes with putty.

If a board bulges or curls outward but is not split, drill a few small holes at the center of the bulge and insert screws. Before you tighten screws all the way, soak the board with water to avoid cracking it. Then countersink the screws slightly and top them with putty.

If a clapboard is damaged beyond repair, replace it. First cut a new clapboard to fit exactly the spot you plan to remove, and paint it on both sides. When it is dry, remove the damaged section by sawing vertically in several spots, as near as you can to the over-hanging edge of the clapboard above. (See Fig. 12-1.) Then remove pieces with a hammer and chisel, being careful not to damage the roofing paper underneath. To remove the section that is under the clapboard above, drive nails all the way through both boards with a nail set—then you can pull out the underneath piece. Now nail the new clapboard in place (drill pilot holes first so you don't split the wood). Countersink the nails slightly and cover heads with putty.

Repairing wood shingle siding is virtually the same as repairing a wood shingle roof. (See Sec. 11.4.) If the shingle is merely warped, you can nail it back in place. First drill holes for the nails so you don't split the shingle. Cap nailheads with putty after they are in place.

Holes and cracks in damaged board-and-batten siding can be repaired with putty or plastic wood, topped with a good grade of exterior paint. (See Sec. 12.5.) If a board needs replacing, rip off

256

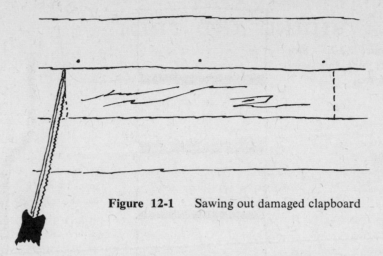

Figure 12-1   Sawing out damaged clapboard

battens on either side, remove the board, and replace it with a new one from your lumber dealer. Have new battens cut and nail them up where the old ones were. Then paint to match other siding.

12.2 | Repairing asbestos cement shingles. If asbestos cement shingles become stained or dirty, they can be cleaned with a solution of ½ cup trisodium phosphate in a gallon of hot water. Then rinse with clear water. If you can't make the shingles look clean again, you can paint with a masonry paint as in Section 12.5.

If an asbestos shingle cracks or breaks, break it into pieces with a chisel and hammer. (Do so carefully, or you'll damage adjoining shingles.) When all pieces of shingle are removed, cut away nails with a hacksaw. Hold the new shingle in place and mark where the nail holes should be. Drill pilot holes, then nail up the new shingle with copper, aluminum, or galvanized nails.

12.3 | Repairing exposed masonry. After many years of weathering, the mortar joints in a brick wall may need some filling up. Masons call this "pointing up." Rake the loose mortar from the worn-out joints to a depth of about half an inch, and then fill with new mortar. Either buy it premixed in a bag or mix one part cement, one-fourth part hydrated lime, and three parts sand. Use a pointing tool (get it at the hardware store or masonry supply dealer) to smooth the joints. (See Fig. 12-2.)

If brick or tile walls leak, they probably leak through the mortar joints and need to be repointed, as in the preceding paragraph. (If

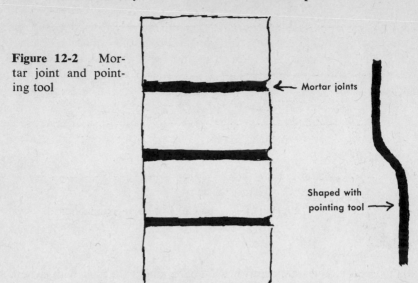

Figure 12-2   Mortar joint and pointing tool

← Mortar joints

Shaped with pointing tool ⟶

you have a brick veneer wall, you don't have to worry about leaks through mortar joints, because water just runs down inside the veneer and out weep-holes in the mortar joint at the bottom of the wall. If you patch joints in a brick veneer wall, be sure not to fill up these weep-holes. (If your wall leaks and the joints look in good shape, check the areas around doors and windows. These should be caulked tight between masonry and wood trim. If they are not, use a caulking compound as in Section 12.4. If mortar joints and caulking at doors and windows are in good condition but the wall still leaks, water is probably coming through hairline cracks in the joints or in the brick or block itself. (Hairline cracks may appear in joints that were made with just cement and sand, no lime. This concrete can shrink just a little and leave a slight crack.) The solution is to spray your wall with a silicone solution—a colorless waterproofing compound. Ask your paint dealer. Silicone will not change the color of your wall but may darken it slightly. Before you apply it, scrub the wall thoroughly with a wire brush (without water) to remove dirt. If efflorescence (a white deposit that comes from salt in the brick) is present, remove it as in Section 12.7 before you apply the silicone solution.

Repairing cracks in stucco is like repairing mortar joints. Clean all the loose stucco out of the joint and patch it with premixed mortar or a mixture of one part cement, one-fourth part lime, and three parts sand. Use a putty knife to get it flat. If the stucco is colored, buy sand-finished colored stucco to put over your patch. Ask your masonry supply dealer.

If stucco is badly damaged, remove old stucco right down to the sheathing underneath. Then put up roofing felt with galvanized nails. Nail chicken wire to it, and mix sand and cement as in preceding paragraph. Apply it with a plasterer's trowel. (See Fig. 12-3.) After

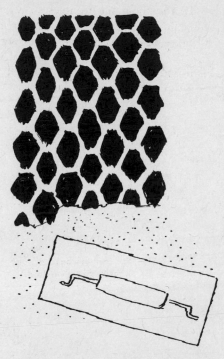

Figure 12-3 Repairing stucco

To patch stucco, put up a layer of roofing felt, then a layer of chicken wire, then apply patching mix with a plasterer's trowel.

it has set about an hour, scratch the coat with a saw-tooth trowel. After seven days, wet down the surface lightly and apply a second coat like the first one—but leave the second coat smooth.

To repair cracked and crumbling foundations, see Section 10.2.

12.4 | Repairing trim and cracks at doors and windows. Cracks between siding and window and door trim, and between siding and foundation, should be closed with caulking. It comes in a tube and is merely squeezed in place. Ask your lumber or hardware dealer. A Thiokol-type of caulking is best. (See Sec. 11.2.) Before applying the caulking make sure cracks are dry and clean. Whether a gun is used or caulking is applied with a putty knife, it should be forced *into* the crack, not just placed on top.

Damaged casings (side trim pieces) at doors and windows can be caulked with a putty knife and repainted if their condition is not too bad. If they are damaged beyond repair, rip them off and replace them with similar pieces from your lumber dealer. Use galvanized finishing nails. Countersink them and putty the nailheads. If jambs themselves are badly damaged, see Section 8.25.

If a window sill becomes so weatherbeaten or damaged by continual moisture that it must be replaced, saw through the old sill as in Figure 12-4. Pry out the pieces without damaging jambs (the sides

Figure 12-4   Replacing damaged sill

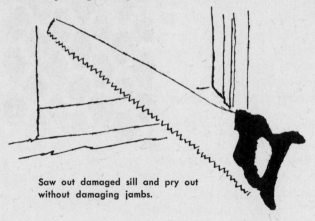

Saw out damaged sill and pry out
without damaging jambs.

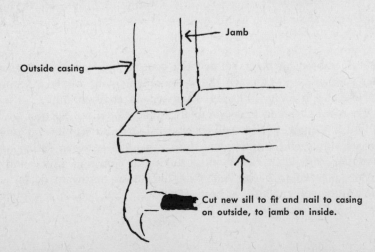

Jamb

Outside casing

Cut new sill to fit and nail to casing
on outside, to jamb on inside.

of the window). You may have to chop out the sill with a hatchet and saw off nails in the opening with a hacksaw. Cut out a new sill, using the old pieces as a pattern. Prime the new sill with a coat of paint before installing it. You may have to remove the outside casing so you can fit the new sill snugly. It must be level in the line of the wall (check with carpenter's level), but must slope from inside to outside walls.

On the outside, nail the sill to the casing by nailing up from underneath. On the inside, nail sill to the jamb with finishing nails. Seal all openings with caulking, then paint.

12.5 | Choose the right paint for your house. If your house needs repainting, you can do the job yourself if you want to. It isn't difficult, and will cost you less than a fourth of what a professional housepainter would have to charge you.

The first thing to do is consult your paint dealer. Tell him what kind of exterior siding you have on your house and what condition the old paint is in. He can tell you exactly what primer (first coat) to use and what finish paints will work best. Paint manufacturers are constantly improving their products, and each year new paints better or more versatile than old ones are coming on the market.

Whatever kind you choose, be sure to get one of the better grades, because good paint will wear longer and better than cheap paint. In other words, an expensive paint is the cheapest in the long run. Most quality paints are made to "chalk": that is, as the paint ages, a little of the top layer washes slowly off, taking the dirt with it. The surface of the paint wears away evenly, leaving no openings where moisture can seep through—and leaving a smooth, even surface for repainting when the time comes.

Older-type house paints require repainting in 4 to 6 years, but some of the newer house paints with alkyd resin in them will last 8 to 10 years, or even longer in some cases.

If you are painting over weathered paint on wood siding, the best paint is a "one-coat" finish paint. This paint is opaque and will cover in one coat over old paint, provided it is in reasonably good condition. If the wood is new wood siding, you should get a good wood primer —a specially formulated paint made to penetrate the wood deeply— and put a coat of that on first. Aluminum paint is usually the best primer for knotty wood, because it seals the knotholes so they can't run and spoil the finish coat. After the primer, you can use a "one-coat" finish. There are also some new water-base paints that can be used on new wood, but most are not recommended for use over old paint.

If you are painting wood shingles, use a special shingle paint. (Or they can be stained, unless they have been previously painted.)

For painting trim, a special trim paint is used in most cases. It has a special glossy finish similar to enamel. Be sure you use a "trim" paint and not an ordinary chalking paint on the wooden trim of a brick or dark-colored house. The "chalking" might cause white streaks on the masonry or painted siding below.

Wooden porches, steps, and railings should be painted with a special porch or floor enamel, designed to withstand heavy wear and scrubbing. New wood in porches and steps must have one coat of primer and two finish coats of floor enamel.

If you are painting masonry, there are a number of different water-base paints, oil-base paints, or clear silicone waterproofing sealers (these protect the surface, but do not alter the appearance of the masonry—see Sec. 12.3) that you can use. Acrylic latex paint designed for exterior masonry is the best choice in most cases, but masonry walls subject to continual dampness should be painted with cement water paints, since they are applied to a wet surface and dry to a hard, strong film. Two coats are usually needed, and the second should be put on after about twenty-four hours—before the first is thoroughly dry. Sand can be added to the paint to conceal defects in the masonry.

Masonry walls previously painted with oil paint (if the surface is glossy, it's an oil paint) must be repainted with oil paint, or else the old paint must all be removed first. If the old paint is flaking off badly, it must be removed in any case before repainting. Use a wire brush and muriatic acid—see Section 12.7. When you have removed it, repaint with a latex paint. Oil paint tends to hold back the water vapor (which is inevitably present in a brick wall) and prevent it from coming out—which would cause the oil paint to crack and peel. Latex paint, on the other hand, lets the water vapor come through, and the wall dries out without affecting the paint film.

If the siding on your house is part masonry or asbestos cement shingles (this is essentially a masonry material, and calls for the same type of paint treatment) and part wood siding, you should use one of the new exterior alkyd latex paints. (Ordinary latex paints are not suitable for wood siding, because they let the wood get damp from outside water and don't expand and contract with the wood.) These combine all the tough properties of alkyd paints with the porous character of latex paints. Ask your paint dealer about them.

Concrete walks, concrete steps, and concrete porch floors should be painted with a tough polyurethane floor paint or one of the synthetic rubber paints manufactured for concrete floors—provided the concrete is waterproof. (That is, provided it has a vapor barrier beneath it to prevent ground moisture from getting into the concrete.) If it doesn't have such a vapor barrier, leave it unpainted because any paint would just peel off.

When painting any exterior metal surface, get a primer especially manufactured for use with the particular type of metal. If you don't, your finish coat will peel off. But with the proper primer the finish coat can be ordinary house paint or trim paint.

12.6 | How much paint will you need? Old paint in good condition that has chalked off to a smooth, even surface can be repainted with one coat, unless you are changing the color drastically. On new wood or old wood in bad condition at least two coats are needed.

In estimating the amount of paint you will need, you can figure roughly that one gallon will cover about 500 square feet in one coat. For very rough or heavily textured surfaces you will need 20 per cent more paint; for very narrow lap siding, about 10 per cent more; for concrete block, 50 per cent more. If two coats are required, of course you will need twice as much paint.

You will also need about one gallon of trim paint for every five gallons of house paint.

12.7 | Preparing to paint. The work you do before you begin painting is perhaps the most important part of the job. First of all, the surface must be clean. If it appears dirty, go over it with a wide scrub brush and detergent, or with a solution of one or two tablespoons of trisodium phosphate in a gallon of lukewarm water. Be careful not to use a stronger solution—it might soften the paint. (Occasionally, paint that looked very dirty looks almost like new after washing, and you may find you don't have to paint. Make a test before you buy the paint.)

When you wash the house, begin at the bottom and work up—otherwise dirty streaks may form underneath that won't wash off. You can rinse it with a hose.

Renail any loose clapboards or shingles, and remove and replace rusty nails. Countersink exposed nails, and fill cracks and nail holes with putty. (Sec. 12.1). Caulk any openings around window and door frames, replace loose putty in window sash, and make any sash repairs needed. (See Secs. 8.24 and 12.4.) Repair leaking roof gutters and downspouts (Sec. 11.8) and coat all unpainted or unvarnished copper and galvanized iron surfaces (such as drain pipes, gutters, screens, etc.) with paint or spar varnish to avoid later staining of your new paint job.

If there is loose and peeling paint on the siding, remove it with a wire brush or scraper—otherwise the new paint won't adhere properly. One of the best ways to do this is to use a wire or hardbristled brush on an electric drill. This makes the work go fast and requires much less effort. You can probably rent an outfit like this from your hardware store.

Paint in extremely bad condition may have to be removed altogether. (If it has merely "chalked" away so much that some spots are bare, you don't have to remove it. But you will have to prime it again.) Before you do anything, read Section 12.10, "Paint Failures and Their Causes," so you can eliminate the cause. If you have to remove paint in only a small area, you can use an electric paintsoftener and scraper. If you have a lot of paint to remove, you will have to hire a professional because this is hard, tricky work.

To prepare a masonry surface for painting, remove dirt and loose paint with a wire brush and wash with water. Whitewash and cement water paint should be thoroughly scrubbed with a wire brush on an electric drill with a buffer—see above—before you paint. Repair all cracks and loose mortar as in Section 12.3. If there is a white, powdery film on masonry, it is due to efflorescence—a white deposit caused by the salt in the masonry. This must be removed before painting by scrubbing with a solution of one part muriatic acid to five parts water. Wear rubber gloves and be extremely cautious, as muriatic acid is very dangerous—especially to the eyes. After the wall has dried completely, treat it with silicone waterproofing to prevent further development of efflorescence.

To prepare metal surfaces for paint, all rust, grease, and oil must be completely removed with turpentine or sanding (with a wire brush, steel wool, etc.) before paint is applied. Then apply a prime coat immediately so no more oil or grease can settle.

12.8 | When and how to paint outside walls. You can't paint just any time—the weather has to be right. The temperature should be between 55 and 90 degrees. Don't paint on humid, dusty, foggy, or windy days. Don't begin too early in the morning, before the sun has dried out the moisture in the air. Don't paint after a heavy rainstorm until several days of sunny weather have thoroughly dried the house and the air. Don't paint if rain is forecast. If it starts to rain and you're painting, stop. Work on north and west sides in the morning, east and south sides in the afternoon, so as to avoid painting in direct sun.

Before you begin, mask windows with tape (you can skip this, if you prefer, and scrape paint off later with a razor blade) and cover shrubs and glass with dropcloths or sheets of polyethylene (a plastic film available at hardware stores and lumber yards), unless you are experienced enough to paint very neatly.

Use a 3½-inch or 4-inch brush for siding, and a 2½-inch or 3-inch brush for trim. When you are ready to begin, set up your ladder (See Fig. 11-1), and begin at one side of the wall. Paint a horizontal strip about 3 feet wide across the top, then move the ladder and continue the 3-foot strip down to the bottom. Brush the paint out thinly at the ends of your strokes to avoid lap marks.

After you have painted all the siding, go back and do the trim. If you have shutters, take them down and paint them across sawhorses for an easier, neater job.

If more than one coat of paint is required, wait at least three days between coats of paint—more if the weather is damp or cold.

12.9 | Painting a house with spray equipment is actually the easiest method in most cases. You can probably rent the equipment from your paint dealer—ask his advice before you decide. You should have a regular air-compressor-operated spray gun. In using this type of equipment, there are a number of basic rules you should follow:

1. Always overlap strokes by one-fourth to one-third the width of each stroke, because the spray will deposit more paint at the center than at the edges.

2. Don't jiggle the trigger.

3. Keep the gun moving. Never stop the gun with the trigger open.

4. Don't tilt the spray gun excessively. If you do, paint from the cup will flow into the cup cover, and the nozzle and air passages in the cover will become clogged and cause gun to sputter.

5. When spraying a horizontal surface, keep the container only partially full. Tilt the gun 30 to 45 degrees and spray the near edge first, working across laterally in successive strokes.

6. When spraying inside corners, spray the adjoining walls instead of the corner itself. The overlapping edges will cover the corner.

7. Don't try to cover in one coat with slow-drying paint. Paint that's too thick may sag before drying, or may accumulate dirt and moisture before drying. Apply coats thinly enough to dry properly even if this means you must put on two coats instead of one. Wait for the first coat to dry thoroughly before applying the second.

12.10 Paint failures and their causes. Paint can fail for several reasons: (1) The surface may not have been prepared properly when the paint was applied. (2) The wrong paint for the surface may have been used. (3) The surface may not have been dry. (4) The paint may have been applied improperly. (5) The walls may leak moisture vapor from inside the house during the winter. (6) There may be a leak in the roof at the eave line, or the gutters may cause water to back up and drip down inside the wall.

If your paint is blistering and peeling off the wall, check for the last condition first, and correct it as in Section 11.8. If that isn't the reason, it may be (5) above. If this is the case, you need a vapor barrier—a watertight film—on the inside wall to prevent moisture vapor from coming through in the winter. You can paper with a plastic-coated paper or paint with a tough oil-base interior paint to waterproof the inside wall. Or you can put midget louvers in the outside wall so moisture vapor can escape that way. Then you won't need a vapor barrier on the inside. (See Fig. 12-5.)

Figure 12-5   Midget louvers in siding

To install louvers, drill holes and set louvers in place.

If your paint film has wrinkled, faded, cracked, crawled, or become spotted, it's due to any combination of reasons (1) through (4) above. The solution is to wire-brush the old paint (Sec. 12.7). If you come out with a reasonably smooth surface, you can repaint. If the old paint is still lumpy and uneven, you should remove it all before repainting. It's best to have a professional do this job.

If your old paint has mildew all over it, wash the surface clean with trisodium phosphate—about two tablespoons to a gallon of warm water—and when completely dry, paint it with an exterior paint with a mildewcide in it. (Ask your paint dealer about this.) If you don't, mildew will form again—it's caused by the atmospheric conditions at that point in your house wall.

12.11 | Natural finishes for exteriors. If the siding on your house is wood shingles, you will probably want to stain it instead of painting. You can buy a ready-mixed stain at the hardware or paint store. New shingles should be stained or painted before they are nailed in place.

If your house is sided with redwood or cypress and you want to leave it natural, your best bet is to do nothing at all to the wood. These woods naturally resist decay, molds, and insects and will gradually "gray" out to the right texture.

No matter what your siding is, do *not* put any varnish or linseed oil on it. These two finishes invite darkening and must be refinished every few years. You can, however, use some pigmented sealers especially made for outdoor natural finishes. Simply brush on one or two coats of sealer and renew it every few years as it weathers down. You can add pigments if needed to get more color in this type of finish. If you do, be sure to follow the manufacturer's directions.

Another good natural finish is a colorless wood preservative, such as Cuprinol or Woodlife, that can be renewed every few years. The wood will gradually take on the weathered gray look of old barns.

In most cases the most satisfactory natural finish is one developed by the Department of Agriculture's Forest Products Laboratory. For a five-gallon batch, you need 3 gallons of raw linseed oil, 1 gallon of mineral spirits or turpentine, 1 pint burnt sienna (oil color), 1 pound paraffin wax, ½ gallon penta concentrate preservative, and 2 ounces zinc stearate. You can get all these ingredients at the hardware or paint store. To mix the stain, pour the gallon of mineral spirits into a 5-gallon can. Put the paraffin and zinc stearate into another pan and heat, stirring until uniform. Pour into the mineral spirits and stir vigorously, keeping the flame away from the mineral spirits. Let cool to room temperature and add the penta and linseed oil. Stir in colors until the mixture is smooth, and stain is ready for use.

12.12 | If your house needs re-siding. Siding that's cracked, broken in spots, and caked with lumpy paint is often not worth repairing or repainting. It can be simply covered up by re-siding. This is a job you can handle yourself if you are very handy, but otherwise is best done by a professional. In any case, it will pay you to consider carefully the various materials you can use—shingles, clapboards, board and batten, asbestos, aluminum, stucco, brick, and so on.

New siding will change the appearance of your house considerably. To be sure you get all the advantage possible out of the change, there are a few points you should keep in mind: First, the best way to make your house look bigger is to make the exterior hug the ground—try to extend your new siding down over a high foundation wall. Don't let it touch the ground though. Next, do away with little patches of contrasting siding—this makes the house look small and scrappy. You can use two kinds of siding (say brick and wood shingle) if the heavier siding is used on the lower portion of the exterior and its area does not exceed the area of the lighter siding.

New siding can be put on over old siding, although in some cases it's better to remove the old siding to get a smooth, flat surface (the sheathing) to work on. If you're going to re-side over the old siding, keep in mind the following things you may have to do: (1) If flashing over doors and windows is inadequate, install new flashing over the drip cap before you re-side. (See Fig. 8-5.) (2) If the new siding will extend out beyond the exterior casing on windows and doors, you can thicken the casings with new moldings or casing boards. (See Fig. 12-6.) Draw a sketch of your casing, showing the distance it now protrudes beyond the old siding, and ask your lumber dealer for the proper trim pieces to use with your new siding.

Before you begin re-siding, loosen or remove the trim board up under the eaves so your siding can fit under it. (If you break or damage this board in removing it, you can simply replace it and the trim moldings that may come away with it.) Cover all old siding (or sheathing if you removed the siding) with roofing felt or aluminum foil from your lumber dealer. Tack the strips up horizontally, with upper strips lapping over lower strips so moisture will drain off.

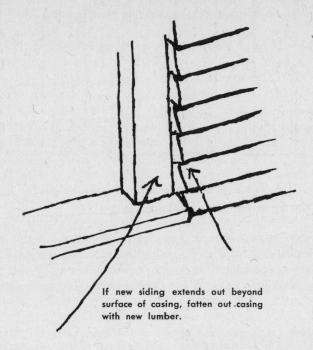

If new siding extends out beyond
surface of casing, fatten out .casing
with new lumber.

Figure 12-6   Fattening old casing out to new siding

Wood shingles, wood shakes (big, rough split shingles), and asbestos cement shingles are the easiest type of siding to apply over
old siding. It's usually best to paint or stain shingles before they are
installed—ask your lumber dealer for his advice. Since shingles and
shakes are a series of small pieces, they can cover misshapen walls
and are easy to fit around obstructions. If you don't get them up
absolutely straight, it doesn't matter. (In fact, they are often applied
in a crooked fashion for the texture they give.) To line up the first
course, use a carpenter's level and stretch a piece of string taut
between nails at the lower corners of the wall. Place bottom edge
of shingles against the string, and nail in place with two galvanized
nails placed about one-third down from the top edge of the shingle.
(Over old siding, nail into the protruding lower side of clapboards or
shingles underneath. See Fig. 12-7.) Make the bottom row double

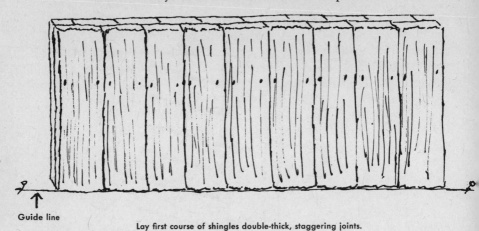

Lay first course of shingles double-thick, staggering joints.

Figure 12-7   Installing wood shingle siding

(staggering joints)—this is called double-coursing, and is sometimes continued all the way up the wall. Ask your lumber dealer's
advice. When you come to a corner, butt shingles up against a corner
board as in Figure 12-8, or cut them so they meet in a tight-fitting
corner.

Figure 12-8   Corner boards for shingles or bevel siding

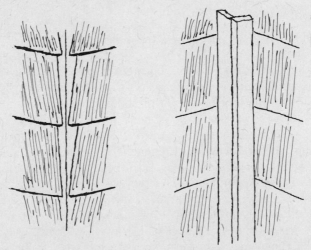

Butt shingles against corner trim at inner and outer corners.

Putting up clapboards, either wood or aluminum, is slightly fussier than putting up shingles, because the boards must be level or the house will look lopsided. To get a level line, snap a chalk line—checked with a level—all along the wall, from corner board to corner board at the top edge of the first or bottom clapboard. The chalk line will show up clearly on the roofing felt. If you're using wood bevel siding, use the same size as old siding and line up the lower edge exactly even with—or just slightly lower than—the lower edge of old siding. Nail it along the lower edge at every stud point. (The newest way to fasten either wood or aluminum bevel siding to old siding is with a new type of clipping device—ask your lumber dealer about this. See Fig. 12-9. Clips for wood bevel

Figure 12-9   Clips for wood and aluminum bevel siding

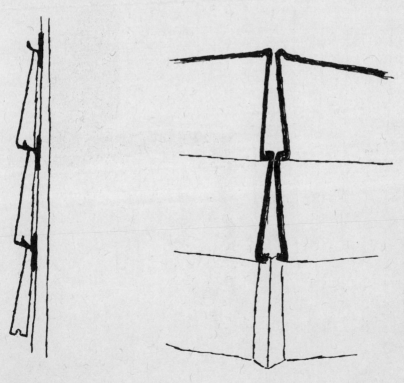

Clips for attaching wood   Aluminum siding fits together and pieces are locked
siding to wall   in place by corner trim.

siding are fastened to the wall as the siding is installed. Aluminum siding usually is made with the top edge of each piece bent over in a clip shape to grab the next piece of siding. The top edge of the aluminum siding is nailed to the old siding. If you are using aluminum siding, you can omit the roofing paper, because the siding forms a watertight surface.)

Board siding (whether board and batten or plywood sheets, like Fig. 12-10) is the easiest of all siding to apply. It simply goes up over old siding in big vertical pieces that span old edges of bevel siding, hiding all imperfections in the wall. It can be nailed to the

Figure 12-10   Plywood sheet siding

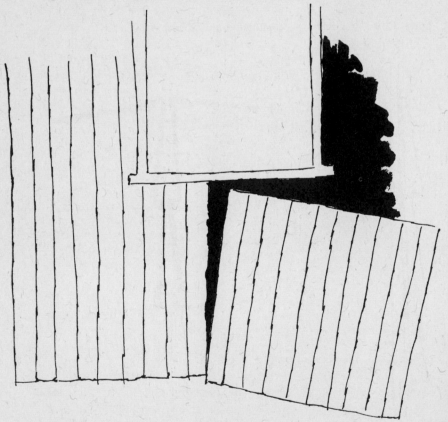

Plywood sheet siding, available in textured finishes, is easiest of all siding to apply.

old wall at almost any point. Joints between sheets of plywood should be caulked, but you need not caulk joints between battens and boards.

Stucco re-siding is applied just as a big stucco patch is applied. (Read Sec. 12.3.)

Brick siding over old siding is a lot of trouble, but it can be done. The easiest way to do it is with one of the new nail-on brick products like that shown in Figure 12-11. You have to fasten clips

Figure 12-11   Brick veneer

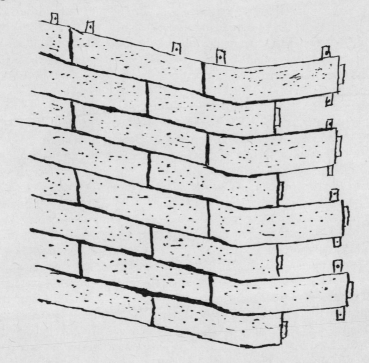

Thin brick veneer comes in both straight and corner bricks. Both are nailed up with special clips.

for every brick in every other course with this system. This means that it's almost essential to remove old siding if it isn't smooth, so you can get a smooth nailing base for the clips all over the wall. (If you just want a piece of brick siding on the front of the house, however, you can nail a plywood nailing base to the old siding. Then put up your nail-on brick so it sticks out the thickness of ordinary brick from the rest of the wall. You can cap this strip of brick with a wood drip cap like a sill, whose rear edge fits under new wood siding above the brick.) To lay up an ordinary brick veneer over old siding, you have to provide a base for the veneer to rest on. This means digging down to the footing of your foundation wall to provide an extra thickness of foundation for the veneer to rest on, or bolting a steel angle ledge to the foundation on which the veneer can rest. Both measures are expensive, but can be done fairly easily by a professional mason if you want the job done. Be sure that there is flashing under the bottom course of brick, and that there are weep-holes through the base at the mortar joint.

12.13 | **Installing and repairing porch floors and steps.** Keeping your outside porches and steps in good shape—and having them big enough—is well worth the effort. If a guest should fall down or through steps, you can be involved in a nasty lawsuit, or if it's a member of the family, some big hospital bills. And wood porches and steps are in contact with the ground and exposed to the weather, so they rot out more quickly than other parts of the house.

If one board or section of a wooden porch floor rots away or is otherwise damaged, it's easy to replace it. Locate the floor joists (from underneath, if you can). The damaged section should be cut out with its ends flush with the joists. If more than two or three boards must be removed, stagger the ends at different joists. Bore holes flush with the joists, then saw out the boards with a keyhole saw. If boards are tongue-and-groove, cut away lower groove side on new board so it can drop into place. Nail boards to supports, countersink nails, and fill holes. Paint boards, or refinish the entire floor if necessary.

If your old porch and steps are completely worn out, and the porch area is small (like a stoop), you can rebuild it quite easily. See Figure 12-12. (If it is large, you should get professional advice and assistance before you tackle it.) The first thing to do is to lay out accurately on a piece of paper exactly what you want to build in the way of porch and steps. Take the measurements—height above the ground and width of your outside doorsill—with a ruler and a level. Be sure they are accurate. Then design your new porch to meet this doorsill just one step down (about 6 inches). If you have porch footings of concrete in the ground, try to design your porch frame to use these footings. If they are inadequate you will have to pour new footings as in Section 10.9.

Design the stringers for your new stairs as in Figure 7-11. Set stringers in or on concrete pads. Have your stair treads overlap the stringers by 6 to 8 inches and fasten them to stringers with galvanized nails. Paint the finish job with three coats of deck paint or floor enamel.

Figure 12-12   Porch framing

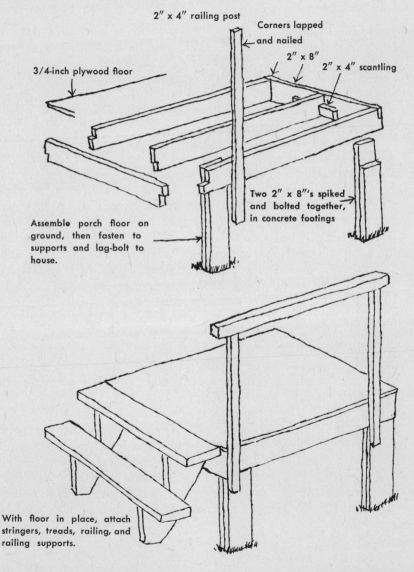

2″ x 4″ railing post

Corners lapped and nailed

2″ x 8″

2″ x 4″ scantling

3/4-inch plywood floor

Two 2″ x 8″'s spiked and bolted together, in concrete footings

Assemble porch floor on ground, then fasten to supports and lag-bolt to house.

With floor in place, attach stringers, treads, railing, and railing supports.

13 OUTDOOR LIVING

13.1 | Planning a patio or terrace. The location of a patio is important from two aspects: its relation to the rest of the house, and its relation to the sun. Ideally, a patio should be accessible from several rooms, among them the kitchen and the living room. A patio accessible only from the kitchen is awkward for entertaining. A patio should seem to extend the size of the house, even in winter when it may do so only visually.

The proper orientation of a patio depends largely on the climate you live in. The warmest patio faces south and west—ideal for cool northern climates and perfect for winter use because it catches the low winter sun. As a matter of fact, a southwest-facing patio that's protected on the sides from cool winds will form a sun pocket that can be warm enough for sun bathing even in March. An east-oriented patio is desirable for a hot climate, for it lets in morning sun but keeps out hot afternoon sun. North-oriented patios are suitable only for hot climates. In other words, if you live in a warm section of the country, you have considerable choice in orienting your patio. If you live in a cool or moderate climate zone, chances are you will prefer a south-facing to a west-facing patio.

When you've decided how you want to place your patio, you're ready to design it. Take the lay of your land into consideration and avoid extensive excavating or the erection of unnecessary retaining walls. Do not remove favorite trees or plantings. In most cases, you can build the patio around them.

In deciding on the size of your patio, consider the size of your family, the size of your house, and the size of your lot. The patio must be large enough to accommodate the necessary outdoor furniture and perhaps large enough for games and toys. However, if you want to relax and entertain on your patio, it's best to relegate the games and toys to some other place so the children won't always be underfoot. A very large patio should be broken up with gardens or planting.

If possible, a patio should be shielded from the street and from neighbors' view. If the house itself doesn't provide this shield, you will need fences to insure privacy. (See Sec. 13.7.) If the house is L-shaped or U-shaped, perhaps the patio can fit into the pocket. This will shield it from wind, neighbors, and noise.

If you must build your patio on a hillside, you will have special problems to solve. Drainage must be properly provided for, and you will need terracing or retaining walls to keep soil from washing downhill. (See next section.) Unless you have done similar work before, you'd better call in a contractor to help you. If your hill is quite steep, you should consider building a wood deck (Sec. 13.4) instead of a regular patio.

If you are going to build the patio yourself, you can do it in stages if you prefer. You can lay the floor one summer, roof it in the next year, and perhaps add screening or other finishing touches the third season.

The choice of materials for your patio depends to a great extent on the style of your house, what materials it is made of, and where you live. (Adobe blocks are a good choice for patio floors in the southwest, but flagstones are better in New England.) The material should also be suitable for the use you are putting it to. A rough surface (such as brick) is not good for children's play or for dancing or games. An overly slick one, like a steel-troweled concrete slab, may be dangerous for children and old people, but is ideal for dancing.

Simple materials are the best choice for a patio: wood, stone, brick, concrete, patio block, gravel, and tile. Metals and plastics should be used for jobs that other materials cannot do. (Plastic, for example, is the only material that can be used for translucent roofs.)

13.2 | How to make steps and retaining walls. You'll have to make steps and retaining walls if you're building on a slope, making a well around basement windows that lie below the level of the patio, or making a wide well around a big tree in the middle of a patio. (If the floor level is more than a foot above the original level of the ground, you'll have to make such a well. If you just build up earth around the tree, it will probably die.)

The simplest and best retaining walls are made of fieldstone laid up at a back slope and backfilled with soil, as in Figure 13-1. The first stones should be firmly dug into the ground, and the earth fill behind is placed as you build the wall up. A wall like this lets

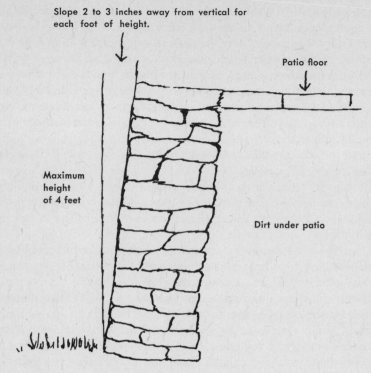

Slope 2 to 3 inches away from vertical for
each foot of height.

Patio floor

Maximum
height
of 4 feet

Dirt under patio

Figure 13-1   Fieldstone retaining wall

the groundwater flow out and drain away. It may shift slightly over
the years, like an old stone wall, but it is easily mended.

The simplest steps to make are also made out of fieldstone, just
like the retaining wall. But in this case, once you have your stones
set, you should put concrete down in and around them. This is
simply to make a good stepping surface, not to bond the stones together—they should be set perfectly firm before you concrete them.
If you prefer, you can top the steps with the same paving material
that you used on the patio floor. Set this material in concrete on the
stones. Mix concrete as in Section 13.10.

Retaining walls and steps of fieldstone laid up like this should
never be more than four feet high. The stones are too hard to
handle and earth pressures from the backfill may knock the wall
down. On walls three to four feet high, be sure to lay the heavy

end of the stone into the backfill to key it into position, and be sure to tamp the fill behind as you build it up. It's a good idea to cap the top course of stone with concrete.

If your steps or retaining walls have to go higher than four feet, or if you want to terrace your patio in a series of levels down the side of the hill, you should call in a contractor to discuss it with you. Local building codes must be met to the letter in big retaining walls, which usually involve reinforced concrete, excavation, drainage provisions, and so on. On a really steep hillside, your best bet is a wood deck instead of a patio. (See Sec. 13.4.)

13.3 | Laying patio floors and paths. The easiest and best way to lay a patio floor is on a bed of sand. You can lay concrete patio block, adobe, brick, flagstones, and pressure-treated wood block this way. Make your sand bed from 2 to 6 inches thick on top of tamped or undisturbed earth. If you're going to need a lot of sand, it will pay you to find out where you can get "dead sand" or "road sand." The first has some clay in it and the second has rocky particles up to ¼ inch in it, so they are both cheaper than clean building sand. Sand comes by the "yard" (a cubic yard, or 27 cubic feet).

Before you put down the sand, you have to make sure the sand cannot wash out of the edges of the patio. This means that you have to have a curb of some sort to hold the sand in. If you're building on level ground, the best solution is to remove the top soil and set the sand bed into the ground, so that soil around the patio forms a curb. Of course, on the house side of the patio the foundation wall serves as a curb. Or you can use a curb of wood. Choose 2-inch stock of redwood or cedar, or a pressure-treated (with preservative) wood. The planks are set on edge in the ground and held in place with stakes driven in at 4- to 8-foot intervals. The top edge of the plank should be level with the top of the patio floor. If the patio is above ground level, you'll need a stronger curb, like stones set in concrete. To make such a curb, dig a shallow trench six inches to a foot deep, and concrete in the foot of the stones to ground level. (For working with concrete, see Sec. 13.10.) If you prefer, you can make the whole curb concrete by building a form of wood up to the proper level and then pouring in the concrete. You don't need to reinforce it because if it cracks it doesn't really matter.

When your curb is in place and any necessary digging and leveling has been done to provide the 2- to 6-inch depth for your sand bed, put the sand in place and level it with a straight board and a carpenter's level. (Place the level on top of the board.) Firm sand down by sprinkling it and walking over it until it is smoothly packed down all over.

Then begin placing the bricks, stones, or blocks in one corner. (You should know exactly how you're going to lay them before you begin. If necessary, make a paper pattern showing how each block will go.) Keep the joints as narrow as you can, for they are easiest to fill later.

You will probably have to cut some of your paving material to fit around edges. To cut a brick, score it all around with a cold chisel or mason's hammer, then set it on edge and tap the chisel along the score mark. To cut a flagstone, rest the stone on a bed of sand, score along the mark with a cold chisel, notch the edges where the line begins and ends, and tap the chisel back and forth along the line until the stone breaks.

When all the bricks or blocks are in place, finish the joints by sweeping more sand into them. If your joints are wide, you may find that the sand washes out readily when it rains. In this case, you may have to put soil in the cracks and plant grass in them. Or, if you want a mossy joint, sour the soil with buttermilk so moss can grow.

If you want a solid patio floor with no cracks in it, you can lay your paving materials in concrete. This type of patio takes a lot of work, but you can do it yourself. First prepare and level the ground for the rough slab by tamping it and rolling it until it is quite firm when you walk on it. Then pour a 3-inch slab over it and float it level to a rough finish. If patio is above ground level, use boards, held by stakes driven in the ground, for a form. You can either mix your own concrete, as in Section 13.10, or if the patio is accessible to a big heavy truck, order ready-mixed concrete. When your slab has set, lay out your paving materials in the pattern you have decided on. Then mix small batches of mortar—one part sand, three parts cement, and one-fourth part lime—to lay one or two stones at a time in a ¾-inch-thick bed of mortar on your slab. Level and seat the stones or blocks as you go, and pack the joints with a slightly dryer mix of mortar.

If you want a plain concrete patio, you can pour colored concrete all in one operation. It's advisable to use reinforcing mesh in your slab to cut down any cracking that might occur. (Cracks around blocks and stones set in concrete are not noticeable.) For an interesting, textured effect, scrub the surface of your concrete slab with a stiff brush about twenty-four hours after the pour. This exposes the rough aggregate. Use a hose to wash away the surface sand and cement. If you plan to do this, use a very dry mix of concrete (see Sec. 13.10) and choose a good-looking gravel aggregate of fairly uniform stones. Pea gravel is very good for this.

13.4 | Making a wood deck. Figure 13-2 shows the typical framing of a wood deck. Working up from the ground on the downhill side, the deck is built as follows:

1. Concrete footings (Sec. 10.9) are placed below frost line at 8-foot intervals along the outline of the deck. Then piers of either concrete or concrete block are brought up to about one foot above the ground. The block is solidly mortared in—see Section 13.10—and the piers are backfilled.

2. With a star drill (a hand drill you hit with a hammer), holes are bored in the tops of the piers so you can set in anchor pins. (If your piers are concrete, pour the concrete with the anchor pins in place.) Fasten the pin solidly in the block with mortar.

3. Bore a 3- or 4-inch-deep hole, the diameter of the pin, in the foot of 4 x 4 posts that will reach the underside of the double 2 x 8 girders. Erect the 4 x 4's and brace them in position with boards nailed to stakes driven in the ground.

4. Toenail the double 2 x 8 girder into position on top of the 4 x 4's. Along the wall of the house a 2 x 6 with its ledger strip should be lag-bolted in place. (Holes are drilled through the siding and into the box joist for the lag bolts, which are turned down tight on the 2 x 6 with a wrench.) The joint between the top edge of the 2 x 6 and the siding should be well caulked to prevent water getting behind it. Be sure to place girder and ledger so the 2 x 8 floor joists that will rest on them will be perfectly level. If the distance between girder and ledger is more than twelve feet, you'll have to use 2 x 10's.

5. Single 2 x 8's are then placed in position and toenailed to the girder and ledger strip. The ends of the 2 x 8's should be notched to rest on the ledger strips. Place the 2 x 8's every four feet.

6. Nail in place the 2 x 6 boards forming the deck, leaving ¼-inch space for drainage between the boards. To finish the job, fasten a railing to the floor deck and the outer 2 x 10 girder.

If you are going to build a wood deck, you will have to get a building permit (see Introduction, "The law and your house") and follow the requirements of your local building department. If the requirements differ from the system described above, you'll be told what changes you have to make.

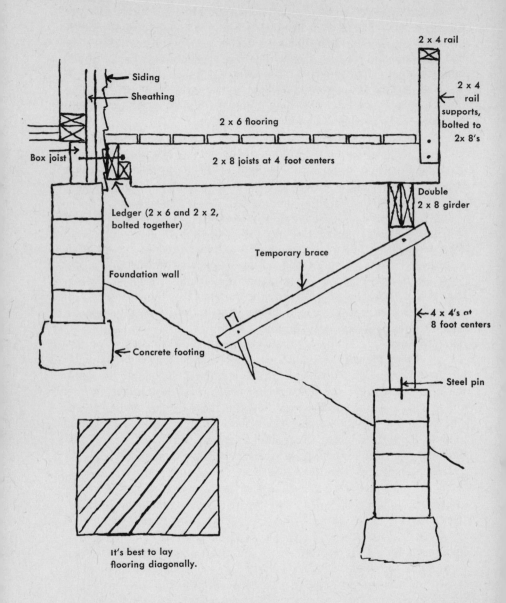

Figure 13-2 labels:

2 x 4 rail

2 x 4 rail supports, bolted to 2x 8's

Siding

Sheathing

2 x 6 flooring

Box joist

2 x 8 joists at 4 foot centers

Ledger (2 x 6 and 2 x 2, bolted together)

Double 2 x 8 girder

Temporary brace

Foundation wall

4 x 4's at 8 foot centers

Concrete footing

Steel pin

It's best to lay flooring diagonally.

Figure 13-2   Wood deck framing

When you've checked with your building department, you should make a careful plan for the work so you can determine exactly the position of each part, and take off an accurate list of materials.

It's often more attractive to lay your floor boards at an angle. Your lumber dealer can give you some pamphlets and suggestions on deck design. Whatever you decide on, make sure all your lumber is treated with a wood preservative (whether you are going to paint the deck or not) and use only galvanized nails.

13.5 | How to roof in a patio or porch. Patio roofs can be built to keep out the rain and the sun, or to keep out the rain and let in the sun, or just to keep out the sun. Reinforced plastics let the light in but keep the weather out. A solid roof of sheathing and shingles can be used to keep out both rain and sun (with the sides open, cooling breezes can come through to keep the patio cool). Or you can build a deep latticework of wide boards on edge to keep all but the overhead sun out of your patio and to make interesting patterns of shade on the patio floor. Or you can build a simple lattice and grow vines across it to get a soft filtered light on your patio all day long. Choose your roof according to what climate you live in and when you want to use your patio. Whatever type you decide on, you will probably need a building permit. (See Introduction, "The law and your house.")

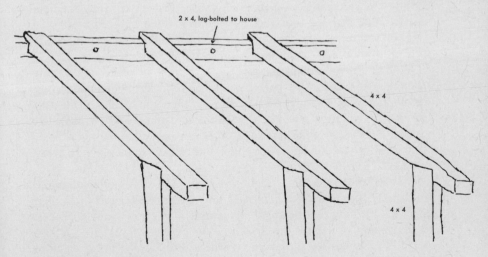

Figure 13-3   Porch roof framing

Figure 13-3 shows the basic framing for any of the patio roof systems mentioned above. It's essentially the same as the framing for a wood deck—see Section 13.4 and Figure 13-2—but it's a lot lighter. The 2 x 4 ledger is lag-bolted to the house and the rafters are notched to fit over it and nailed in place. If your roof is to be waterproof you will have to flash the joint between roofing and siding. (See Fig. 11-2.) If your roof will be an open lattice, be sure to caulk between the ledger and the siding. Figure 13-4 shows a few kinds of both open and closed patio roofs.

13.6 | Screening in a porch or patio. In most climates screening is necessary for complete protection from insects. Even if you have open roofing, you can use screening in combination with it—the screening is merely stapled to the top of the roof framework. The best screening to use for porches and patios is plastic—it won't corrode, and it comes in rolls up to 6 feet wide.

When you get ready to screen in the sides of your porch or patio, you will have to provide a wooden frame at the base to which you can attach the screen, if there isn't a base there already. Framing for screening is roughly like framing for a simple porch roof (Fig. 13-3). It's best to staple screening every 3 feet along the wall, even if you are using screening 6 feet wide. If your posts are every 6 feet, you can install intermediate supports at mid-points by nailing them to the wooden base. (If you have posts every 8 feet, you can get by with stapling up screening at 4-foot intervals. Just install intermediate supports, and buy a 4-foot-wide screening.)

You will also need additional framing members around door openings. Buy ready-made doors and install the framing to fit.

When you're ready to staple the screening in place, it's easiest if you have a helper. One person can hold the roll of screening while the other staples. Put a broom handle through the center of the roll and pull the roll tight after one end of the screening has been fastened in place—then staple the rest of it. You can rent a stapling gun from the hardware store if you don't have one. Place staples about every 6 inches.

If you want removable screening, have your lumber yard make up big screen panels (like giant window screens) that will fit against stops in your framed openings. Of course, if you are an experienced carpenter you can do this yourself.

13.7 | Fences for patios and gardens. You may want a fence to give privacy, to provide decoration, to serve as a windbreak, or to

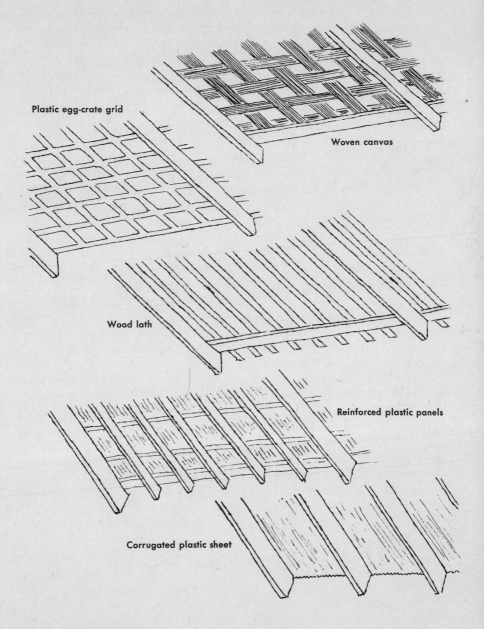

Plastic egg-crate grid

Woven canvas

Wood lath

Reinforced plastic panels

Corrugated plastic sheet

Figure 13-4   Types of patio roofs

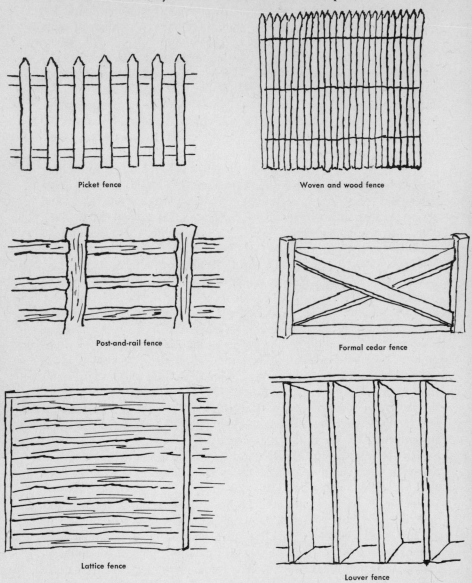

Picket fence

Woven and wood fence

Post-and-rail fence

Formal cedar fence

Lattice fence

Louver fence

Figure 13-5   Fences

give shade from the late afternoon sun. A good masonry fence will even keep out the street noises. Figure 13-5 shows a number of types of fences.

The big chore in building wood fences is setting the posts. They should be set down about 2 to 3 feet in the ground. If you are using wood posts, put some wood preservative on them before you set them in place, and use a level to be sure they're absolutely vertical. Many types of wood fences can be purchased ready to be assembled from your lumber dealer, but you may find it just as simple to assemble your own.

For fences of masonry block (which may be laid in interesting designs to admit light and air), the concrete footing must go down below the frost line. It should be twice as thick as the wall, and about as deep as the wall is thick. See Section 13.10 for working with concrete and masonry. In soft areas, footings should settle a week or two before the fence is built. Be sure the footing is level before you begin. (If it isn't, bring it to level with mortar.) Lay blocks with mortar, checking alignment with a carpenter's level as you work.

13.8 | Landscaping, flower boxes, and borders. Trees, flowers, and shrubs are the best decoration a patio can have. If you have a good tree or two where you're going to place the patio, don't move it or cut it down. Build a well around it—Section 13.2—if your patio floor will be above existing ground. Or, if the floor will be at ground level, be sure the paving around the tree will let plenty of water get to the tree. Usually bricks or stones laid concentrically around the tree, with no earth or sand in the joints, will do the job well and attractively.

The easiest way to handle shrubs and flowers is to build simple planter boxes. These are usually simple surrounds of 2 x 12's. They look like a box made of 2 x 12 stock (see Fig. 13-6) but the bottom of the box is left out so water can leach down through the soil and out under the patio floor to keep the soil fresh. (A tight bottom in the box would make the soil sour and soon kill the plants.) When making your planter boxes, be sure to treat wood with a wood preservative. Drill nail holes (slightly larger than your nails) so you don't split the boards. Use galvanized nails, and paint the boxes with exterior house paint. If you prefer, you can of course buy clay pots or other ready-made planters at your nursery.

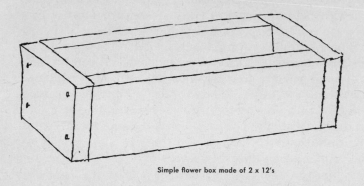

Simple flower box made of 2 x 12's

To edge flower border, use carpenter's square to lay out corners and fasten guide lines to stakes in ground.

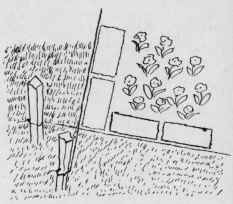

Dig up sod with edger, along guide line, to depth of block. Then lay blocks in place.

Figure 13-6   Flower boxes and borders

If you want flower borders at the edge of your patio, or other flower beds in the yard, you can edge them with the same type of paving material that you use on the patio floor. For instance, a patio block edge, shown in Figure 13-6, is simply installed with an edger, a line, and a square. The topsoil is removed with the edger to the depth of the block's thickness, and the line of blocks is installed. The lawn mower can run right up on the blocks, too, which eliminates clipping the edges around the border.

13.9 | Outdoor wiring for the patio. If you plan to use your patio at night, you will need extra outlets. (You may want them for cooking and for other appliances, too.) For technical information on installing outdoor outlets, see Section 2.12.

Over-all lighting for your patio should be placed high, shining as straight down as possible to avoid glare. Flower and shrub lighting should be from low lamps near the ground with mushroom-type caps to reflect light back down to the flowers.

If you want to enjoy hi-fi outdoors, you can install a waterproof jack in your outside wall so that a small outdoor speaker can be plugged into your regular system.

An electric bug trap—there are a number now on the market—plugged in to an exterior outlet is a good idea if your patio is not screened. In many climates these will actually take the place of screening.

13.10 | Fireplaces and barbecues. An outdoor fireplace is not only useful for cooking—it can also raise the temperature just enough to make you comfortable outdoors on a cool evening.

Plan the location of your fireplace so it doesn't interfere with foot traffic, so wind will carry smoke away from the house, and so there is plenty of room for accessory equipment around it. The design of a barbecue can be extremely simple, but be sure to make the cooking surface movable—or have more than one—so it can be adjusted up or down as required. Plans for barbecues and fireplaces are available from your masonry supply dealer as well as in shelter magazines and how-to books.

When you have decided on a plan you like, probably the first thing you should get or borrow is a mortar tub. This is a big steel tub about 1 foot deep, 3 feet wide, and 5 or 6 feet long, with sloped ends. It's an invaluable aid in any masonry or concrete job you decide to tackle.

For the base or slab of your barbecue, you will use concrete. Concrete is usually mixed one part cement, two parts sand, and four parts gravel, plus enough water to make it workable. Cement comes in 80- or 90-pound sacks roughly equal to one cubic foot. Sand and gravel are sold by the cubic yard (27 cubic feet). All are available from your masonry supply dealer.

Mortar is used for laying in the bricks or blocks. Mortar is mixed one part ready-mixed mortar to three parts sand. If you can't get ready-mixed mortar, or already have a bag of cement, you can use cement but add ¼ part hydrated lime to it. Add only enough water so you can trowel the mixture out to shape and have it hold the shape. (Mix your mortar with a hoe and get a mason's trowel, for spreading, at your hardware store.) Using an 80-pound sack of mortar, this mix will give you about enough mortar to lay 250 bricks or 40 concrete blocks. With a little practice with the trowel—placing mortar on edges of brick or block, then setting the next one in place —you'll be doing good masonry work in no time.

When you are ready to begin, remove topsoil so your barbecue slab will be at ground level. If your soil is well drained, you can pour a 4-inch slab on undisturbed soil. Use boards held in place by stakes to get a good straight edge. If the soil is not well drained or if it's filled in, use a layer of expanded metal lath or wire mesh for reinforcing the slab. An alternative is to tamp the soil firmly, lay

Figure 13-7　A simple barbecue

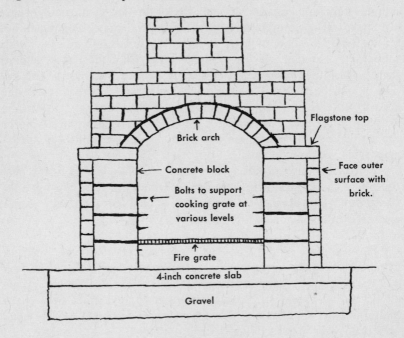

down a 6-inch gravel base, and then pour the 4-inch slab without reinforcing. Another alternative: Lay out bricks in the tamped soil about 2 inches apart, then lay small, ⅜-inch steel reinforcing rods between the bricks. Finally, fill the space between the bricks and around the rods full of concrete.

Float the concrete to a fairly smooth surface and smooth it with a steel trowel. Leave it rough at the outside edges, where the walls of the fireplace will be.

After twenty-four hours, you can put boards down on the slab to walk on while you build the barbecue. Build the solid masonry masses with concrete block and mortar, facing them with brick. Fill the holes in the block with sand and mortar to give the barbecue mass that will hold the heat in for good cooking and let it radiate heat out on cold nights long after the fire itself has died down. Smooth the joints between bricks with a joint tool. (See Fig. 12-2.)

Figure 13-7 shows a typical simple barbecue. The front of the chimney over the grate can be made with an angle iron supporting the brick and spanning from side to side of the base, or it can be

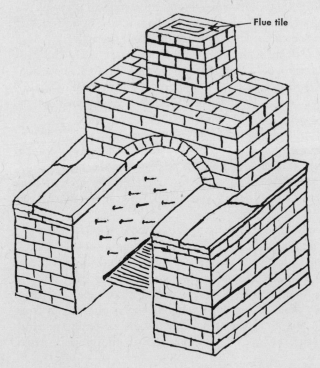

Flue tile

made of an arch of bricks. In this case, make a wood form for the arch and lay the first course of bricks around the wood form. After the chimney is completed, the arch is withdrawn.

13.11 | How to make a patio cooler. In hot climates, or in patios that soak up the hot sun all day, you may need to make some provision for cooling. The first thing to do is to provide shade. (See Sec. 13-5, "How to Roof in a Patio or Porch," and 13.7, "Fences for Patios and Gardens.") In the long run, shade from trees may prove more satisfactory, for trees let in the winter sun but screen out summer sun with their leaves. Ask your local nursery for advice.

When planning roofs and fences for shade, be sure to provide sufficient ventilation so air can circulate freely. If there is a prevailing breeze, your patio should make the most of it. If you are installing a solid roof, use a reflective surface, such as aluminum or white asphalt shingles, to bounce much of the sun's heat away.

Another thing you can do to make the patio cooler is to build a wading pool or fish pool. (See next section.) Evaporative cooling can take away as much as 50 per cent of the sun's heat energy. You can increase this cooling effect even more by installing a sprinkling nozzle (like a small fountain) in the pool. The nozzle can be fastened to the end of a plastic pipe that is embedded through the floor of the wading pool, rising slightly above the top water level. The plastic pipe is run underground to come out near an outdoor faucet. Connect plastic pipe to the faucet with a short length of hose and turn the sprinkler off and on at the faucet. (See Sec. 1.40 for instructions on working with plastic pipe.)

13.12 | Wading or fish pools and sandboxes. To make a wading or fish pool successful you must make satisfactory drainage arrangements. This is easy if you can plan the location of the pool so that the bottom of the pool is still higher than some nearby ground—see below. If your ground is all level, you will have to make more complicated drainage arrangements.

Figure 13-8 shows how a simple wading pool is built. First the earth is carefully dug out and shaped by hand, using a shovel. Disturb as little as possible of the soil you want to leave under the pool. You can dig to a prearranged shape or, if you have very big rocks in your ground you may want to let these dictate the shape. Dig deep enough so that the finished depth of water in the pool will run from 8 inches to a foot. Dig a narrow trench for the plastic drainpipe from the pool to a nearby ditch, drain, or low spot in the ground. Make

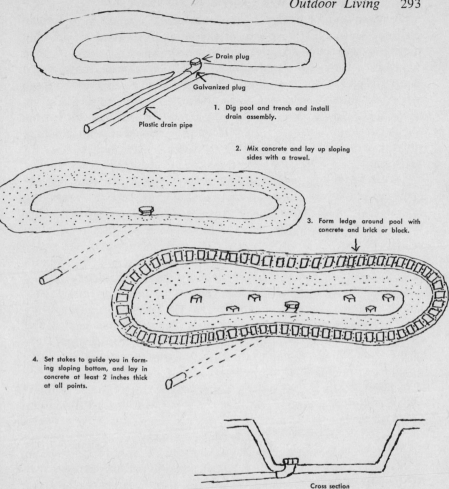

Drain plug

Galvanized plug

Plastic drain pipe

1. Dig pool and trench and install drain assembly.

2. Mix concrete and lay up sloping sides with a trowel.

3. Form ledge around pool with concrete and brick or block.

4. Set stakes to guide you in forming sloping bottom, and lay in concrete at least 2 inches thick at all points.

Cross section

Figure 13-8   A simple wading pool

sure the trench slopes away from the pool, and keep its length as short as possible. If the pipe is to empty into a low spot in the yard, you'll need to install a splash block to keep the water from washing away the grass.

When you've finished digging, install the galvanized elbow, drain plug, and plastic pipe drain in the bottom of the pool and to the end of the trench. Be sure top of elbow is 2 inches above soil level in bottom of pool.

Then mix cement and sand one to three in a mortar tub—see Section 13.10—and start laying up the sloping walls of the pool with a trowel. Then place the ledge around the pool, setting into it patio block or stone. (If you want absolutely vertical sides, you'll have to make forms for them before pouring the concrete.) When the sides and ledge are formed, set stakes in the bottom to guide you in placing concrete. Arrange the stakes so there will be a pitch from every point down to the drain plug. (Check stakes with a level.) Then put in your concrete, bringing it to an even depth above the stakes. (It should be at least 2 inches thick at all points.)

Wait two weeks before using the pool. The next season you can paint it with epoxy pool paint—ask your paint dealer. When you fill the pool, add some Chlorox to keep down marine growth.

A sandbox flush with lawn or patio can be built in exactly the same way, omitting the drain and the concrete bottom.

13.13 | Swimming pools. You should not try to build a swimming pool yourself. (You would find it easier to build a summer cottage.) Get a good contractor and a good contract. If you don't know much about contracts, have your lawyer examine it for you.

When planning a pool remember that level ground, not too low, is the best location. (Hillside pools can be very expensive.) If you have a lot of groundwater you will need extra underground drainage around the foundations of the pool. Pools should not be built on filled land—they should rest on undisturbed firm ground. Try to get the pool into the sun so you can enjoy it earlier in the spring and later in the fall. Keep it away from large trees or it will be full of sticks, leaves, and bugs.

Plan for at least 4 feet of walking space around the sides of the pool, more if you can. Locate it close to utilities so that it is easily accessible from the house. You should have high fences to insure privacy and safety. (Fences serve as windbreaks, too.)

Provide space for and be sure you get a filtering, skimming, and vacuum system with your pool. These should be housed not more than twenty feet from the pool. If you don't filter your water, but replace it every two weeks, your water bill may run over the cost of a filtering system in two seasons.

If you want to take all the headaches out of pool ownership, you should consider getting a maintenance contract with a swimming pool company.

If you already have a pool but its sides are badly worn, ask a contractor about getting a sprayed-on, reinforced plastic surface. If it needs patching in just a few spots, use a good pool-patching compound and paint it with epoxy pool paint.

14 USING YOUR ATTIC

14.1 | Planning to use attic space. If you have an unfinished attic in your house you are not taking full advantage of the space you have. Attics are usually more desirable as living areas than basements, because humidity, ventilation, and lack of sunlight are not the problems they are in basements. An attic fan with a ridge vent (or an air conditioner in hot climates) can keep the attic comfortable even on hot days. An attic can provide ideal space for bedrooms, playrooms, or studios.

If you have a so-called "expansion attic" you are lucky, because the necessary dormers are probably already in, and the builder may have provided wiring and rough plumbing. If you have an unfinished attic in an old house there will be more work, but you are likely to have a lot more choice in laying out and planning rooms and windows.

There are a number of points you should keep in mind at the planning stage. If the attic is to be divided into more than one room, you should not have to go through one room to get to another. If attic space is limited, you can get more space by planning to have beds and dresser drawers that slide out of built-in pockets under the eaves or edges of the attic. (See Chap. 16.)

Attic living space will be satisfactory only if the roof ridge is at least nine feet above the floor, because there must be a ventilated air space above the attic ceiling to keep the attic cool under the hot roof in summer. (See Section 14.4.)

If there isn't enough light and air in the attic, you can increase the size of the gable-end windows (Sec. 8.34), or you can put gable-end windows in if you don't have any (Sec. 8.31), or you can put in skylights (Sec. 8.35). Or you can get increased space as well as increased light by adding dormers (Sec. 14.5).

If there is no provision for heating in the attic now (look to see if there are any floor registers up there), the cheapest way to provide heat in most cases is to have a qualified electrical contractor install radiant heat. This requires only a new cable from your service entrance up to the attic—there is no chopping and patching to install new ductwork to the attic. If you live in a mild climate, you may be able to omit heating the attic—just insulate heavily and keep the attic door open on cold days—warm air rises.

Don't forget to plan on some electrical outlets and switches in your new attic space. Usually a complete new circuit is necessary to serve the attic, and a licensed electrician should put it in for you unless you're pretty good with tools. (See Chap. 2.)

Although a bathroom in the attic can be expensive if you don't have an expansion attic with the rough plumbing already there, it can be installed. In planning the location of the attic bathroom, remember it should be accessible to all the bedrooms in the attic. To cut plumbing costs as much as possible, it should be placed over an existing bathroom. If you are handy at plumbing, and your community codes allow it, you can do the work yourself. (See Secs. 1.39 and 1.40). Otherwise, have a plumber install the rough plumbing, and put the fixtures in yourself if you want to. If you are planning a full bath, remember that the minimum size is 5 feet by 7 feet. (See Sec. 17.4 for ideas on bathroom planning.)

Before you begin any work on the attic, you should have planned every step, from the installation of windows and dormers to the treatment of finished walls. Don't rush into it. Finishing an attic is a big job, one which will cost you several hundred dollars, but it should increase the value of your house by far more than you put into it.

14.2 | Access to the attic. An attic stairway should open from a hall downstairs, not from a bedroom. It should open into a foyer or hall in the attic—not into a bedroom. (If the attic is to serve as a one-room playroom or studio, of course this isn't important.)

If your present stairway doesn't fit these specifications, you may want to remodel or build a new stairway—or have a carpenter do it for you. (See Secs. 7.9 and 7.10.) In most cases you shouldn't attempt to create the staircase opening yourself, because this involves major structural changes. If you can use the opening that is already there, you can design and cut your own new stairway or have it precut at your lumber dealer's.

If your only attic access is through a trap door, and there isn't room to install a regular stairway, you can put in a folding stairway from your lumber dealer's or mail-order house. (This type of attic probably won't be suitable for living space, but can be much im-

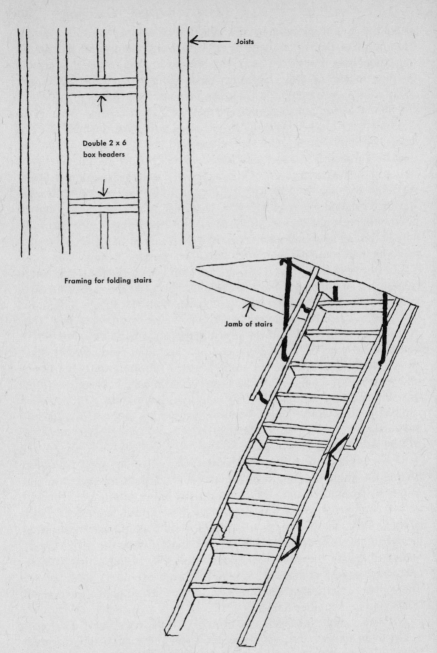

Joists

Double 2 x 6
box headers

Framing for folding stairs

Jamb of stairs

Figure 14-1 Folding stairs

298

proved as a storage area by the addition of folding stairs.) Folding stairs are installed by nailing the jamb sections (that come as part of the completely assembled unit) to the joists that frame in the box opening in the ceiling. (See Fig. 14-1.) Hangers on the stairs are adjusted for variations in ceiling height. A ceiling panel of plywood covers the ceiling opening when the stairs are folded up.

14.3 | Putting a floor in the attic. If your attic doesn't already have a floor, but has only exposed ceiling joists, of course the first step is to install a subfloor that you can walk on and work on. Low-cost 1 x 6 tongue-and-groove boards or rough plywood will serve very well for this. Nail the 1 x 6's diagonally across the ceiling joists. If you are using plywood, be sure to us "H" clips (ask your lumber dealer) to hold the end edges of ⅜- and ½-inch-thick plywood subfloor together where the edges do not lie over joists. The long side edges of plywood sheets should meet over joists

. If the attic is being made into children's bedrooms or a playroom, you will probably want to deaden the noise as much as possible. The best way to do this is to use a number of layers in your floor, alternately hard and soft—and they should be glued together, not nailed. Over the subfloor you might put down a layer of fiberboard sheathing material, then another layer of ⅜-inch-thick plywood, each glued to the layer beneath with mastic from your flooring supply dealer. For the top layer use resilient flooring or wood blocks set in mastic—see Sections 7.10 through 7.19.

Leave the installation of finish flooring until the end of your remodeling job so it will not be scarred by the carpentry work that will be done to finish the attic.

14.4 | Ventilating the attic. When the floor is in, make provision for attic ventilation before going ahead with remodeling plans. No attic can be really comfortable unless the parts of the attic behind and above walls and ceilings (as well as within the finished attic space) can be ventilated. Figure 5-1 shows the ridge vent that should be used to insure ventilation of the hot space above the attic ceiling. Section 5.1 details other measures you can take to ventilate the attic. Louvers should be used in the small gable ends of the space above the ceiling so air can rush through the louvers and up out of the ridge vent.

In many homes built within the last few years there are vents at the soffit of the roof. (See Fig. 11-10.) These supplement louver vents in the gable ends. Air enters through the screened soffit vents, rises up behind the walls of the attic rooms and out the ridge vent. When you are insulating the attic be sure you do not cover these soffit vents if you have them.

14.5 | Adding windows and dormers, or enlarging those that are already there, is the next phase in attic remodeling. To put in a new gable-end window, see Section 8.31. To enlarge a gable-end window that is already there, see Section 8.34. To put in a skylight, see Section 8.35.

If you need more space as well as more light, you can add dormers. Placing new dormers in your attic will depend not only on room arrangement—each room should have at least two windows, to provide for cross ventilation and light—but on the appearance from the outside. Your house won't look the same after you have added dormers and windows. A dormer should not be too big for the roof, and should be set in from the ends of the roof. Make a drawing of how the finished house will look; if you can't do this yourself, have someone do it for you, or make an enlarged photograph and trace over it before you decide. Any dormers you add will require a building permit. (See Introduction, "The law and your house.") Unless you are extremely competent you should not attempt to install a dormer yourself; call in a contractor.

If you have sufficient space in the attic, but need additional light and air, you will probably want to install at least two small dormers. If you lack sufficient headroom, it is possible to install a shed dormer along one whole side of the house. If this is visible from the street, however, you should consider it carefully, for the appearance of your house will be drastically altered (and in most cases, it won't be for the better).

Figure 14-2 shows how a shed dormer is installed. Any smaller dormer is installed the same way. Your old roof is left in place, except for holes at the peak and eave and one on each side, until the new dormer gets a weatherproof roof on it. At night, roofing felt is draped over the holes to keep out rain or snow.

Briefly, here is how the job is done: First, the eave edge of the old roof is cut away with a power saw to reveal the top plate of the wall beneath. Then the front studs for the dormer are erected with their top plate. The side-wall top plate is then installed—it ties the front studs to the existing roof rafters. Then the ridge of the old roof is opened up and dormer rafters are put in alongside the old rafters and nailed to the ridge beam. Next, the dormer is roofed over and

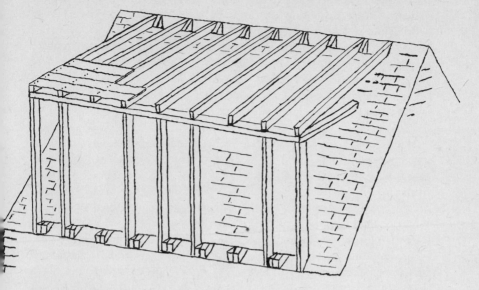

Figure 14-2   Framing a shed dormer

vent pines extended up through it and flashed (Fig. 11-2) if there
are vent pipes. Shingles are applied as in Chapter 11.

If the dormer is a small dormer whose rafters do not reach the
ridge, they are nailed to a header running between the two side
rafters. This is just like the framed opening for a stairway (Fig. 14-1)
or for a skylight (Fig. 8-24). The studs for the front wall of a small
dormer rest on the lower side of this framed opening rather than
on the top plate of the wall below.

Existing rafters at the sides of the dormer are usually doubled,
because the side wall of the dormer rests on them.

When the dormer roof is finished, the old roof and rafters within
the dormer are cut out and removed. Then windows, sheathing, and
siding are installed. (See Secs. 8.31 and 12.2.) The dormer side-wall
siding is carefully flashed into the roof shingles as shown in
Figure 11-2.

**14.6 | Framing ceilings, knee walls, built-ins, and wall parti-
tions.** Figure 14-3 shows how framing is installed for attic ceilings
and knee-wall partitions (which usually are about 4 feet high) under
the sloping attic ceilings. The framing members are nailed to all

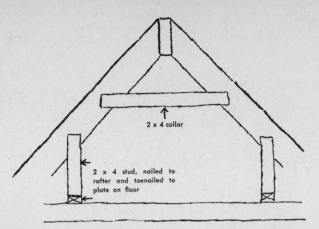

2 x 4 collar

2 x 4 stud, nailed to
rafter and toenailed to
plate on floor

Figure 14-3   Attic framing

existing rafters, which means they should be at 16-inch intervals.

At this point, make provision for any built-in furniture you plan to have by building it right into the knee wall. Dressers, bookcases, closets, and so on may be designed so that their front is part of the wall—the storage unit extends behind into the knee-wall space, saving valuable floor area. Chapter 16 describes how you can build in this type of unit.

When the knee walls are in place, prefabricate and install the framing for wall partitions, if there are to be any. (See Sec. 6.31.)

If plumbing, wiring, and heating work has not already been completed, make sure it is finished at this stage. (See Sec. 14.1.)

14.7 | Insulating and finishing. Ask your lumber dealer's advice about what insulation to use. The heavier the insulation, the cooler the attic will be in summer and the warmer in winter. Fit the insulation carefully in every stud space in your knee-wall partitions and ceiling, and around pipes and electrical boxes. You don't actually have to insulate behind built-in furniture (they provide a certain amount of insulation themselves), but it's better to do so.

You can use batt-type insulation with a vapor barrier flange, which is stapled to the faces of the studs (Fig. 14-4), or you can use a new type of insulation that simply comes as a semirigid blanket of glass fibers. You can tear this with your hands and stuff it into any crack or stud space. With this type of insulation it may be necessary to use drywall with an aluminum-foil backing to serve as a vapor barrier—but if the space behind walls is properly ventilated with ridge vent and louvers or soffit vents, you probably won't have to.

302

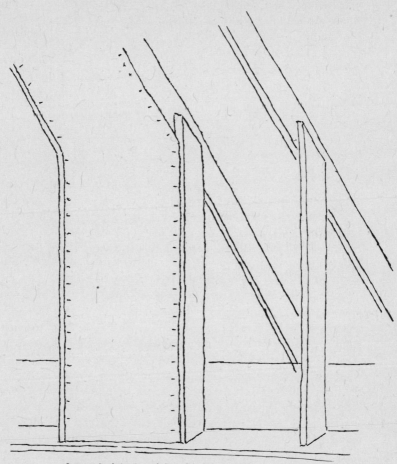

Batt-type insulation is stapled in place between knee-wall studs, collar beams, and sloping ceiling rafters.

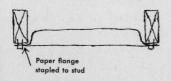

Paper flange
stapled to stud

Figure 14-4   How to insulate

When all insulation is in place, install ceiling tiles or drywall (Secs. 6.26 and 6.27) and surface the walls with drywall (Sec. 6.32) or paneling (Secs. 6.19 through 6.21). Install doors as in Chapter 8. Then finish and decorate as in Chapter 6.

Finally, install finish flooring as in Chapter 7, Sections 7.15 through 7.21.

15 USING YOUR BASEMENT

15.1 | Planning basement space. If you have a basement that is partially above grade, it's quite possible that it can be put to excellent use as a family room, playroom, hobby area, etc. The amount of use you can get from it depends principally on two things: its freedom from dampness and the amount of daylight it has or can be made to have.

If your basement is dry and light and you can spend several hundred dollars on it (no matter how thrifty you are, it will be a fairly expensive proposition). The first thing to do is to plan the use of the space. If it's a full basement, you can divide it into several rooms if you want to. If a bathroom or darkroom are included in your plan, locate these at existing plumbing lines to save trouble and expense. If possible, the bathroom should be near the outside door.

Remember that the main area—the family room or playroom in most cases—should be the most accessible from outside and from upstairs. The stairway should open into it so you don't have to go through any unfinished areas to get to it.

If there are to be room partitions, try to place them under the center girder so the lally columns will be hidden. If there are no wall partitions, you can still enclose or decorate lallys to make them look like part of the decoration.

15.2 | How to keep the dampness and water out. If you have dampness in your basement all the time, or if you have water there seasonally, read Sections 10.1 through 10.3. Cracks and holes must be sealed with mortar, and you may have to waterproof the foundation on the outside. If the entire floor leaks, you will have to cover it wall to wall with waterproofing compound and pour a new concrete slab over it.

Even with all these measures, most basements have a relatively damp atmosphere part of the time—particularly in the summer. If yours does, you will certainly have to install adequate ventilating fans, an air conditioner, or a dehumidifier if the basement is to be used as a living area. If you don't want to go to this expense you may as well forget about doing over your basement. In some cases, no matter what you do, you just can't entirely get the musty atmosphere out of the basement.

Don't try to use a damp basement. Damp basements are not even suitable for photographic darkrooms, because the moisture will rust your expensive equipment and ruin your photographic paper.

15.3 | Making more light in a basement. No matter how good a job you do on artificial lighting, no room is ever satisfactory unless it is well lighted by natural light during the day. If yours is an old-fashioned basement with small, high windows, it probably will never be satisfactory as a playroom or family room. A dark, dingy room is never attractive and will not be used much, no matter how much you spend to decorate and equip it.

If your basement is partially above grade, you can probably enlarge windows or add new ones to get the needed window area, and unless your basement is unusually light you will certainly want to increase the window area.

You can enlarge a basement window by removing the old window and using a cold chisel and hammer (on concrete block) or an electric hammer (on poured concrete). You can probably borrow the electric hammer from your hardware dealer, or rent it. You will probably destroy the old window in removing it, but be sure you don't damage the continuous sill of wood that supports the wall framing above. (The sill runs along the top of the foundation wall.) Be sure that the new sash you get is suitable for use in the basement, and find out from your lumber dealer just how it should be installed. Most basement sash can be concreted (with a trowel) into the new opening with a 3-to-1 mix of sand and cement (plus enough water to make it workable). Keep the mix as stiff as possible so you can work it freely. For some sash, it is necessary to concrete in a wooden surround to which the sash is later attached.

It's also possible to cut new windows into your foundation walls. Average-sized windows and doors can usually be placed in any foundation wall; wider ones can be made only in the two foundation walls that run in the same direction as the floor joists. Large openings in the other two walls require placing a girder at the top of the opening. Don't attempt this yourself. In fact, if you are at all doubtful of your ability to make even a small window in a foundation wall, you should have a contractor do it for you.

If the space above grade does not give you enough room for satisfactory window openings, you can grade back the earth outside the foundation wall so it is about a foot below where the bottom of the window opening will be. But you must be sure this doesn't form a pocket where water can collect—you'll have to continue your grading until you come to a spot where water can run off.

If you have a basement wall entirely above grade, or nearly so (so that it can be graded as above), you can convert the entire area into a glass wall. This work should be done by a qualified contractor, and a building permit may be required—see Introduction, "The law and your house."

15.4 | Refurbishing basement stairs. If you make your basement into a living area, the stairs will get a lot more traffic. Make sure they are completely safe and sound (Secs. 7.7 through 7.10) and that they are well lighted. If there are no risers, install them. Just cut risers out of pine boards and nail them through treads from above and below the stairs. Then put up a railing—you can get the parts ready-made at any lumberyard. Boxing the stairs in underneath can also give you an attractive storage area.

15.5 | Basement walls, ceilings, and floors. When you are ready to decorate, the first thing to tackle is the walls. The cheapest solution, which you should use only if you have a very dry basement, is simply to paint the walls with emulsion paint—a water paint that "breathes," or lets moisture in the wall get through. Pick a paint specifically recommended for basements.

However, your basement will be far more finished if you fur out the walls (Sec. 6.19 and Fig. 6-14) and install drywall or paneling. Be sure all framing is absolutely true and straight. Box in unsightly pipes and meters (be sure you leave access where needed, though) and frame in any built-in closets or other storage units. (See Chap. 16.) Insulate pipes to eliminate condensation (Fig. 1-19). If additional wiring is to be installed, do it at this stage. If there are any wall partitions, prefabricate them as in Section 6.32.

Install drywall or paneling and finish as in Chapter 6.

After the walls have been completed, you can do the ceiling. The best way to handle ceiling ducts and pipes is to hang furring strips below them as in Figure 15-1. If this would make the ceiling too low, you'll have to box them instead. Install outlet boxes and wiring for ceiling light fixtures before installing finish ceiling material. If the room is to be a playroom, the best choice is acoustic ceiling tile. (See Sec. 6.26.)

Floors can be finished with wood flooring, with asphalt tile, or with a masonry floor. (See Chap. 7.) Be sure to tell your flooring supply dealer that the material is to be used in a basement, and he'll tell you the proper method of installation.

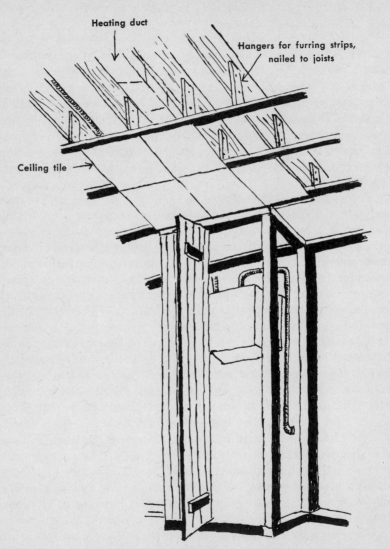

Figure 15-1   Framing basement ceiling and walls to conceal ducts, pipes, and utilities

16 STORAGE

16.1 | **If you need more storage space,** the first thing to do is to look over your existing closets, cabinets, and other storage units. Chances are you can increase storage by at least 50 per cent merely by getting maximum use out of the space you already have. Adding adjustable shelves, vertical dividers, drawers, or closet accessories (there is a special hook, rack, stand, or hanger for practically every item you own) can make a closet twice as useful. If you have empty spaces above books, cans, or china, you're not making the most of your shelf space.

The secret of good storage is in figuring out exactly where every item in the house should be stored, and then providing a suitable place for it. Everything should be stored at or near the place where it is used—toys in the playroom, table linens in the kitchen or dining room, outdoor clothes in the hall closet. In the kitchen, store foods, appliances, dishes, and linens where they are used. (Remember, however, that certain items, such as herbs, spices, starchs, and fruits keep best in a cool, airy spot, away from cooking steam.) Divide food and cleaning supplies by size as well as categories, so you can use tall shelves for tall cans and boxes, short shelves for smaller items. Remember that frequently used items should be easily accessible.

Figure out what kind of items you don't have room for, and then see if you can fit them into your existing storage facilities by adding shelves and accessories. If not, you can design new storage. In either case, the following sections will show you how to go about it.

16.2 | **Building storage is basic woodworking.** You can do some of the simplest things in this chapter with only a few simple tools and only a little knowledge. If you get very far into cabinet work, however, you will quickly learn how to work with tools and woods, and you'll want a set of basic woodworking equipment. It should include:

Claw hammer and nail set (tapered steel punch used for setting nails below surface—Fig. 7-2).

Carpenter's saw, keyhole saw (Fig. 7-9), hacksaw (Fig. 1-14)

Backsaw and miter box

Block plane (a short plane for trimming edges of boards)

Jointer plane (a big plane for getting flat edges on boards)

Surform (this looks like a plane but works like a rasp to smooth wood)

Wood rasp, rattail file, flat file, triangular file

Rachet brace and set of bits, including screwdriver bit (Fig. 7-5)

Hand drill and set of twist drills

Set of ordinary screwdrivers, rachet screwdriver, Phillips screwdriver for crosshead screws (Fig. 3-1)

Needlenose pliers, ordinary pliers, wirecutting pliers (Fig. 3-1)

Whittling knife, awl (to start screws in soft wood), sanding block, woodscraper, putty knife (Fig. 6-2)

Star drills for cutting holes in plaster and masonry

Woodworking vise, wood clamps

Adjustable square, carpenter's square (Fig. 12-6)

Carpenter's level (Fig. 8-20), plumb bob (Fig. 6-10), folding ruler

Chisels—2″, 1″, and ½″ wide (Fig. 6-2)

(Figure 16-1 shows most of these tools that have not already been illustrated in a previous chapter.)

If you plan to do a lot of woodworking and cabinetry, you should seriously consider buying a few power tools. They take all the drudgery out of the job. The most useful power tool you can buy is a radial saw. (See Fig. 16-1.) All-in-one tools are good, but they are hard to use. A radial saw can cut at any angle on a horizontal or vertical plane—and it can groove, shape, sand, drill, rout, plane, grind, buff, and even do jigsaw work with a special attachment. You'll find that you will use a radial saw on every job you tackle, once you get used to it.

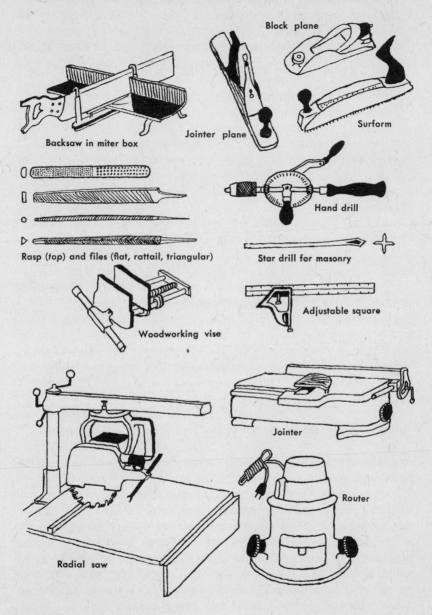

Block plane

Jointer plane

Surform

Backsaw in miter box

Hand drill

Rasp (*top*) and files (flat, rattail, triangular)

Star drill for masonry

Woodworking vise

Adjustable square

Jointer

Router

Radial saw

Figure 16-1   Woodworking tools

The next most important power tool is a jointer. This is essentially a motorized plane. It gives a true flat surface to any board. When you get the knack of it, you'll find that after every saw cut you'll put the board through the jointer to get a perfectly smooth edge. The jointer is also used for tapering boards and legs and for beveling edges of boards.

The third most useful power tool is a router. It's like a big power drill permanently set on a base. When cutting bits are put in it and pulled along as you move the router, you can shape moldings, cut grooves, make mortises, and (with a special jig) dovetail joints for cabinets and drawers.

Once you can use these three power tools and the hand tools listed above, you can make virtually any piece of cabinetry, and enjoy doing it.

16.3 | Joints and fasteners. The critical point in woodworking is the joining of two pieces of wood. Figure 16-2 shows the typical wood joints used in most cabinetry and storage units. The butt joint is obviously the easiest to make, the rabbeted miter joint the hardest.

The best way to fasten a joint is with glue and wood screws. Dry powdered glue or one of the new plastic glues from your hardware store is best. It is simply mixed with water. You can only glue surfaces that are quite smooth and evenly matched.

The next best fastener is wood screws alone. You should always drill a hole in the wood, slightly smaller than the screw, before inserting the screw. This prevents splitting the wood and shearing off the screws. In soft wood you can use an awl rather than a drill to make the holes, if the screws are small. For most cabinetry and storage, screws alone, without glue, will make perfectly satisfactory joints.

Nails are the easiest fasteners to use. The best kind are galvanized nails or cement-coated nails—their roughness makes them hold well. You can make simple but perfectly good wood drawers by butt-jointing front to sides and sides to back, and fastening with cement-coated nails. If you use finishing nails, the drawer may pull apart. (Finishing nails are slim nails with almost no head on them. They are used principally for tacking on finish moldings and in places where you will later putty over the heads.) In simple work, like bookshelves, big finishing nails can do a perfectly adequate job of butt-nailing through the uprights into the end of shelves.

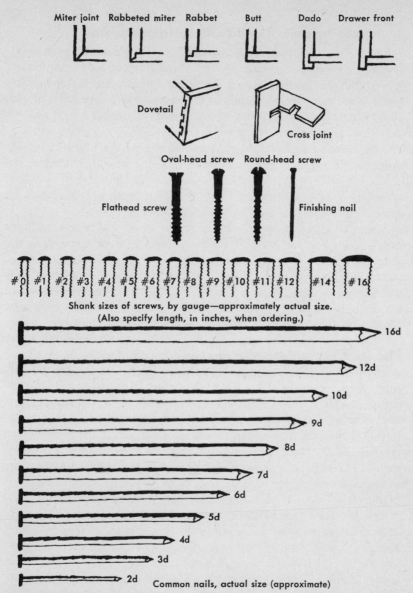

Figure 16-2   Types of joints and fasteners

In nearly all cases, hardware (hinges, handles, slides, knobs, angle brackets, etc.) should be screwed, rather than nailed, in place.

16.4 | Using stock units and hardware. Ready-made drawers, door, cabinets, and other storage units of steel, plastic, and wood

—finished or unfinished—are available to solve nearly any storage problem. But you will save money if you select just a few key units and build the rest of your storage around them. Mail-order houses, hardware dealers, and lumber dealers all carry ready-made cabinets and storage units, and they are easy to install.

If you are buying steel cabinets, make sure the cabinet doors are well insulated so that when you close them you don't hear a lot of noise. (Look for rubber bumpers near the catch.) Check the fit of drawers and try to get units with drawers that slide on nylon rollers. Find out if the cabinets have a baked-on finish. Don't install steel cabinets where they will be near moisture all the time.

In selecting ready-made wood storage units, remember that the thicker the wood, the better. The best wood is a lumber core with veneer on both sides. Its edges look like 3-ply plywood with a thick middle ply and thin exterior plys. This kind of wood is the least likely to warp. Check the fit of drawers and doors to see that there is no binding and no wide cracks. If cabinets are prefinished, be sure they are finished inside as well as out.

Of all the stock storage units you can buy ready-made, the most useful and handy are plastic drawers and their sliding hardware. You can build them into anything and they are one item that you cannot make yourself. (You can duplicate any ready-made wood storage unit in your own workshop, if you have the right tools and know how to use them.)

16.5 | Shelves. The easiest way to get more storage in the kitchen, pantry, or utility area, or for books or *objets d'art* or toys, is to add shelves. The best shelf material for the price is No. 2 shelving pine from your lumber yard. Figure 16-3 shows the basic ways of mounting shelves on the wall. Shelves supported by angle brackets fastened through plaster to the studs are good for utility rooms and workshops. Shelves supported by end-cleats are used in closets. The end-cleats can be nailed to studs or fixed to plaster with toggle bolts (Fig. 6-6).

In kitchen cabinets, shelves are usually hung by back cleats and front hangers that are tied to nailers bolted to the ceiling. The cabinet doors are mounted on the same hangers. Workshop shelves can be hung the same way, or their front edge can be supported by front hangers resting on the floor. Full-height cabinet doors, like broom closet doors, can be mounted on the front hanger if you want to close the shelves off.

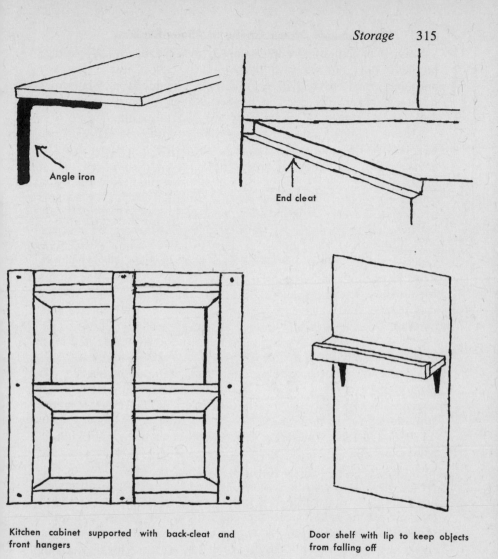

Angle iron

End cleat

Kitchen cabinet supported with back-cleat and front hangers

Door shelf with lip to keep objects from falling off

Figure 16-3   Mounting shelves

Shelves mounted on the inside of closet or cabinet doors should be fastened with small angle brackets and should be narrow. A small lip of wood nailed to the front of the shelf, before you put up the shelf, will keep things from falling off.

Figure 16-4 shows the basic methods for putting bookshelves together. Bookshelves should generally be made as a unit, like a

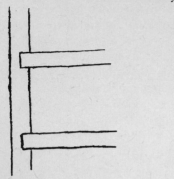

Dadoed shelf requires
power equipment.

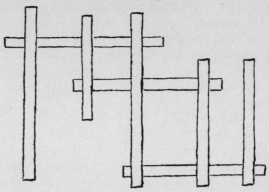

Cross-jointing is best way to make complicated shelf
designs. Only plywood can be used.

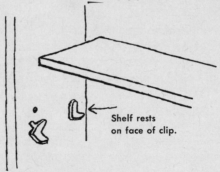

Shelf rests
on face of clip.

Use adjustable-shelf hardware for easy-to-
make shelves.

Figure 16-4   How bookshelves are made

piece of furniture, rather than being built in place. To make bookshelves in which the ends are dadoed into the uprights, you should
use either a power saw with a dado set of blades, or a router. If you
have no power equipment, you'll find it easiest to use adjustable shelf
hardware. This is simply screwed to the uprights and the shelves
are cut to length. You can also make adjustable shelves by boring
¼-inch holes in the uprights and setting the shelves on pins that fit
into the holes. If you make shelves by cross-jointing the various parts,
be sure to use plywood—pine will split open when used this way.

16.6 | Wall cabinets. You can convert a shelf to a cabinet merely by installing doors on it. If there are wood hangers simply nailed to the facing edge of the shelves, you can let them serve as the exposed cabinet front and hang doors between them. If the hangers are set into the facing edge of the shelves, you can make the cabinet front just one door after another, using pin hinges. A pin hinge swings a door out and open so it doesn't bind the adjacent door edge.

Cabinet doors can be either swinging or sliding. The best type of swinging door has rabbeted edges that lap over the cabinet frame, or front. (See Fig. 16-5.) If this type of door doesn't fit exactly, no one will ever know. Minor sags won't show either.

The best material to use for doors is regular cabinet door stock. This is called lumber-core stock—it has a core of boards glued together edge to edge, and faced with veneer on both sides. It takes a fine finish and is not likely to warp at all. Plywood doors will not warp either, but they don't take a good finish. For inexpensive doors you can use N. 2 shelving pine. If the door is to be wider than the stock, you can nail a piece about 4 inches wide to the back side, extending it an equal distance over the edges of the pieces to be joined. Drive in finishing nails that reach almost (but not quite) to the front of the door pieces. Or you can edge-glue two boards. If you do this, put both edges to be glued through your jointer to make them absolutely smooth, and use a two-part epoxy glue. Use clamps to hold them together tightly while the glue sets. (If pine doors warp, it is possible to straighten them out by fastening a stiff piece of plywood to the back of the door with screws in slots a little bigger than the screws themselves. This lets the door expand and contract through the seasons.)

Hinges, latches, handles, and knobs are available in a wide variety of styles for cabinets. Tell your hardware dealer the type of door you're using, so you get the right hinges. Rabbeted doors take "semi-concealed" hinges. Doors mounted in the opening, flush with the front of the cabinet, take cabinet, piano, antique, cottage, or plywood hinges. Plywood hinges can be used with any door stock, but of course are designed specifically for plywood doors.

When hanging cabinet doors in the winter—when wood has shrunk—allow the width of a paper match between paired doors. When hanging them in midsummer, the edges can touch because the doors are at their fullest width.

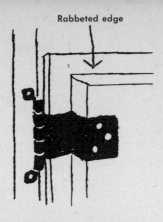

Rabbeted edge

Rabbeted door with semiconcealed hinge (door in open position)

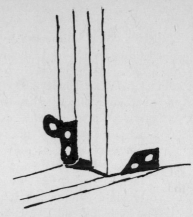

Flush door hung on recessed hanger with pin hinge

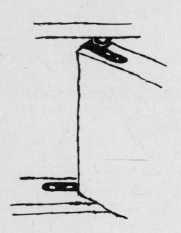

Flush door with cottage hinge

Flush door with pivot hinge

Figure 16-5   Cabinet doors

Sliding doors are useful for cabinets if you don't need the inside of the door for storage and never need to open both doors at once. They can be set in plastic channels, dadoed wood channels, aluminum channels, or equipped with a fiber shoe that rides on a fiber track. You can make dadoed wood channels yourself if you have power tools. Tracks are usually placed right on the top and bottom edges of the cabinet opening and covered on the front with a small piece of wood trim. Drill pilot holes for nails before installing the channel and the trim, so the wood doesn't split. (See Fig. 16-6.)

318

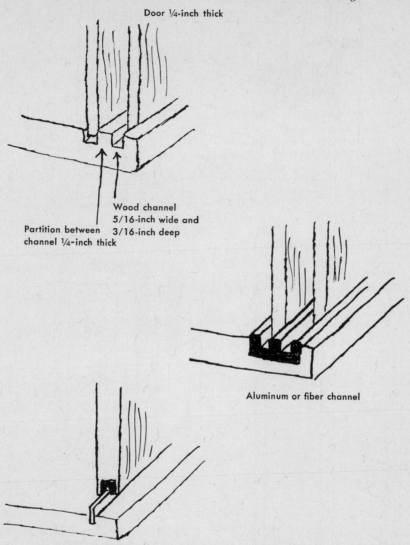

Door ¼-inch thick

Wood channel
5/16-inch wide and
3/16-inch deep

Partition between
channel ¼-inch thick

Aluminum or fiber channel

Fiber shoe (on door) and fiber track

Figure 16-6 Sliding doors

16.7 | Dividing cabinet space for better use. Most kitchen cabinets can store almost twice as much if the shelves are arranged properly. A good method of dividing a deep cabinet for food, glass-

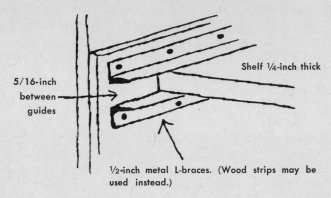

Figure 16-7   Sliding shelves

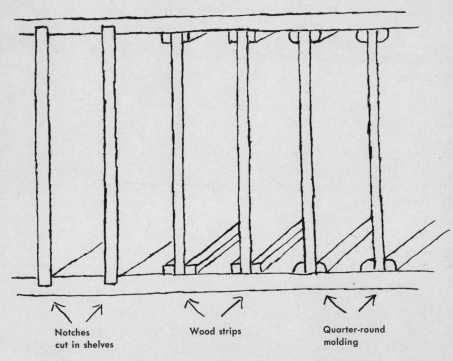

Figure 16-8   Vertical dividers and how they can be attached

ware, or china is to build a half-shelf in the rear. This is simply a miniature bench of ¼ - or ½ -inch plywood set at half the height and half the depth of the regular shelf openings. It can sit on small wood ledges screwed to the sides of the cabinet. If it fits snugly it isn't necessary to nail it in place.

Adjustable shelves for a cabinet or closet can be made like adjustable bookshelves—see Figure 16-3.

Sliding shelves are useful for placemats, platters, and linens— anything that must be stored flat. The sliding tracks may be of wood or metal. (See Fig. 16-7.) In existing cabinets you must build out the inside of the cabinet walls flush with the door opening so the shelves can slide out.

Vertical dividers often provide the best storage for trays, large plates and platters, record albums, magazines, and other flat objects that require large, thin storage. (See Fig. 16-8.) They can be made of hardboard or ¼ -inch plywood cut to fit. They can be full depth or slanted across the front for easier access. You can cut slots in top and bottom of cabinet to install dividers, or you can nail wood cleats in place.

16.8 | Building between the studs. If you have an interior partition with unused wall space, you can make it into a narrow shelf for one-deep storage of canned goods, glassware, toys, or other objects by opening up the wall and using the area between the studs. (See Fig. 16-9.) Don't use an outside wall this way because you will disturb the insulation.

To locate studs in the wall, see Section 6.7. If you want to build just a small cabinet, between only two or three studs, you can simply cut through the drywall or the plaster with an old keyhole saw. (Try to make sure before you begin that there are no plumbing or electrical lines in the wall.) If your cabinet is wider, so that it is necessary to remove more than one stud, you'll have to install a header and cripples to support the wall and floor above. (See Fig. 16-9 and Sec. 8.31.)

Construct your cupboard framework to exact measure and set it in place complete. Trim out the face of the cupboard with molding or casing to cover the raw edges of the wall. If you want a deeper cupboard, use wider boards for the top and sides, so they extend out in the room. (Cover the ragged edges of wall with quarter-round molding.) Nail the completed cupboard in place to studs or cripples. If it is to have doors, install them as in Section 16.6.

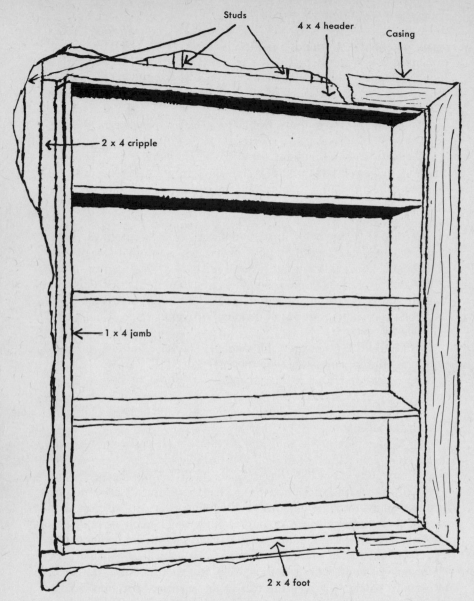

Figure 16-9   A shelf between studs

16.9 | Base cabinets. Figure 16-10 shows the basic structure of a base cabinet. It's essentially a box set on a low platform to form a toe space at the bottom front. (This is necessary so you can stand

322

Figure 16-10   Base cabinet

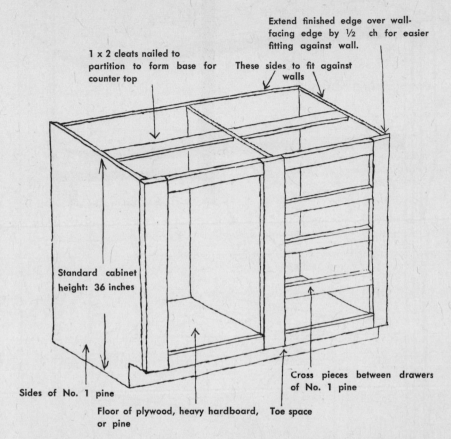

1 x 2 cleats nailed to partition to form base for counter top

These sides to fit against walls

Extend finished edge over wall-facing edge by ½ ch for easier fitting against wall.

Standard cabinet height: 36 inches

Cross pieces between drawers of No. 1 pine

Sides of No. 1 pine

Floor of plywood, heavy hardboard, or pine

Toe space

right up against the cabinet to use the counter top.) The back and sides of the box that are not exposed can be made of plywood or left open (against the wall) with framing members serving to hold the rest of the cabinet in place. The floor of the cabinet should be plywood, heavy hardboard, or pine boards. Exposed parts should be of No. 1 pine. Kitchen cabinet tops are usually covered with Formica or other durable, hard-surfaced material before being fastened in place —see next section. Doors are best made of regular cabinet door stock—see Section 16.6.

The interiors of cabinets are furnished with shelves (Sec. 16.5), dividers (Sec. 16.7), drawers (Sec. 16.11), or other accessories in any combination you select. Typewriters, mixers, sewing machines,

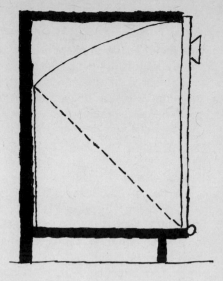

Figure 16-11 Pulldown bin

Make curved sides of pulldown bin same
height ((measuring from hinge) as front
opening, less ½-inch for clearance.

Wooden stop nailed to underside of
top cabinet

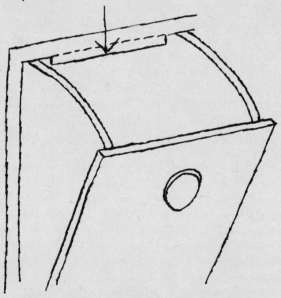

To keep bin from falling out of cabinet when opened, attach
wooden stop to center of top of opening. When closed, front
of bin will cover stop.

324

and other heavy appliances can also be installed permanently on pop-up shelves in base cabinets. Hardware for such an installation can be purchased at the hardware store and comes with complete instructions. Be sure it fits the unit and cabinet exactly, or there'll be a lot of waste space.

Pulldown bins in an open-front base cabinet—Figure 16-11—can provide handy bulk storage for laundry, toys, and other items. They're quite easy to make out of plywood or pine, and all joints can be butted. (See Fig. 16-2.) Long wood screws are the best fasteners to use on any base cabinet work, but cement-coated nails can also be used. Half-inch plywood is sufficient for sides and back, but use overlaid ¾-inch plywood for the front.

16.10 | Counter tops. Kitchen and bathroom cabinets need a durable surface that is not easily scratched, stained, or damaged by water. Ceramic tile, hard plastics such as Formica, and laminated hardwood all serve the purpose beautifully.

Ceramic tile is usually applied to a ¾-inch-thick plywood top with a tile adhesive, and the joints are grouted in. Be sure to use exterior-grade plywood and screw the backsplash tightly to the plywood counter before installing the counter. Apply the tile with the adhesive your dealer recommends after the counter is fitted and in place. The easiest way to handle the front edge of the counter, and the top edge of the backsplash, is to install a stainless steel counter edging (from your hardware or tile dealer) after the tile is in place, but before grouting. An alternative method is to glue and screw a strip of wood under the front edge of the counter (to make a lip to support tiles), and then adhere tile to the edge of the counter too. You can tile the top of the backsplash, too, in this case. When you grout between the tiles you can also grout corners and gaps between tiles and stainless steel or wood edging.

The most often used counter-top material is the rigid plastic laminate commonly referred to as Formica. (It goes by a number of other trade names, too.) If you want a de luxe type of counter top with rounded corners (no sharp edges to bump against) and rounded edges and joints (no place for dirt to collect), you must have it made by a good millwork shop.

But you yourself can make handsome plastic counters with square edges and joints. It's easiest to apply the plastic before you fasten the backsplash to the counter, and before you place the counter on the cabinet. For a new cabinet, use ¾-inch exterior-grade plywood. Be sure it's perfectly smooth. If you are refinishing an old surface, be sure that it's clean, dry, and smooth before you apply the plastic.

Support the plastic carefully and solidly while cutting it to fit your counter, because it is fragile before mounting. Cut it with the surface side up (unless you are using a portable electric circular saw) and use a fine-tooth saw held at a low angle. Cut it ¼ inch larger all around than you need, to permit final finishing with plane and file.

Use the contact cement recommended by your dealer and follow manufacturer's directions for application. Apply to both surfaces and let dry until a sheet of wrapping paper can be pressed on the surface and easily pulled away without bringing any cement with it (at least 40 minutes). When ready to bond, place a series of overlapping slip-sheets of heavy wrapping paper on the counter surface. Put the plastic in place (if the area is large, you'll need a helper) and get it exactly right, for you can't move it once it's stuck. Now remove the end slipsheet and press the plastic in place with a rolling pin. Gradually work along the sheet, removing one slipsheet at a time and pressing plastic in place.

Next, cut plastic to fit the backsplash, attach it as above (using a hammer and wood block to bond it), and then screw backsplash in place. Use a metal cove molding to finish off the joint, and trim off plastic on front and edges with a file, block plane, or surform. You can apply a metal edging strip, or sand plywood edge smooth and leave it exposed, painting it if you like. Or you can edge counter with the same plastic you used on the counter top. Ask your dealer for an instruction sheet.

Laminated hardwood counters are practical for kitchen use, extremely good-looking, and should last a lifetime. They can be used like a butcher's block for cutting and chopping. They need no finish. You can buy hardwood counters ready-made at most millwork shops and large lumber supply houses, or you can have them custom made.

If you prefer, you can make your own hardwood counters. Buy maple or ash boards, planed on both sides, at your lumberyard and have them ripped into strips 2½ inches wide. Then cut the strips to the length of your counter. With a waterproof glue (two-part epoxy), glue the strips face to face (planed surfaces to planed surfaces) and clamp the whole assembly together. (See Fig. 16-12.) The best clamps to use are plumber's clamps on pieces of ¾-inch pipe—ask

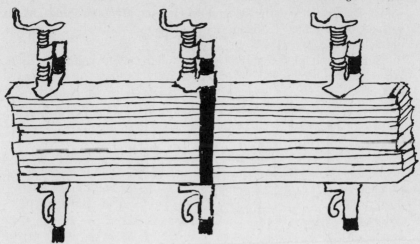

Figure 16-12   Pipe clamps on hardwood counter

your hardware dealer about them. It's best to use three clamps, one at each end on the same side, and one in the middle on the other side. (This will prevent the assembly from jumping out of the clamps.) When the glue has set, you can smooth the rough surface with a floor sander, or if it's less than 24 inches wide, take it to a millwork shop and have it put through a 24-inch planer.

Finish the counter by screwing and gluing a hardwood backsplash to the back.

16.11 | Drawers. If you are building new drawer units or want to include drawers in a base cabinet, it's easiest to use plastic drawers of a stock size and build your unit to fit. These are available in a wide variety of sizes and styles. They also come with their own framework that you can simply cover with a shell of wood to make a dresser or other cabinet. Ready-made drawers are also available in metal and wood. All types are carried by your hardware dealer, lumberyard, and mail-order house.

If you want to make your own drawers, the easiest way is to build them as shown in Figure 16-13. The best drawers are made with dovetail joints, but this requires a router, a dovetail jig, and a considerable amount of skill. Dovetail joints are shown in Figure 16-2.

Sliding drawer supports are also shown in Figure 16-13. Most drawer cabinets, however, are made just like a bookshelf (Fig. 16-4)

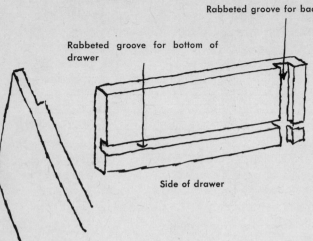

Rabbeted groove for back of drawer

Rabbeted groove for bottom of drawer

Side of drawer

Front of drawer

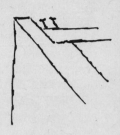

Use glue, then nails, to join front to sides.

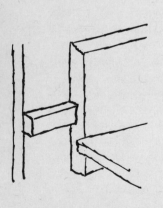

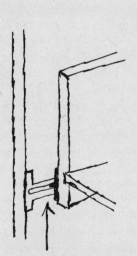

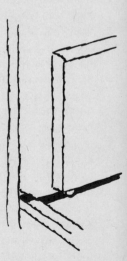

Wood guide on cabinet side, with rabbeted groove in drawer side

Metal guide on cabinet side, metal runner on drawer side

Metal guide attached to front and rear rails of cabinet, with roller assembly on bottom of drawer.

Figure 16-13   Drawers and drawer guides

with butt or dado joints, spacing the shelves just a little farther apart than the height of the drawers. The advantage of sliding supports is that they can be installed so that there is no space, except clearance, between drawer fronts. This eliminates the waste space used up by boards between drawers.

If many small items are being stored together (sewing accessories, makeup, office supplies) you may want to install drawer dividers. You can cut slots in the sides of drawers to accommodate the partitions, or you can merely glue the divider strips and fasten them in place with finishing nails. Dividers can be made of ¼-inch plywood or ³⁄₁₆-inch hardboard.

16.12 | Closets. If you lack sufficient closet space, it may be that you merely need to reorganize the closets you now have. There should be a special place for everything that is stored in a closet. Shoes, pocketbooks, hatboxes, sporting equipment, should each have their own niche. You can install new shelves (Sec. 16.5), dividers for the shelves you now have (Sec. 16.7), and you can build in drawers (Sec. 16.8). You may be able to install another closet pole beneath the shorter garments in a closet, if you group all short items together. Many special closet accessories are also available—consult your hardware or department store, or your mail-order catalogue.

In planning closet space, remember that folded garments should be stored in shallow drawers to avoid wrinkling and to provide easy accessibility. Hats are best stored on open shelves. Shoes can be stored on shelves, racks, or drawers. Except for walk-in closets, doors should be arranged so that the entire front of the closet is easily accessible.

If you can spare the space, you can install a closet wall. (If you are planning to put up a wall partition, you might want to make it a closet wall.) One closet wall can serve two adjacent bedrooms, with half the closet opening into each room. It can also be useful in a family room, basement, or kitchen—or any place where you need storage and can spare the space from your living area.

A free-standing wall, or one that takes the place of a room partition, is made approximately the same way as a room-high base cabinet (Sec. 16.9). If the closet is to be built in place against an existing wall, the shelves can be hung like kitchen shelves (Sec. 16.4), the closet poles installed with pole hangers from your hardware store, and the doors installed as in Section 8.10 or 8.11.

16.13 | Pegboard walls. If you have unused wall space but can't spare the depth needed for shelves or cabinets, you can install a pegboard wall. You can get the pegboard (perforated masonite) and fixtures (for hanging things on it—there are many different fixtures available) from your hardware store or lumber dealer.

To mount pegboard, first locate the studs in the wall. (See Sec. 6.7.) A full-height pegboard wall should have three big nails in every other stud. Before you nail up the pegboard, fasten small spacers (of the pegboard material, or other wood of the same thickness) to the back of the pegboard, using Scotch tape, at every point where you are going to nail it. The spacers leave sufficient space behind the pegboard so the hanging fixtures can be inserted easily. Nail the pegboard in place and cover edges with trim or molding if you like. Then paint the pegboard and its trim.

16.14 | Providing storage in unused areas. If you look carefully around the house for unused corners, you can probably find a number of excellent storage areas. Here are some suggestions:

1. *Under beds and couches.* This is ideal space, seldom used, for storing toys, linens, and clothes. A frame like a base cabinet frame (Fig. 16-10) can be made to fit right under the bed, fitted with ball casters so it rolls out easily. The top of the frame or drawer should be covered so lint and dust don't filter down into it.

2. *Under-sink cabinets.* These will conceal unsightly pipes and provide useful storage for cleaning supplies, towels, and so forth. They are basically base cabinets in which the sides are made to fit the contour of the sink. This makes such a cabinet a little harder to build than a base cabinet, but if you lay out your work first on paper you can assemble it quite easily. Build it with the back open so it can be simply shoved under the sink into position. Don't fasten it permanently in place—you may have to remove it for plumbing repairs.

3. *Under-the-eaves cabinets.* If you have bedrooms or attic rooms with sloping ceilings and knee walls at the sides, you have a wealth of storage space that can be utilized without any sacrifice of floor area. There is plenty of room behind the knee walls for shelves and drawers, and you can design a unit to fit your particular needs. Frame the opening for the cabinet as you would for a between-the-studs cabinet (Fig. 16-9). The interior is equipped with shelves (Sec. 16.5), dividers (Sec. 16.7), and drawers (Sec. 16.11), as needed. Ready-made drawer units are available which are designed especially for this use. They have finished fronts and are easily installed.

4. *Window seats.* A window seat provides seating space and storage for linens, toys, or sporting goods. The basic unit is built as in Figure 16-14. The top can either be flush with the front or it can

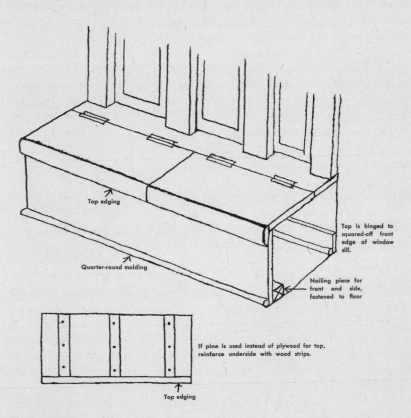

Top edging

Quarter-round molding

Top is hinged to squared-off front edge of window sill.

Nailing piece for front and side, fastened to floor

If pine is used instead of plywood for top, reinforce underside with wood strips.

Top edging

Figure 16-14   A window seat

project beyond it. The top should be reinforced with strips of hardwood screwed on underneath. The window seat is basically a base cabinet fastened to the floor.

5. *Lazy Susans for corner storage.* A lazy Susan is the best way —in fact, the only good way—to make useful storage areas out of corners between two kitchen base or wall cabinets on adjoining walls. Figure 16-15 shows how to make a good sturdy lazy Susan.

You can get the threaded steel rod, nuts, and big washers at most hardware stores. The shelves should be made of ¾-inch plywood if they are to hold heavy canned goods. The nuts should be turned down hard on the shelves with a wrench. The bottom end of the rod should rest in a hole bored in a crosswise framing member on a bed of nuts and washers (Figure 16-15), not directly on the floor—

Figure 16-15   A lazy Susan

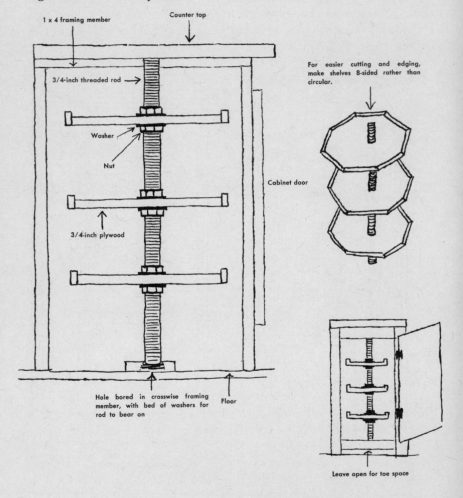

1 x 4 framing member

Counter top

3/4-inch threaded rod →

For easier cutting and edging, make shelves 8-sided rather than circular.

Washer

Nut

Cabinet door

3/4-inch plywood

Hole bored in crosswise framing member, with bed of washers for rod to bear on

Floor

Leave open for toe space

it might grind a hole in the floor. The cabinet for a lazy Susan is a base cabinet with top bracing set across the top to position the top end of the rod.

6. *Corner cupboards.* A corner cupboard can convert an unused corner into an attractive display space for china, glassware, toys or practically anything else. You can use glass or wood doors, or leave the cabinet open if dust isn't a problem. Figure 16-16 shows how to build a basic corner cupboard. It's framed like a triangular base cabinet with shelves in the top half. You can buy corner cupboards all assembled and ready to finish from lumberyards and mail-order houses if you prefer.

Figure 16-16   A corner cupboard

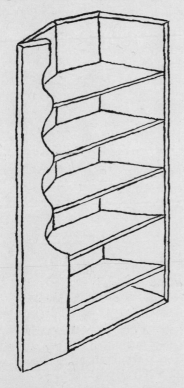

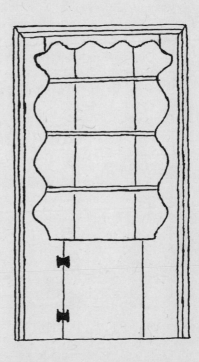

Frame cupboard sides and back to fit corner, then add shelves and scalloped front.

Finish off with hinged door on lower portion and place molding around top and side edges.

17 REMODELING

17.1 | How much should you remodel? Sooner or later, every homeowner does a certain amount of remodeling—even if it's only a new coat of paint or a few new kitchen cabinets. If you are considering a major remodeling job, however—one that involves many structural changes or new additions to the house—you will want to give it careful thought beforehand, to make sure the remodeling will prove worth while.

If you and your family like the location of your house, like the neighborhood and the lot you are on, you have a good reason to consider remodeling. Or, if you have investigated and discovered that moving to another, larger house would be too expensive, remodeling may provide the best solution.

Remember, however, that what you spend on remodeling is not always reflected in the price you can get for the house if you should decide to sell it later. (Of course, you should repair obvious bad points before trying to sell, but don't go in for major remodeling.) Kitchen and bathroom improvements usually add substantially to the sale value of the house, but in most other cases you must consider the money as spent for your family's enjoyment—not for a possible profit later.

You should remodel only if the house is basically sound. You shouldn't remodel to such an extent that your house is very much bigger or better than other houses in the neighborhood—because it will be absolutely impossible to sell it for what is is worth. You shouldn't remodel too much in a rundown neighborhood, unless you are sure it is going to make a comeback. (You can get good advice on this point from your bank or lending institution.)

17.2 | Making plans for more space. If you are thinking of remodeling, you probably have a fairly good idea of what you want and where you want it. There may be other possibilities, however, that you have overlooked. The first thing you should do is draw a careful plan to scale of your present room layout. Then, with tracing

334

paper laid over this plan, begin working out possible additions or rearrangements.

Consider first of all whether you can possibly achieve what you need by rearranging the space you have. A lack of bedroom space can sometimes be solved by finishing the attic (see Chap. 14) or by dividing one oversized room into two smaller ones. (Don't forget to provide separate access to the hallway from both rooms.) If you need a family room or larger living room you may be able to convert the garage or carport. (This will probably involve the addition of a new carport.) Or you can make a screened porch into an enclosed room to give you extra inside living area. Sometimes you can use the basement—see Chapter 15. For suggestions on kitchen and bathroom remodeling, see the following two sections.

In rearranging your existing floor plan, you must bear certain factors in mind: (1) Interior nonbearing walls can be easily removed. (See Secs. 6.30 and 6.31.) Bearing walls can be removed, too, but this is more complicated. (2) You can make doors into windows, windows into doors, close up existing openings altogether, or make new ones. (See Secs. 8.31 through 8.35.) (3) You can move light fixtures and outlets fairly easily (Chap. 2) but heating ducts are more difficult. If you can possibly avoid it, do not cut into any wall containing plumbing lines—they are costly and difficult to move. (4) If new plumbing fixtures are being added, locate them near existing plumbing lines to save money.

If rearranging existing space will not give you the room you need, you'll have to enlarge the house. In some cases you can do this by installing a shed dormer. (See Figure 14-2.) Or, if there is already a one-story wing on a two-story house, you can extend your second floor out over the wing—see Figure 17-1. This is usually cheaper than a ground-floor addition, because no foundation work is involved. If you plan on a ground-floor addition you will need a plot plan, and you must find out from your local building inspector how close you can build to the front, rear, and sides of the lot, and other restrictions that may affect your plans. You must also consider the location of the septic tank—you can't build over this without installing a new one elsewhere (a costly proposition at best).

If you have any choice in the matter (there may be only one possible place where you can build), look for a corner where you need add only one or two walls and a roof. When you tear out a wall, you may be able to salvage doors, windows, or framing to use

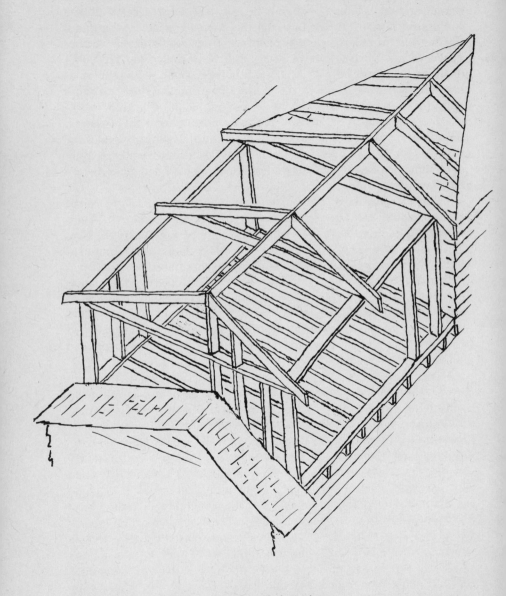

Figure 17-1 Building out over existing wing

in the new addition. Try to avoid tearing out a wall containing plumbing—the plumbing alteration will add hundreds of dollars to the cost of your project. Consider in advance whether your present heating system is large enough to heat the new addition, or whether a new unit will have to be added. (Your fuel dealer can tell you.) Your addition will have to meet local building code requirements as to plumbing, wiring, and heating, and for ceiling heights and room and window sizes.

The appearance of the new addition from the outside is also an important consideration. New roof lines must harmonize with the existing roof. Window lines and styles must match up. Be sure everything about the new addition ties in architecturally with the old part of the house.

Consider also how the new addition will affect the layout of the existing house. Will you convert part of an existing room to a corridor by adding the new room? If you are adding a new living room, what will you do with the existing living room? If you need a new bedroom, it may be smarter to convert your present living room to a bedroom, and add a new and larger living room. The possibilities for remodeling are endless; only you and your family can decide how best to remodel your house. Try to create a good traffic pattern, so that children don't have to go through the kitchen when they come in from outside, so that guests don't have to go through a bedroom to get to the bathroom, and so forth.

Finally, be sure to plan for adequate ventilation and lighting.

17.3 | Kitchen remodeling. If your present kitchen is inconvenient or is not large enough, you have probably thought about remodeling it. Kitchen remodeling can run into a lot of money—thousands of dollars in some cases—especially if you install the newest and latest appliances. A modern kitchen usually adds substantially to the value of your house, however, and makes life much simpler for the cook.

Home economists and expert kitchen planners have put a lot of time and effort into designing the most efficient kitchen arrangements. It is the housewife, however, who should have the last word in planning her kitchen. She has her own work habits, is used to her kitchen, and knows what is wrong with its present arrangement. Expert guidance and planning can be a help if you can afford it, but the housewife herself should do most of the planning.

If your kitchen is too small for efficient operation or allows insufficient space for family dining, perhaps you can get additional space from a hallway, pantry, or other adjoining room. You may be able to enclose a back porch. If not, perhaps you can remove a wall and extend the kitchen out. (Before you proceed with any such project, however, you should thoroughly plan the new arrangement of your kitchen.) It's possible, too, to move the kitchen from its present location to another part of the house, but because of the extreme expense involved this usually isn't feasible. If you do consider this possibility, remember a kitchen must be located conveniently to the dining area, to the outside dining area, to service or delivery area, to carport or garage (for unloading groceries), and to family room or playroom.

The best way to plan your kitchen is to make an accurate drawing (using a scale of $\frac{1}{4}''$ equals $1'$) of your present room, showing windows, doors, radiators, registers, fireplaces, and any other immovable objects. Then you can make sketches on tracing paper, held over the original drawing, to consider possible enlargements of the kitchen. Cut out rectangles of cardboard or paper (to scale) to represent appliances, so you can plan their rearrangement.

It's easiest when planning your kitchen if you work around three basic "centers." The food storage and preparation center includes refrigerator, counter for mixing and food preparation, and sink. (For storage and cabinet suggestions, see Chap. 16.) The cooking and serving center includes the range and oven, counter space for cooking appliances and for serving, and storage space for pots and pans and other cooking utensils. The clean-up center includes the dishwasher, disposal unit, sink, counter space for dish racks, and so forth, and storage for soap and other cleaning supplies. If you have the room and can afford the extra expense, two sinks will make your kitchen more efficient: a single sink for the preparation center, a double one for clean-up. If you can have only one sink, obviously your preparation and clean-up centers will have to overlap. Remember in planning the clean-up center that even if you don't have a dishwasher or disposal unit now, you may want to add them later.

Essentially, the important thing in planning a kitchen is to arrange the sink (or sinks), refrigerator, and range as efficiently as possible—with sufficient counter and storage space in between. Basic arrangements are the U-shape, the L-shape, the two-wall kitchen, the one-wall kitchen, and the island kitchen (Figure 17-2.).

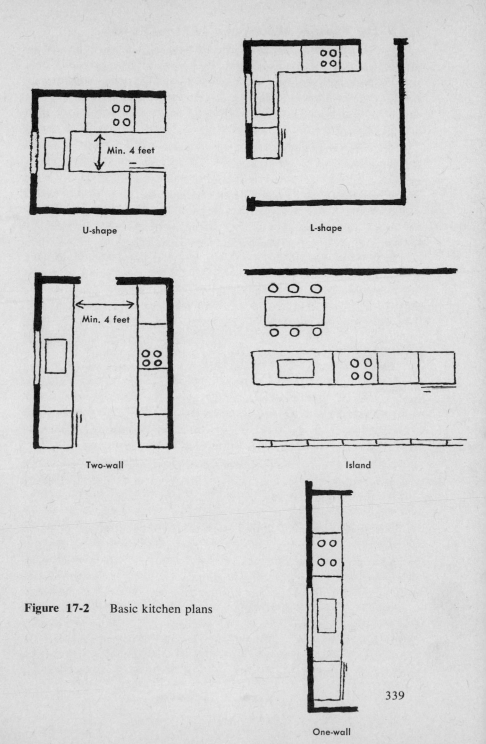

U-shape

Min. 4 feet

L-shape

Two-wall

Min. 4 feet

Island

Figure 17-2   Basic kitchen plans

One-wall

339

Obviously, this is just another way of saying that you can put the three basic units in just about any arrangement so long as the sink, refrigerator, and range are not too far apart. The three units should form a rough triangle (except in a one-wall arrangement, of course) which isn't more than 22 feet around. Otherwise, too many steps will be wasted.

Early in the planning stage, decide what other centers—besides the three basic ones—your kitchen will include, and work them in as best you can, A planning center with telephone and desk is always a convenience. Many kitchens must include the laundry equipment too. If you have room, you may want to plan a sewing or hobby center as well. What your kitchen includes depends on its size and on your family's needs and preferences—especially the housewife's.

Here are some rules of thumb to keep in mind as you plan:

Work around existing plumbing lines if you possibly can—moving them will add considerably to the cost of remodeling.

Window area should equal at least one-fifth of the floor area, and window sills must be at least 36½ " high to accommodate standard counter height of 36".

Minimum counter space is 15" at the refrigerator, 36" at the mixing counter, 36" on right of sink, 30" on left of sink (unless you have dishwasher), 24" on both sides of the range. This can actually total up to as little as 66" of counter space, depending on your arrangement.

At least 6 cubic feet of storage space should be allowed for each member of the family, with an extra 6 cubic feet if you entertain often.

Wiring is of special importance in a kitchen, for as much as 80 per cent of your total electricity may be consumed in this one room. You must have separate circuits for freezer and refrigerator, a heavy-duty (220-volt) circuit for range and oven, a separate heavy-duty circuit for the dryer, and another separate circuit for the washing machine. You need a number of outlets for portable appliances and other outlets for lighting the kitchen. This means you should have, ideally, from six to eight circuits for the kitchen alone.

Be sure to have plenty of light, both daylight and artificial, or the kitchen won't be a pleasant place to work in. Lights under wall cabinets give good work light. General illumination is best provided by ceiling fixtures or a luminous ceiling. (See Sec. 6.28.)

Finally, good ventilation is essential in a kitchen. The best way to provide freedom from cooking steam and odors is by a range hood and fan. (See Sec. 5.1.) In hot climates, you may also need an air conditioner in the kitchen if the house isn't completely air-conditioned.

When you reach the final decorating stage, be sure to choose durable, easy-to-clean materials. For information about resilient floors, see Sections 7.17 through 7.21. For wall treatment, see Chapter 6. For storage suggestions and directions for installing new counter tops, see Chapter 16.

17.4 | Adding and remodeling bathrooms. If your house is short of bathroom facilities, or you are adding a new room to your house that will require new plumbing, the first thing to do is decide exactly where the new bathroom is most needed and makes most sense. Do you lack a downstairs bath? Need a master bath or a separate bathroom to serve children or guests?

Since the space occupied by a bathroom is small, you can usually find the room you need by taking over a large closet, part of a hallway, or part of a good-sized bedroom. For a full bath, allow a minimum of 5' x 7'. (Remember that an outside window is not a necessity. Ventilating fans make the inside bath just as acceptable.) Be sure the bathroom location will be convenient for everyone who will use it, and that you will not be creating additional problems by reducing a small hall or bedroom space to less than the minimum required. (See Figure 17-3.)

In addition, you will save money if your new bathroom can be located near existing plumbing lines—if possible, the new bathroom should be adjacent to, or directly above or below, the old one. You will need a plumber to advise you on this point and then tell you how much the job will cost. New plumbing work is not inexpensive by any means. Unless you are really handy and experienced, it will be absolutely necessary to have a plumber install waste and water lines for you. (Read Secs. 1.39 and 1.40.) If you want to, you can install the fixtures yourself. You can also do the tiling (Sec. 6.25) and decorating.

A bathroom is far more useful if it is divided so that two or more persons can use it at the same time with privacy and convenience. The simplest way to achieve a compartmented bath is to have the

Figure 17-3 Minimum full bathrooms

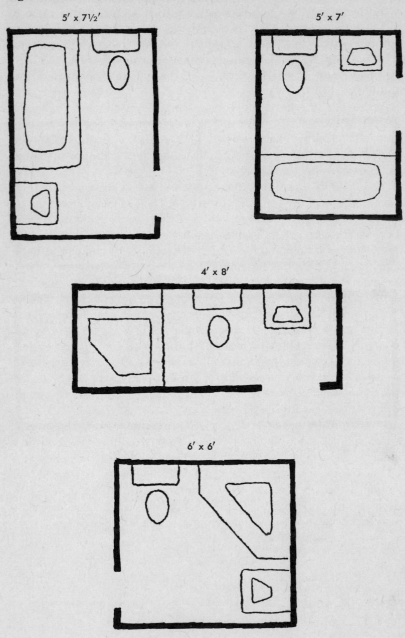

5′ x 7½′

5′ x 7′

4′ x 8′

6′ x 6′

lavatory (or two, if there is space) just inside the door, with the tub and toilet completely closed off in the farther section of the room by a sliding door. Or the tub or shower can be compartmented at one end, the toilet at the other. Better yet, provide separate access from the hallway to each compartment. However you plan it, the compartmented bathroom will go a long way toward relieving the morning rush hour. (See Fig. 17-4.)

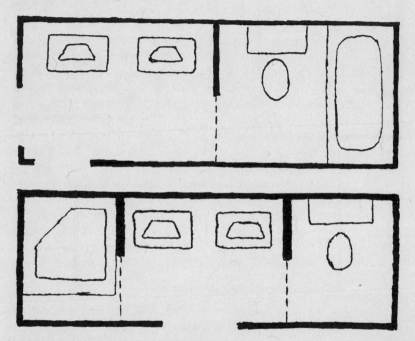

Figure 17-4 Compartmented bathrooms

If you lack space for a full bath, perhaps you can squeeze in a half-bath somewhere. If you're adding a powder room, this may be all you really need anyway. Or you can install a shower, toilet, and a lavatory in three separate locations. (Usually, however, this would raise plumbing costs.) If an extra lavatory is a necessity and it can't be fitted into your present bathroom or the new one you are installing, you can build it into a bedroom vanity or dresser, preferably so that it backs up on a plumbing wall.

If your existing bathroom is hopelessly inconvenient or outmoded, you can make it more functional and attractive by replacing old fixtures (Sec. 1.46), redecorating, installing additional storage, compartmenting (if it is large enough and suitably arranged), and adding a second lavatory if there is room.

When you have decided on your bathroom arrangement, call in a plumber to give you an estimate. If he is doing only the rough plumbing, be sure to add in the cost of fixtures, tiles, additional storage units, and other raw materials you plan to install yourself. Be sure to include plenty of storage facilities—the traditional medicine cabinet is not enough (but install the largest one you can find). Storage cabinets and counters can be built around traditional lavatories—see Section 16.10—or you can get storage units with modern lavatories built into the top. Every bit of unused wall space in the bathroom is a potential cabinet or counter top. Be sure to provide adequate mirrors—a full-length one and a three-way dressing-table mirror if you can. In choosing wall and floor materials, make absolutely certain they are all waterproof and easily washable. Tile or other hard-surfaced material should be placed to the ceiling on all sides of the tub, and at least 12 inches above and to both sides of the lavatory. If carpet is used, it must be stainproof and washable. Don't forget safety precautions: Install grab bars in shower stall and tub, and arrange light switches well away from lavatory, tub, and shower. If extra heat is needed in the new bathroom, you may be able to run a new duct or have a heating contractor do it for you. But the easiest way is to use an auxiliary electric heater built into the wall or ceiling.

Finally, remember that bathroom privacy is affected not only by location, but by soundproofing as well. Ideally, inside bathroom walls should be double-framed—actually, two stud walls back to back, arranged so studs don't touch. Then ⅝-inch gypsum board is applied to both sides. When planning a downstairs powder room, try to place a coat closet between powder room and hall.

17.5 | Getting better light. Whether you are remodeling the kitchen or bathroom, opening up the living area, or adding a new wing to your house, don't forget to plan for good lighting. Every room in your house should have comfortable all-over lighting as well as concentrated lighting for reading and working.

One of the most effective ways to provide general illumination in any room is to build in valance or cornice lighting on the window walls. (See Fig. 17-5.) Since the light comes from the same direction as daylight, it looks more natural, and will make a room look larger

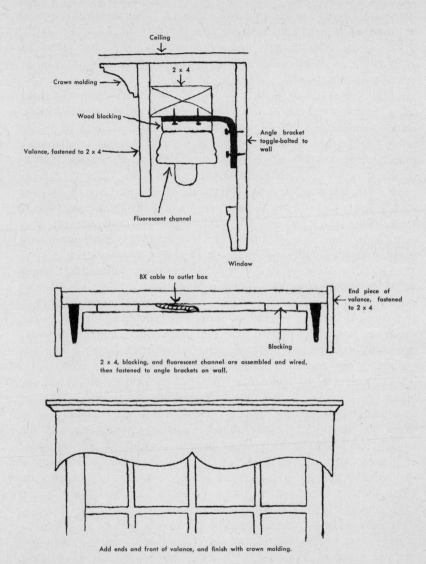

Ceiling

Crown molding

2 x 4

Wood blocking

Angle bracket toggle-bolted to wall

Valance, fastened to 2 x 4

Fluorescent channel

Window

BX cable to outlet box

End piece of valance, fastened to 2 x 4

Blocking

2 x 4, blocking, and fluorescent channel are assembled and wired, then fastened to angle brackets on wall.

Add ends and front of valance, and finish with crown molding.

Figure 17-5   Valance lighting

than it would with just ceiling light. It isn't difficult to install the fluorescent lights—you can probably do the work yourself. (See Chap. 2.) You can make your own valances, order them ready-made, or have a carpenter make them for you.

In kitchen, bathrooms, and other utility areas, you need an especially high level of illumination. One way to achieve it is to install a luminous ceiling. (See Sec. 6.28.)

17.6 | How much work can you do yourself? Naturally, your remodeling job will cost you less if you do part of the work yourself. Don't attempt to do *all* of the work on a new addition or major inside job yourself, however, unless you are thoroughly experienced. In many communities, building codes require that wiring and plumbing be done by licensed professionals.

By far the most sensible approach, if you are trying to save money, is to hire a general contractor to do the major part of the work (foundation, framing, roofing, plumbing, and wiring), but save all the finishing—painting, decorating, laying finish floor, and possibly the installation of bathroom fixtures—for yourself.

The alternative method is to do your own contracting, hiring individual contractors to do each phase of the job: foundation, carpentry, wiring, plumbing, and so on. This is a risky method at best, and one which rarely works out well. You can't possibly tell in advance just how much the job will cost, because you may miscalculate materials or labor. Furthermore, the subcontractors may take advantage of you because you are an amateur.

The best way to figure out what the job will involve and how much you can do yourself is to know what the various stages of construction will involve. (Even if your contractor is doing *all* the work, you should know just what he is doing at each stage of the work.) The first thing to be done in a new addition—after drawing up plans and getting a building permit—is to excavate for the foundation, whether you are going to have a basement, crawl space, or slab. (You should not attempt this part of the work yourself under any conditions.) If your present house has a basement or crawl space, then your addition should have a crawl space, too. But if your present floor level is only inches above the outside ground, then you can use a slab so the new floor comes out level with the existing floor.

In slab work, the soil is excavated about 1½ feet below the finished floor level. Around the perimeter of the slab, a footing trench is dug below the frost line and form boards are placed for pouring a concrete foundation wall. This is usually a 6-inch-thick wall poured with a 2 x 4 sill set into the top with anchor bolts. The top of the sill is placed at finished floor level. When the foundation sets, forms are stripped, the trench backfilled, and a subgrade of graded gravel is placed inside the foundation to the proper level to take a 4-inch slab on top of it. Before the slab is poured, heating ducts, waste lines, and forms to leave openings under bathtub traps are set. Rigid insulation is installed inside the foundation wall to keep the floor warm. Then a vapor barrier of polyethylene film, to keep the ground water out of the slab, is set down on top and the slab is poured. (It should be reinforced with welded wire mesh.)

In crawl space work, soil is removed to a depth 2 or 3 feet below the bottom of the floor joists and a foundation trench is dug all around to a point below the frost line. A continuous concrete footing is poured in the trench and a concrete block wall is laid with mortar to sill level. A sill in this case is usually a 2 x 6 bolted to the top of the foundation wall by setting the bolts in mortar between the blocks in the top course. Floor joists are placed on the sill and an intermediate beam supported by piers inside the crawl space if the span is big. Box joists—the same size as regular floor joists—enclose the open sides. A 2-inch ground cover of concrete is then poured over the dirt floor of the crawl space to keep rodents and water out. Subflooring is installed over the joists and the outsides of the foundation wall are usually "parged"—this is like plastering, but done with mortar—and the trench is backfilled on the outside. Now the walls are ready to be framed. Fireplace and chimney is now installed if there is to be one.

Very often the contractor will frame the walls in a flat position on the subfloor—or the slab—and raise them into position and then nail them to the sill on the top of the foundation wall. (See Figs. 6-22 and 8-19.) The wall is then sheathed with plywood or fiberboard sheathing, or, if there is corner bracing, they can be covered directly with one of the new types of siding materials that also double as sheathing.

When the walls are all up, ceiling joists and roof rafters—or roof trusses—are placed and the roof is sheathed. If a ridge vent is to be used (Fig. 5-1), an opening in the roof sheathing is left on either side of the ridge. Doors and windows in the wall openings are placed now. Stairs are installed if there are any.

Up to this point you should let the contractor do all the work, unless you have done it before yourself. You should also have him take care of the mechanical elements: heating, electrical work, and rough plumbing. This work is hard and critical, and mistakes are difficult to correct.

You can do all final finishing and decoration and install bathroom fixtures, if you want to. This will reduce your costs considerably.

17.7 | How much will the job cost? Before you can get an estimate from your contractor you must have a fairly accurate, scaled drawing of your remodeling plan. If you can't do this yourself, the contractor can do it for you. Or you can hire an architect if you feel you need one, though this will add considerably to your remodeling costs.

In addition to a scaled drawing, you should have a list of "specifications," telling exactly what work is to be done, what kind and quality of materials to be used. Be sure to state how much finishing work will be included. (See next section.)

Here are some rough figures to guide you in making your own preliminary estimates, or in checking those the contractor gives you. New additions should cost between $15 and $25 a square foot (including finishing), exclusive of kitchens or bathrooms. Add to the per-square-foot cost $1,000 for a new bath and $3,000 to $6,000 for a completely new kitchen. The bigger your addition, the lower the per-square-foot cost will be. (Adding over an existing wing is cheaper than a ground-floor addition, because no foundation work is involved.) Remember that a contractor's charge includes not only materials and labor (averaging $2 to $6 an hour) but also his overhead (covering office expenses, estimating expenses, insurance, and so on.)

When you are ready to take bids for your job, by all means have two or three contractors give you an estimate, making sure all are using the same specifications. In most cases, a bid is a definite commitment to undertake the job at the stated price, provided the contract is signed within thirty days after the bid is made. Don't automatically choose the lowest bid. You must be sure you are dealing with a reliable contractor. If you don't know him yourself, check with someone who does. Or you can consult your bank or chamber of commerce for its recommendations.

To the contractor's bid you must add (to get the total cost) your own estimate of whatever finishing work you are going to do your-self. To make such an estimate, use a specification—see next section —to check the amounts of materials and products you'll need for each job. You can get prices at your building supply store or from a mail-order catalogue. Buy only from reliable dealers and avoid un-known products and brands.

If you decide to accept the contractor's bid, you must get a signed contract with him. This can be simply a letter, but be sure it refers to your specifications. This will protect both of you from future problems and disagreements. Read all agreements carefully before signing. Most contracts call for payments at specified intervals as the job progresses, and you should be prepared to pay your bills on time.

If changes are made during the course of the work, written orders should be drawn up and signed. Never try to deal directly with the workmen—this is the contractor's job.

17.8 | Simple specifications. Specifications are necessary to get good bids on any job—if your bidders are just looking at a plan, they may not understand exactly what you want. If you are going to do the finishing work yourself, you will need two separate specifications— one for the contractor's part of the job, one for your own part. The following elements should be on the contractor's specs:

Trees and shrubs to be moved

Existing plumbing, electrical ducts, pipes, doors, windows, and walls to be moved

Cubic yards of earth to excavate, or fill

Linear feet of footings to be poured

Square feet of concrete block foundation walls

For slab floors: cubic yards of gravel backfill
square feet of 4-inch slab, with reinforcing mesh, including vapor barrier

For crawl space: square feet of 2-inch ground cover, concrete square feet of floor framing—including sill, joists, box joists, intermediate piers, and beams

Linear feet of 8-foot high exterior wall to frame and sheath

Number and size of windows, including flashing and hardware

Square feet of roof framing—either ceiling joists, rafters and collar beams, or trusses

Another furnace or boiler, if needed

Heating, ductwork, registers; radiation, or piping

Fireplace and chimney, with flashing, if to be included

Waste, vent, hot- and cold-water lines

Electrical outlets, hardware, and fixtures

Stairs, railings

You can put all or some of the following items on your own list of specs, depending on how much of the work you plan to do yourself:

Square feet of shingles, color and type

Gable-end louvers and ridge vent

Linear feet of soffit, cornice, rake boards, and moldings

Linear feet of gutters and downspouts

Square feet of siding, type of siding

Square feet of exterior paint, colors and coats

Square feet of insulation, type of insulation

Linear feet of interior wall framing

Number and size of interior doors with hardware

Square feet of drywall, including ceiling and closets

Tape and spackle

Paint (number of coats, type of paint) or paper

Linear feet of interior base, toe, cornice, and casing moldings

Cabinetry, built-ins, shutters, counters, shelves, sliding closet doors

Bathroom fixtures, hardware

Square feet of bathroom tile

17.9 | Financing the job. If you don't have the cash to pay for your remodeling job, the next cheapest way to finance it is by borrowing the equity from your insurance policies, if you have any equity. You can take your time about paying it back, and the interest is usually a straight 5 per cent. If this isn't possible, there are several other things you can do. They all involve working through your bank, and you will have to have complete plans and estimates before you approach them. You must be working through a reliable contractor; banks don't like to lend money for amateur building operations, for there are too many unforeseen problems involved. Before you take out the loan, figure out exactly what it will cost you in the long run. Here are some types of loans available for home improvement:

FHA Title I. Under this plan you can borrow up to $3,500 to be repaid in a 5-year period. The interest and service is discounted from the face value of the loan when you get the money. The discount is $5 per $1,000 loaned per year; any portion over $2,500 is a $4 discount per $100.

FHA 203k. Under this plan you can borrow up to $10,000 for 20 years at a straight 6 per cent amortization, just like a mortgage. This is a very good loan—if you can get a bank to give you one.

Home Improvement Loans. These conventional loans, by lenders, banks, loan companies, credit unions, are usually discounted loans—and therefore not cheap—but they are more flexible. You can do just about anything you want with the money. Under FHA loans you cannot do swimming pools and patios, but you can with an improvement loan.

Mortgage Financing. Whether you have an FHA mortgage, conventional mortgage, or an open-end mortgage, you can refinance it, if your credit is good at the bank. This method spreads the payments out, but often involves the cost of instituting a whole new mortgage at a slightly higher interest rate than you had with your original mortgage.

INDEX

353